Introduction to Memory Development During Childhood and Adolescence

Introduction to Memory Development During Childhood and Adolescence

Michael Pressley
State University of New York at Albany

Wolfgang Schneider
University of Würzburg

 LAWRENCE ERLBAUM ASSOCIATES, PUBLISHERS
1997   Mahwah, New Jersey   London

Lawrence Erlbaum Associates, Inc., Publishers
10 Industrial Avenue
Mahwah, New Jersey 07430

Library of Congress Cataloging-in-Publication-Data

Pressley, Michael.
    Introduction to memory development during childhood and adolescence / Michael Pressley, Wolfgang Schneider.
        p. cm.
    Abridgement of: Memory development between two and twenty / Wolfgang Schneider & Michael Pressley. 2nd ed. 1997.
    Includes bibliographical references and indexes.
    ISBN 0-8058-2705-6 (cloth : alk. paper). — ISBN 0-8058-2706-4 (pbk. : alk. paper)
    1. Memory in children. 2. Memory in adolescence. I. Schneider, Wolfgang, Dr. phil. II. Schneider, Wolfgang, Dr. phil. Memory development between two and twenty. III. Title.
    BF723.M4P73 1997
    155.4'1312—dc21   97-1849
                                                                              CIP

Books published by Lawrence Erlbaum Associates are printed on acid-free paper, and their bindings are chosen for strength and durability.

Printed in the United States of America
10 9 8 7 6 5 4 3 2 1

To our colleagues, students, and friends who were the sources of our fondest long-term memories, the people who caused memory traces that we love to activate into consciousness.

Contents

Preface

Memory development has been a centrally important topic in developmental psychology for the past 30 years. This volume summarizes the research achievements during that era and relates those achievements to work on memory development conducted throughout the 20th century.

Although there are now substantial literatures on infant memory and memory changes during adulthood, the term *memory development* typically has been used to describe research conducted on participants between the ages of 2 and 20. We follow that convention in this volume, consistent with the title of our longer book, *Memory Development Between Two and Twenty, Second Edition*, by Wolfgang Schneider and Michael Pressley (1997). Indeed, this volume is very much an abridgement of the longer work, although there was considerable reorganization and rewriting in order to make salient the themes that are most important for the beginning student of memory development.

This book is intended as a text in undergraduate and beginning-level graduate courses covering the topic of memory development. After completing this text, readers will be in a good position to understand the newest studies on memory development appearing in the leading journals, for great care was taken to make certain that the issues that are driving contemporary memory development research were not only included but highlighted. This textbook is not a history, but rather it provides a framework for understanding the many memory development studies now appearing in the literature.

The 700 references that are cited in this text were selected carefully to provide introductory students with guidance to the most important work of the past. For those students who want to go beyond an introduction to memory development, they need only head to the campus library with the reference list from this book in hand. The most important articles and all of the lead figures doing research on memory development are contained on that list. Of course, another option is to read our longer book, which we emphasize contains better than 100% more information than could be placed in this volume.

We anticipate that there will be a revision of this text from time to time. Both of us welcome input from readers, especially with respect to information that would make sense to include in a next edition. Feedback in reaction to the first edition of *Memory Development Between Two and Twenty* very much colored our thinking about and writing of the second edition of that book, which in turn affected the development of this book. We take

pride in being open to constructive criticism and responding to it construc-
tively in turn.

Both of us are enormously indebted to our families for their patience as
we pursue matters academic, including the writing of this book. We are also
grateful to the group at Lawrence Erlbaum Associates, who agreed that a
shorter version of our longer book made a lot of sense, and that it would
make our ideas about memory development accessible to a much larger
audience. Finally, we are indebted to our past readers who have assured us
repeatedly that our previous summary helped them sort through a difficult
literature. We play the guides again, confident that there are new readers
out there who will cut new research paths once they have journeyed
through this volume.

—*Michael Pressley*
—*Wolfgang Schneider*

Chapter 1

A Brief History

The aim of this book is to give an integrative introduction to theory and research on memory development during childhood and adolescence. For more than a century, scholars have investigated what children can remember and how they do it, with the result being a large, well-organized database about children's memory. Even so, this is a database that is often ignored. For example, the last decade witnessed many cases in which children's memories were critical in criminal trials. In particular, children's memories often were given great weight in deciding the fates of accused child molesters. Although children's memory data were accepted uncritically in the middle 1980s, by the mid-1990s the courts were much more discerning. This was due in part to a great deal of research on the development of autobiographical memory (i.e., memory of events in one's life), which was inspired by the legal community's need to know about children's memory abilities, and also by an increasing understanding of children's memory in general based on a century of data. Moreover, the accumulated understandings of the last century did much to inform those carrying out the studies of autobiographical memory.

In this introductory chapter, we briefly review the "ancient" history of memory development—memory development research from 1885 until about 1965. An overview of the conceptions driving modern memory development research is provided in anticipation of the remainder of the book, which is mostly about memory development as studied since 1965. We continue the chapter by considering work on autobiographical memory, because that work has garnered so much scholarly and popular attention in recent years. The chapter concludes with a brief commentary on the good information processor perspective, which is our overarching theoretical perspective with respect to memory development.

1885–1935: GERMAN STUDIES

Research on memory development has a long and distinguished history. It begins in the 19th century in Europe.

Investigations of Immediate Memory

Most of the developmental memory studies in the late 19th and early 20th centuries were concerned with memory span, that is, the size of immediate memory. Much of the memory development research at that time was conducted in Germany. Many studies were conducted in which children were exposed to lists of meaningless syllables, single-syllable words, or numbers with recall required immediately after one presentation. In general, these studies revealed that memory span increased with age, although there were some other important findings. For example, meaning played a significant role in determining the amount recalled in Binet and Henri's (1894a, 1894b) study in which preschoolers exhibited substantially better memory for sentences with many words (e.g., 38 words in length) than for short lists (e.g., 7 items) of meaningless words. Lobsien (1902) and Netschajeff (1900) found that memory span performance was better for objects and labels describing sensations than for sounds and abstract concepts. Lobsien's analyses of the exact recall sequences yielded another important result: Memory of items in order develops later than simple free recall of list items.

Individual Differences in Memory Development

The majority of the early studies attached great importance to the identification of interindividual differences in memory development. At the time these studies were conducted, demonstrations that adults produced superior recall than children were by no means trivial, for there were hypotheses that children would learn some types of material (e.g., nonsense syllables; Meumann, 1907) better than adults would. In addition, there was a great deal of concern with sex differences. Many of the opponents of coeducation sought to win the cause of separate education by arguing that girls had inferior intellectual aptitudes. Because women were portrayed as not being able to keep up with men, coeducation was considered a "sin against nature" by some (Braunshausen, 1914, p. 95f). The memory development literature failed to confirm this idea, with only small and inconsistent differences in the performances of girls and boys. When there were sex differences in memory, small differences favoring females occurred more often than small differences in favor of males (e.g., Brunswik, Goldscheider, & Pilek, 1932; Kesselring, 1911; Netschajeff, 1900; Pohlmann, 1906; Vertes, 1913, 1931).

The early studies also dealt extensively with the possibilities that there are important relationships between memory and intelligence. An informal observation of the day was that bright students did not always have good memories. This issue was investigated empirically by cross-classifying subjects in terms of relative academic achievement and relative memory performance. In a study of memory span, Bolton (1892) and Ebbinghaus (1897) found evidence in support of the everyday observation. The correlations between academic achievement and memory span were low. Others, however, found more striking relationships between simple memory performance and achievement (e. g., Binet, 1909; Bourdon, 1894; Meumann, 1912; Pohlmann, 1906; Winch, 1906). Meumann's and Binet's studies were particularly noteworthy in that academic ability was not inferred from school achievement but was instead measured using psychometric and experimental techniques. Not surprisingly, the more meaningful and complex the materials to be memorized, the greater the correlation between memory and intelligence (Brunswik et al., 1932; Vertes, 1913, 1931). When all of the data were considered, the relationship between intelligence and memory performance proved positive, although the correlations were not particularly high in many cases.

1936–1965: SOVIET STUDIES

The great progress made by German researchers in the early 20th century came to a halt as war exploded over Europe. Theoretical perspectives that predominated in Germany in the immediate postwar period (i.e., Gestaltist, phenomenological) did not encourage analytical research on memory or memory development. But others were now interested in memory development.

American learning research during this period was most often conducted in simple learning paradigms, with studies of classical conditioning, instrumental conditioning, and discrimination learning. There were a few studies of children's learning of verbal material. Unfortunately, most of the verbal learning studies with children were descriptive, with studies often conducted at a single age level (Goulet, 1968; Spiker, 1960). In short, research on children's memory was rarely programmatic, with single-shot studies common. Developmental changes were not central concerns of North American researchers in the middle third of the 20th century.

In contrast, Soviet researchers were particularly interested in the development of meaningful memory (i.e., memory mediated by prior knowledge) compared to rote, "mechanical" learning. A prototypical example of Soviet thinking is provided by Smirnov's (1973) analysis of rote versus logical memorizing at different age levels. In particular, Smirnov evaluated the hypothesis that logical memory begins to predominate at about 13 or

14 years of age, and thus, differences in learning that favor meaningful material over nonsense material should increase with age during childhood. Smirnov evaluated this claim by examining studies that used nonsense syllables as indicators of rote learning and meaningful word materials to tap logical memory, a methodological approach that was generally consistent with European thinking in the first half of this century (Brunswik et al., 1932; Lobsien, 1911; Pohlmann, 1906). In fact, the results were very different than expected. The efficiency of memorizing nonsense material increased more rapidly with age than did the efficiency of learning meaningful material. That is, the superiority of "logical" over rote memory (i.e., memory of meaningful materials over nonmeaningful materials) was more pronounced in elementary school children than it was in adolescents.

Smirnov explained that in older children, rote memorizing without consideration of meaning is only rarely found. With age, children show a greater ability to give meaning to meaningless material, and thus, they transform what could be a mechanical and rote process (i.e., learning of nonsense materials) into a meaningful one. A great deal of modern data support this latter conclusion (e.g., development of uninstructed use of elaboration; see chapter 4 of this volume).

Two major concerns can be distinguished in the empirical studies conducted by the Soviets during the 1930s (see reviews by Leontjev, 1977; Meacham, 1977; Smirnov & Zinchenko, 1969). One was the study of involuntary memory, which occurs when the ultimate goal of the subject is not memory, but something else—often, in the Soviet studies, comprehension. In such cases, memory is involuntary in that it is a byproduct of comprehension. The second focus was voluntary memory, which is a product of activities that are driven by a goal to remember. The Soviets assumed that superior forms of memory develop on the basis of the transition from natural and involuntary memorizing to subject-controlled and voluntary memory involving the use of mediating processes and cues (Leontjev, 1931; cited by Leontjev, 1977).

Involuntary Memory. A study by Zinchenko (1939; cited by Smirnov & Zinchenko, 1969), produced a striking set of results, and can be used to illustrate research on involuntary memory. Illustrations of various objects depicted on 15 pieces of cardboard were presented to schoolchildren and adults. A 2-digit number was recorded in the right-hand corner of each piece of cardboard. Subjects in one experimental condition were asked to categorize the picture objects. In the second experimental condition, subjects were asked to arrange the cardboard pieces in sequence on the basis of the numbers. Immediately following completion of the task, subjects in both conditions were unexpectedly instructed to describe and list the items. The findings were clear-cut. The adults who had been asked to categorize the materials recalled many more pictured objects than numbers. The second group (who had sequenced the cards) recalled many more numbers than pictures. The pattern of results was similar with children. From these findings, Zinchenko concluded that active intellectual participation determines what is remembered.

Voluntary Memory. Children's learning from text was examined in a large number of studies of voluntary memory. This research was stimulated both by theoretical concerns about the development of organizational processes that could be applied to text and by the pragmatic possibility of providing guidelines for educators. For instance, Korman (1944, 1945; cited by Yendovitskaya, 1971) studied preschool children's memory for connected material (fairy tales). Korman was impressed by the children's ability to recall the main events of the stories correctly. Although he noted that the children frequently departed from the original sequence of events, the deviations were often logically consistent with the story. The recall differences found between groups of 4- to 5-year-olds and 6-year-olds were primarily quantitative. The younger children recalled the skeleton of the story, whereas the older children gave a more detailed and precise recall of the fairy tale.

In a more analytical study, Smirnov (1973) presented second, fourth, and sixth graders with the goal of determining which cognitive processes influence encoding and intentional memorizing of text. In general, there were age-related increases in text recall. There were also developmental increases in the use of increasingly complex and flexible coding strategies. Only a few of the most capable second graders evidenced a process like self-checking, which was observed more frequently in older children. Selective repetition of material also increased with age.

Correlation Between Voluntary and Involuntary Memory. The relationship of voluntary and involuntary memory as a function of developmental level was analyzed in a number of studies (Smirnov, 1973; Smirnov & Zinchenko, 1969). The relationship varied considerably with the age of subjects: Aggregated across tasks, it was very high for 3- to 4-year-olds, moderate with 5- to 6-year-olds, continuing to decrease until Grade 8, when the relationship was very small. The younger preschool children typically behaved the same way when given involuntary and voluntary memorization instructions and hence, the similar performances with the two sets of instructions. Older children's memory behaviors differed considerably when given voluntary instructions compared to involuntary directions, with more memorizing activity and higher performance when voluntary memorizing instructions were provided. Hence, with older children, voluntary and involuntary memories were less correlated.

Summary. Relative to Western researchers of the day, Soviet scientists emphasized more the development and evaluation of particular theoretical positions (see Meacham, 1977, for an extensive overview of these theoretical positions). The Soviets believed that qualitatively distinct memory processes and learning activities are prevalent at different age levels. The support for this position was provided principally by studies of involuntary and voluntary memorization.

A number of conclusions followed from this database:

1. Three- to 4-year-olds generally did not show intentional memory behaviors when instructions to remember were provided. That these children were not very active when attempting to memorize was apparent in a number of analyses. More optimistically, preschoolers' memories could be improved by manipulations that increased their meaningful processing of material.

2. The first signs of goal-directed activities in the memorization of objects, pictures, and words were observed among 5-year-olds. They appear to set goals about what they want to remember and try to achieve these memory goals. Unfortunately, they usually did not possess means by which to accomplish most memory goals.

3. Six- to 7-year-olds more frequently possessed methods that facilitated the recall of objects and pictures. Nonetheless, the repertoire of memorizing methods was observed to be limited to simple repetition. Conscious reorganization strategies were rarely observed.

4. Additional improvements in performance were noted between the second- and fifth-grade levels, with development greater during this period than during the fifth- to seventh-grade interval (Smirnov & Zinchenko, 1969).

There are many problems in appraising the Soviet literature, however. In general, Western reviewers in the 1990s must rely on secondary sources, for the primary sources either are not available at all or not readily accessible. These secondary sources are often incomplete with respect to designs, procedures, and results. Even more disheartening, when primary sources either are located and translated, they, too, are often vague about how studies were conducted and analyzed, given a different emphasis in the Soviet Union than in the West on the importance of the methods and results sections compared to the discussion section in scientific articles.

When Westerners can peruse the methods of Soviet experiments, it is clear that Soviet experimental studies are not as well controlled as U.S. studies, with this conclusion especially compelling for studies conducted before 1960. Even so, many of the Soviet conclusions were not arrived at by Western researchers until decades later. Soviet scholars were doing important work on memory development during the middle third of the 20th century.

THE MODERN ERA: WESTERN RESEARCH

Most of the rest of this book is concerned with research conducted since 1965. Most of the research that is taken up in the subsequent chapters was carried out in the West. The most influential theoretical perspective by far is the general information-processing approach. The modern conception of memory is in terms of interacting information-processing components, with memory development a product of developing components in ever more complex interactions.

For readers who are not familiar with information processing, a few simple distinctions should help as advance organizers for what is to come. Many information-processing models divide memory into short- and long-term components (e.g., Atkinson & Shiffrin, 1968). Information that is in short-term memory is currently in consciousness. Thus, when a person reads a story, he or she may be aware at any given instant of the exact wording of the last sentence read and a few other pieces of recently encountered information. Perhaps one or two points covered a while back in the text are activated as well—maybe because they were associated with information that was processed recently. Only a limited amount of information can be consciously processed at any one time—that is, short-term capacity is limited. (Development of short-term capacity is discussed in chapter 2.) If nothing is done with information held in short-term memory, it is usually forgotten quickly. (Short-term memory is short term in that what is there usually does not stay there for long!)

In contrast to short-term memory is a long-term store that contains virtually everything that the person knows. Particularly relevant here, this long-term store contains knowledge of procedures (e.g., strategies) that can operate on information in short-term storage. The development of strategy use is taken up in chapter 4. In addition to knowing strategies, people know many others things—concepts, associations between concepts, hierarchical classifications of concepts, schemas, and so on. This nonstrategic knowledge (world knowledge) often has direct effects on the memorability of newly encountered content, as well as profound influences on whether strategies operate efficiently or can operate at all. This knowledge base as a determinant of children's memory and memory development is considered in particular in chapter 3. Whether strategic procedures are used correctly depends on knowing when and where to use particular procedures, a form of metacognition (i.e., knowledge about thinking). Metacognitive knowledge is also stored in long-term memory, with the metacognition (metamemory in particular) the topic of chapter 5. In relegating strategies, nonstrategic knowledge, and metamemory to long-term memory, we emphasize that when these components are activated, they operate in consciousness, and thus, short-term capacity determines their use in part. This interaction between short-term memory and long-term components is just one of many interactions that will be considered in the chapters that follow, but it is a very important one.

As important as all of the analytical work on memory has been, popular attention to memory development in the media has been spurred less by theoretical analysis of components than by whether and when children can remember what has happened to them at all. This fascination with children's autobiographical memory, as memory for personally experienced events is now called, has come about because children's memories of their lives are often probed in courts of law, with potentially grave implications if and when children's memories err. We conclude this chapter on history by considering the research on autobiographical memory that has done so much to place memory development in a limelight not previously enjoyed.

AUTOBIOGRAPHICAL MEMORY

Autobiographical memories are of particular events that happened at a particular place and time (Brewer, 1986; Nelson, 1993b). That is, although every Western adult knows what happens to them when they go to McDonald's, that is not autobiographical memory. Recall of a visit to a McDonald's in South Bend in spring, 1982, when a fire broke out is an autobiographical memory.

Autobiographical memories can be based on a single event in the past (e.g., the one baseball practice an 8-year-old attended that resulted in the child's decision not to play Little League that year) or repeated events in the past (e.g., memory of what went on at Little League practices before the season started).

Infantile Amnesia

For a century (Dudycha & Dudycha, 1941; Howe & Courage, 1993; Wetzler & Sweeney, 1986), there has been little dispute that adults cannot remember what happened to them during the first few years of their lives. On average, adults do not recall events in their lives before about the age of 3½ years (Pillemer & White, 1989). This inability to recall early life events has been referred to as *infantile amnesia.*

It is not that the adult never knew about some of those things that happened very early in life. Preschoolers do have memories of events that occurred in their life. Nelson's work (e.g., 1993a), for example, is telling on this point. Beginning at about 21 months of age, Nelson listened in as a little girl named Emily laid in her crib. What Emily did was talk to herself a great deal, recounting the events that had occurred during the day and in her life. For example, at 32 months of age, Emily recalled for herself a happy event:

We bought a baby, cause, the well because, when she, well, we thought it was for Christmas, but when we went to the store we didn't have our jack but I saw some dolly, and I yelled at my mother and I said I want one of those dolly. So after we finished with the store, we went over to the dolly and she brought me one. So I have one. (Nelson, 1993a, p. 6)

Even though Emily could recall these events when she was 32 months old, she probably would not be able to do so years from now, or remember much of anything else that happened during her first 3 years of life (Eisenberg, 1985; Hudson, 1990; Miller & Sperry, 1988; Nelson, 1988). That is infantile amnesia—the inability to remember what happened early in life.

Schema and Long-Term Memory. One possibility is that young children form memories, but these memories are inaccessible years later. How could that occur? Particularly critical in being able to recall an event is that it is encoded in an organized way rather than as jumbled pieces of information. For example, one of the reasons that an adult can remember a trip to a Superbowl 20 years ago is that when the event occurred, the adult had much generalized knowledge (schema) of football games and the Superbowl in particular. This generalized knowledge was helpful in encoding the original Superbowl event. It is also helpful now in retrieving information about attendance at that game.

In contrast, a 2-year-old making a trip to a Superbowl with a parent would not have the same schema when the game was experienced, with the result fragmentary coding of the experience when it happened, so much so that the impressions of that day are difficult to access and reorganize once understanding of football and Superbowls is acquired in the ensuing years. Because a young child experiencing a Superbowl may pay attention to very different elements of the experience than an adult, the fragments of the experience that are encoded may be idiosyncratic and unrelated to the types of information an adult would go looking for in memory when asked to recall what happened when she or he went to the Superbowl as a 2-year-old. This explanation seems plausible, given that young children's encoding of once-experienced events is fragmentary. When very young children remember things that happened to them several months before, their memories often are disorganized and unstable (Fivush & Hamond, 1990).

Thus, one necessary ingredient for enduring autobiographical memories is some generalized knowledge of the world (i.e., schema). It is a necessary but not a sufficient ingredient, however: There is strong evidence that children 1 to 3 years of age can and do encode schematic information with respect to events they encounter often (see chapter 3, this volume), yet, years later they will not recall these events.

Narrative Skills and Autobiographical Memory. Although even 1-year-olds can sometimes represent the order in which activities they observed occurred, with the recall of ordering more certain the more the activity is consistent with schematic understandings possessed by the child, free recall of such events is often fragmentary and disorganized (Bauer & Fivush, 1992; Bauer & Mandler, 1989, 1992; Bauer & Thal, 1990). Nelson (1993a, 1993b) and like-minded memory developmentalists believe (Fivush, 1994; Miller, 1994) that one explanation of increasing memory for particular episodes after the first 3 or 4 years of life is tied to increasing communication skills during the preschool years. That is, children need to learn how to talk about the experiences they have had before they form enduring memories of the events.

Learning to talk about one's past seems to be a language skill that is acquired with experience. Adults are always telling stories about themselves and the child in the presence of the child, always telling stories about what has happened to them and the child. That is, adults are always modeling autobiographical remembering for children (McCabe & Peterson, 1991; Miller, 1994). But parents do more than that. They also spend a great deal of time talking with their children about things that happened to them, assisting the child in learning how to be tellers of their own autobiographies. Such parent–child dialogues are filled with maternal questions and responses. Through experiencing such dialogues, a child learns how to talk about things that happened to her. When the child cannot structure recall of an event, the mother asks questions, providing a scaffold for the child's recall of the event. As the child becomes increasingly familiar with what should be told in recalling an event and, in fact, begins to recall with greater completeness, adult scaffolding in the form of leading questions is reduced.

As a result, by the end of the preschool years, children who have had rich verbal interactions with parents are able to recall fairly complex events with a minimum of parental support in the form of leading questions (Hudson & Shapiro, 1991; Peterson & McCabe, 1983). They have learned that they do know more about events they have experienced than comes to mind immediately, that much can be recalled and reported given a little systematic searching of memory (Price & Goodman, 1990). That dialogical experiences are critical in development of autobiographical recall is supported by a variety of analyses relating the amount and quality of adult–child interaction about events and a child's ability to recall events (Engel, 1986; 1991; Nelson, 1993a, 1993b; Pillemer & White, 1989; Ratner, 1980, 1984; Reese, Haden, & Fivush, 1993; Tessler, 1986). Much of the development of autobiographical memories and memory skills can probably be explained as development of narrative language skills.

Other Mechanisms of Autobiographical Memory. There are a variety of other mechanisms that have been identified as potentially contributing to the development of autobiographical memory (Fivush, 1994; Nelson, 1993a, 1993b): First, children hear others telling stories about them (e.g., mother tells about how Susie liked to pick flowers every time she saw flowers). Such storytellers help the child understand how to define his or her autobiography. Much can be learned about the structure of autobiographical memories from what storytellers do and do not include in retellings, what they do and do not emphasize, and how they interpret the actions of the child. Second, sometimes children tell tales about themselves to themselves. Rehearsing and retelling particular experiences as a child lays in her or his crib can affect memory of the events. Finally, events that occur only once are not remembered as well as ones that are reinstated by actually re-experiencing the event again. Thus, Fivush and Hamond (1989) demonstrated much greater memory of a play opportunity 3 months after it occurred when there was a second opportunity to experience the play event 2 weeks after the original event (see also Howe, Courage, & Bryant-Brown, 1993).

One thing is certain about autobiographical memory. Our memories of our experiences are never perfect. A little bit of reflection on the mechanisms underlying autobiographical memories that have been reviewed thus far makes clear that there is ample opportunity for changes in memories as time passes (Brewer, 1986): (a) Aspects of an event covered in dialogues or heard in retellings of the event will be remembered better than aspects of the event that are not discussed or re-experienced, either actually or through a retelling. (b) When people have an experience, perception of the experience is colored by prior knowledge. Thus, the child encountering a fast food restaurant for the first time pays attention to and considers important very different features than does a person who has had many visits to fast food restaurants (Nelson, 1993a, 1993b). During recall of an experience, people reconstruct a memory of a past event in light of what they know now (Brewer, 1986). (c) Even re-experiencing an event has potential to change memory of an event, for experiences the second time around are rarely the same as the first time. Autobiographical memories are not static but rather dynamic memories.

Summary. The point emphasized as we conclude this section on infantile amnesia is that developmentalists believe that as children begin to participate in dialogues, they acquire powerful understandings about how to represent the events of their lives. As they become more proficient in dialogue, there are more and more opportunities to dialogue with others about the events of one's life. When no one is around, the child who has internalized narrative skills can tell a better tale to herself or himself than the younger child. The ability to talk about events and the actual talking about events probably goes far in determining what events are remembered years later. That what happened earlier in life was talked about less and less completely than events encountered later in life may go far in explaining why so little of what was encountered early in life is remembered. That is the thinking driving much of contemporary research on infantile amnesia and the development of long-term memories of early and later childhood.

Autobiographical memory is reconstructive memory, with long-term knowledge affecting original encodings of events and later recollections of the events (Farrar & Goodman, 1990, 1992; Hudson, 1986; Mistry & Lange, 1985; Nelson, 1986). If a child attends a birthday party with no party streamers decorating the ceiling, do not be surprised if later recall includes party streamers!! Because party streamers have been at so many birthday parties, the child might remember them at this one, even though the ceiling was bare.

The century-old mysteries concerning infantile amnesia seem to be yielding to new insights about memory development produced in the past 10 years, although there is also plenty of mystery left (Howe & Courage, 1993). As becomes obvious during the course of this book, some issues in memory development are never resolved fully but rather challenge generations of researchers. Even so, attempting to resolve these issues does much to increase understanding of memory development.

Children's Eyewitness Memory

The stimulus for much of the most recent research on children's memory, and certainly the stimulus for research that has been in the public eye, have been concerns about the credibilities of children as witnesses in legal proceedings. In this section, we review the research evidence with respect to several important types of memories that were explored in eyewitness memory research.

Face Memory. A variety of paradigms have been used to study children's face recognition (Davies, 1993). These paradigms yielded somewhat contradictory outcomes.

There have been a number of laboratory studies involving the presentation to children of a set of pictures of faces. These presentations were followed by tests in which the children were asked to identify which faces occurred previously and which did not. Performance on this task does often increase between 5 and 10 years of age (Davies, 1993). There is a peculiar, and at this time, inexplicable, dip in performance in making discriminations between previously presented and new faces after age 10 (e.g., Carey, Diamond, & Woods, 1980; Flin, 1980).

An advantage of this paradigm, which is purely an in-the-laboratory approach to the study of face recognition, is that it permits fairly easy evaluation of a number of variables that might affect face recognition, with some potentially important practical findings emanating from this research: (a) The developmental improvement in recognition that is apparent at short testing intervals (e.g., the test occurs immediately after the original presentation of the pictures) is much less apparent when the test is delayed (e.g., by a week; Ellis & Flin, 1990). (b) Children are better able to identify faces of their own race than of other races, with this ability increasing with age (Chance, Turner, & Goldstein, 1982; Cross, Cross, & Daly, 1971; Feinman & Entwisle, 1976). (c) Some facial features are more important in affecting subsequent identification of a face than others. Thus, upper facial features provide a better basis for discrimination than lower facial features, with the ability to identify familiar people on the basis of upper facial features alone increasing between 4 and 10 years of age (Goldstein & Mackenberg, 1966). (d) When a previously seen face is disguised in a test picture, or even if the faces bear a different expression, or the person wears different clothing, or the face is shown in a different pose, children's recognition of the face declines. Such changes reduce the recognition of children younger than 10 years of age more than they do the recognition of older children (Carey, 1978, 1981, 1992; Diamond & Carey, 1977; Ellis, 1990, 1992). In summary, children's memory of faces often varies as a function of situational factors.

The laboratory studies of face memory are criticizable for their lack of ecological validity. Researchers responded to this criticism with eyewitness bystander studies, in which children witnessed events, with memory for the participants in the events then tested. In most of these studies, the child was a bystander to an event, in contrast to other studies, taken up subsequently, in which the child was a victim.

When children are asked to describe individuals they observed in an event, a consistent finding is that older children report much more information than do younger children, although the proportion of incorrect information often does not increase as the amount of information reported (Davies, 1993). Young children seem to attend more to what people do than what they look like, with recall of actions witnessed accounting for a greater proportion of the information remembered by younger compared to older children, who remember more than younger children about what actors looked like (Davies, Tarrant, & Flin, 1989; Dent & Stephenson, 1979; King & Yuille, 1986; Yuille, Cutshall, & King, 1986). Posing more specific questions intended to produce information about descriptive details (e.g., to tell about the eyes) increases the amount of information children provide, but often at the expense of more errors, especially with younger children (King & Yuille, 1986; List, 1986; Parker, Haverfield, & Baker-Thomas, 1986; Yuille et al., 1986).

Rather than ask open-ended questions at all, an alternative tactic is to ask a child witness to select the picture of the actor in the event from an array of pictures or to select the actual actor from a lineup of people. There is little if any developmental improvement on such recognition tasks (Davies, 1993), but there is one important developmental difference. In the studies revealing this difference, children were presented sets of test pictures; sometimes the test set contained the target actor and other times it did not. When the test set contained the target item, there was little evidence of an age effect. In striking contrast, errors of a particular sort are particularly likely when young children are presented a set of test pictures that do not include the original actor: Younger children are more likely than older children to identify one of the pictures in the set as the individual they had witnessed (e.g., Davies et al., 1989; Parker & Carranza, 1989). That is, younger children are more likely than older children to identify a "suspect" in a lineup of possibilities, even when it is certain that the individual who was seen previously is not included in the lineup.

Children are often the victims of crimes, such as sexual assaults. Of course, it is not possible to carry out well-controlled studies of witnessing as victim. Goodman, Aman, and Hirschman (1987) thought of a clever analogue situation, however. They studied children who were victims of an individual who took their blood, an invasive, physical procedure that is often considered painful by children. They studied memory of professional encounters at the doctor's office. A few days later the children were asked to select the picture of the person who drew the blood from an array of pictures. About half the time, the 3- to 6-year-olds in the study selected the correct picture from a set of six pictures. However, at a longer retention interval (1 week later), the younger children in the study performed at chance, whereas the 5- and 6-year-olds still were correct about half the time.

Summary.   Whether there are developmental differences in face recognition depends. Developmental differences are more likely when verbal recall is involved. Developmental differences are striking when the individual who was witnessed is not actually in the test array. Young children are more likely than older children to claim that a witnessed person is included in a target-absent array of pictures.

One of the most striking aspects of these data, however, is that although recognition is often above chance levels, it is never perfect, and often far from perfect. That is, children often do not make accurate identifications of faces. Those who have great confidence in children as eyewitnesses must confront this fact, which is consistent with far lower than 100% accuracy in other eyewitness studies, including the ones discussed in the next section.

Memory of Physical Contacts With Adults

Others besides Goodman and her colleagues have used memory of medical procedures as a proxy for victim memory of assault, because medical procedures share many of the features of assault events. They are stressful, involving others looking at and touching parts of the body, sometimes including private parts. Medical procedures are sometimes painful. Looking and touching occurs as part of a complex sequence of events.

Consider an important investigation tapping children's memories of medical procedures. Research by Baker-Ward, Gordon, Ornstein, Larus, and Clubb (1993) involved 3-, 5-, and 7-year-olds who visited a medical clinic for a routine physical examination. The intent of the research was to determine how well children encode what happened during the medical procedure and the effects of delayed testing (up to 6 weeks) on the accuracy of memory.

During the exam, each child interacted with a nurse and a doctor, each of whom performed the particular aspects of an examination typically carried out by nurses and doctors. The nurse, working alone, went through her regimen with each child, followed by the doctor who also worked alone. After the doctor finished the exam, necessary innoculations were given. The nurse also deviated from the normal routine in order to introduce an unexpected event into the examination. She took a photograph of each patient. The children received stickers and other small rewards for their participation. The nurse and physician rated how stressed each child was during the examination on a 1 (*no anxiety*) to 5 (*very anxious*) scale.

Most participants were interviewed about their examination experiences immediately after the examination. These immediately interviewed participants were then re-interviewed either 1, 3, or 6 weeks later. In contrast, participants in a control group were not interviewed immediately after the examination, with the only interview that they experienced occurring 3 weeks after the physical examination.

The interviews consisted of a set of standard questions, beginning with very general ones (e.g., "Tell me what happened during your checkup") to more specific ones (e.g., "Did the doctor check any parts of your face") and even more specific ones still (e.g., "Did (s)he check your eyes? Did the doctor shine a light in your eyes?"). Children were consistently prompted to elaborate their answers (e.g., "Tell me how the doctor checked your eyes"). In addition to the questions tapping things that actually happened during the exam, children were also asked questions tapping things that definitely did not happen, things that would never happen during a medical examination ("Did the doctor cut your hair? Did the nurse sit on top of you?").

As was true for recall of faces, there was a clear developmental trend in children's memory when recall demands were high—that is, in response to more open-ended questions. Age differences were much less dramatic when all of the data were considered. For example, given specific questions, at immediate testing, even the 3-year-olds remembered 80% of what went on during the examination. One of the more surprising outcomes was that delayed testing had little (at age 3) to no (at age 7) impact on memory of the examination. Another unexpected finding was that the perceived level of anxiety did not correlate with recall.

Because not every child experienced every aspect of the examination regimen (i.e., nurses and doctors did not perform every checklist item for every patient), it was possible to assess whether children would report whether particular things happened, ones that could happen during a medical examination, even though they were absent. Again, consistent with the face recognition data, 3-year-olds were more likely than older children to claim that a procedure occurred that had not occurred. This outcome was paralleled with respect to the responses to questions about events that could never occur during a medical examination: Three-year-olds were more likely than older children to claim that the doctor cut the child's hair or the nurse sat on top on the child. At all age levels and for all very specific questions, however, the children were much more likely to answer correctly than incorrectly. Yes, the younger children were more prone to errors, but even the young children knew a great deal about what had happened during the examination procedure (see Merritt, Ornstein, & Spicker, 1994, for another demonstration of young children's accurate memory for distressing events).

Susceptibility to Suggestion

An important topic in children's eyewitness memory concerns age differences in susceptibility to suggestion. In most suggestibility paradigms, participants witness or experience an event and are later either presented with some postevent information that contradicts events observed earlier (misinformation) or are asked sets of misleading questions, suggesting an inaccurate "fact" (e.g., Cassel & Bjorklund, 1995). There is little doubt that people of all ages are susceptible to both misinformation and misleading questions. The primary concern of developmental researchers has been whether or not there are age differences in suggestibility. Although this has been a controversial area of research, most studies that have looked for age differences in suggestibility have found them, with preschool children being particularly susceptible to suggestion (e.g., Goodman & Clarke-Stewart, 1991; Goodman & Reed, 1986; Poole & White, 1991, 1995). Particularly important, age differences in suggestibility were confirmed in studies that simulate repeated questioning in a legal context (Cassel & Bjorklund, 1995; Cassel, Roebers, & Bjorklund, 1996), because such repeated questioning is common in legal proceedings.

General Conclusions About Children's Memories
of Stressful Experiences

Many questions have been addressed in studies of children's memories of medical procedures and other stressful or shocking experiences. The most important conclusions from these studies are as follows:

- In general, children typically do not report that they have been touched in suggestive ways by adults, or had sexually suggestive interactions with adults when no such interactions occurred (Rudy & Goodman, 1991; Saywitz, Goodman, Nicholas, & Moan, 1991). Even so, the false report rate typically was not zero in these studies, so there were some false reports. False reports were more likely from preschoolers than older children (Baker-Ward et al., 1993; Gordon, Ornstein, Nida, Follmer, Crenshaw, & Albert, 1993; Ornstein, Shapiro, Clubb, & Follmer, 1996).

- It is much more likely that children will omit information about suggestive contact than claim suggestive contact happened when it did not (Saywitz et al., 1991). The more open-ended the question, the more likely the omission, with preschoolers less likely to report suggestive contact (e.g., genital contact during a medical exam) than slightly older children (Ornstein et al., 1996).

- Delayed recall has a greater negative impact on preschoolers than older children (Baker-Ward et al., 1993; Ornstein et al., 1996). More striking, however, is that the effects of delay are typically not very great, especially when responses to less open-ended questions are considered (Baker-Ward et al., 1993; Gordon et al., 1991; Ornstein et al., 1996).

- In general, the younger the child, the greater the susceptibility to suggestions from interviewers, with preschoolers consistently more open to interviewer suggestions than older children (Ceci & Bruck, 1993, 1995; Goodman & Clarke-Stewart, 1991, Experiment 6; Goodman & Reed, 1986). Nonetheless, in general, children are not easily misled (i.e., through suggestive questions) to report physical contact that did not occur (Rudy & Goodman, 1991; Saywitz et al., 1991).

- An aggressive interviewer can intimidate children into providing errant answers to misleading questions, answers implied by the wording and tone of the interviewer's questions (e.g., "Are you afraid to tell? You'll feel better when you tell"; Goodman, Wilson, Hazan, & Reed, 1989). A high status interviewer, such as policeman, has greater potential for misleading a child witness than a person of lower status (Tobey & Goodman, 1992).

- Use of anatomically correct dolls does not seem to increase completeness or accuracy of children's reports of what happened to them (Goodman & Aman, 1990; Gordon et al., 1993). In fact, there are reports of increased tendency to report suggestive physical contact that did not occur when dolls are used during an interview (Bruck, Ceci, Francoeur, Renick, 1995; Saywitz et al., 1991). The purported potential of such dolls to enhance the memories of young preschoolers, who may have difficulties verbalizing about suggestive contact, is questionable, for young preschoolers often do not understand the symbolic value of such dolls— they do not understand that a doll can be a model of themselves (DeLoache & Marlzoff, 1995).

In general, all of this data would suggest that children often can provide believable reports about things that have happened to them. This is true, even in some cases when they are subjected to practices that are sometimes suspected as coercive, such as leading questioning.

That is not to say there is not reason for concern with respect to distortions of children's memories in reaction to questions posed to them. Distortions in children's reports occur, even when the interviewer does all possible not to pressure or mislead the child—forensically serious distortions, such as the reporting of bones and blood in a setting in which there were no bones or blood (Rudy & Goodman, 1991). In general, the younger the child, the greater the risk of such outrageous inaccuracies, with preschoolers particularly suspect. Yes, children, even preschoolers, are often accurate in their memories, but inaccuracies occur as well, with the likelihood of really egregious errors (i.e., reports of blood and guts when there was no blood and guts) greater the younger the child. Thus, scientific research on children's eyewitness memory has provided an idea of how competent children can be and a warning that children's memories are often wrong.

Summary

Memories are never perfectly reliable. That said, there are clear developmental improvements in memory. The research of the past decade, in particular, has made clear that there is very great development during the preschool years and into the elementary years with respect to the accuracy and completeness of event memories.

Situational variables affect children's memories of events. Claims about children's memories of events are consistently qualified by concerns about specifics, such as when the memory is tested relative to when the event occurred (e.g., a long time ago vs. a short time ago), the familiarity of the situation witnessed, the types of features being recalled (e.g., action elements vs. actor descriptions), the types of questions being used to tap memory (i.e., open-ended vs. more suggestive), and the stress experienced by the children when the event occurred.

The most salient research on the situational specificity of children's event memories concerns the susceptibility of children to postevent suggestions. Although there is some evidence that the younger the child, the greater the potential susceptibility, the more general conclusion that comes from this literature is that children can be misled through questioning to believe that something happened that did not happen and can be bullied into reporting events that did not occur through aggressive and misleading questioning. There have been concerns about children's testimonies being distorted through postevent suggestions throughout this century (Whipple, 1912), with the most recent research simply bolstering the historical case that children's testimony can be affected by events other than the witness event (Ceci & Bruck, 1993). The research on memory development at the beginning of the century is meeting the research on memory development at the end of the century, reflecting the enduring importance of many of the issues studied by memory developmentalists.

WHAT FOLLOWS?

In the chapters that follow, we review the major components of memory and how they develop. This organization reflects our beliefs that memory development is well understood in terms of basic capacities, knowledge, strategies, and metamemory and the reality that much of the research on memory development occurred with respect to problems of capacity, knowledge, strategies, and metacognition. These components are also at the heart of memory at its best.

Memory development makes more sense when the endpoint of development is understood. In our view, that endpoint is *good information processing* (e.g., Borkowski, Carr, Rellinger, & Pressley, 1990; Pressley, 1986; Pressley, Borkowski, & Johnson, 1987; Pressley, Borkowski, & Schneider, 1987, 1989; Pressley, Goodchild, Fleet, Zajchowski, & Evans, 1989; Pressley, Johnson, & Symons, 1987). The components that are the focus in this volume are at the heart of good information processing.

The good information processor has more than average short-term capacity—that is, a good information processor can juggle a half dozen pieces of information in mind rather easily. That capacity is required to use the many memory strategies used automatically and consciously by the good information processor (e.g., Baron, 1985, chapter 3; Campione & Armbruster, 1985). The good information processor has had many opportunities to use and practice strategies, and thus, their application in appropriate situations has become habitual. The good information processor also has extensive knowledge about strategies, being especially aware of when particular strategies are effective, which motivates the good information processor to use the strategies she or he knows (e.g., Black & Rollins, 1982; Borkowski, Levers, & Gruenenfelder, 1976; Cavanaugh & Borkowski, 1979; Jackson & Gildemeister, 1991; Kennedy & Miller, 1976; Lange, Guttentag, & Nida, 1990; Lawson & Fuelop, 1980; Paris, Newman, & McVey, 1982; Ringel & Springer, 1980; Weed, Ryan, & Day, 1990). Good information processors possess much knowledge about when and where to use the strategic procedures they know (e.g., Duffy et al., 1987; Paris, Lipson, &

Wixson, 1983; Pressley, Borkowski, & O'Sullivan, 1984, 1985; Roehler & Duffy, 1984).

In summary, good information processing is complicated, because it involves the coordinated development and use of strategies, metacognition, and the nonstrategic knowledge base, all operating in the confines of limited capacity. We emphasize that a global good information processor is something of an idealized endstate. More optimistically, there is a good deal of evidence that children in fact do make substantial progress toward good information processing, with substantial development with respect to all of its components, as documented in the following chapters.

In general, we restrict our coverage of memory development during childhood to memory development after the age of 2. A fair representation of infant memory would require many pages, with most work on infant memory addressing very different issues from those addressed with children and adolescents. Work on infant memory belongs in a different book. We end coverage of memory development at about age 20. The literature on adult development of memory is very large, with the issues in that literature very different from the ones reviewed here. Work on adult memory development also is for a different book.

Chapter 2

Basic Memory Capacities and Mechanisms

This chapter examines an extremely simple hypothesis about the development of memory— that memory perhaps improves because of neurological development. Two specific possibilities are considered—that neurological development increases short-term capacity and that it increases children's inhibition and resistance to interference.

SHORT-TERM CAPACITY

It is important to understand the nature of *short-term capacity* and its development, because all strategies, metacognition, and world knowledge that is used by the child must operate within the constraints posed by short-term capacity: Short-term capacity determines how much can be consciously contemplated at any moment, that is, how many pieces of information can be mentally juggled at once. Short-term capacity is attentional capacity. Complex cognition is easier and more certain to be accomplished by those who can contemplate relatively more than others, by those who can attend to more information at a time than can others. Short-term capacity has been conceived of as including both capacity to hold and manage information in memory in a speech-based form (e.g., silently saying things over) as well as in a visual imagery form (Baddeley & Hitch, 1974).

Research on this topic is directly related to the earliest studies that examined memory development, the work on memory span conducted at the turn of the century and reviewed briefly in the last chapter. Memory span tasks are structured simply. Subjects are usually presented sequences of stimuli at a constant speed (e.g., one item per second). Short sequences (e.g., three items) are used first, with subsequent presentations increased by one item at a time until the subject can no longer produce the entire sequence. Regardless of the type of material presented for learning, there are clear developmental increases in memory span (see Fig. 2.1), which was traditionally assumed to reflect developmental increases in short-term memory capacity.

There are a number of possible explanations for the apparent developmental increases in short-term (working memory) capacity, however (Dempster, 1985). The traditional explanation was that developmental increases on measures such as digit span reflected increases in neurologically determined "slots" (Miller, 1956) with development. The alternatives to the structural change explanation include developmental changes in strategies and increases in speed of processing. Like Dempster (1985), we believe attributing developmental increases in memory span to developmental increases in the number of storage slots should occur only if age differences cannot be reduced to differences in strategies or processing efficiency as reflected by measures such as speed of processing.

Strategies and Skills Potentially Determining Memory Span

There is research support for several strategies that potentially affect and determine developmental improvements in memory span.

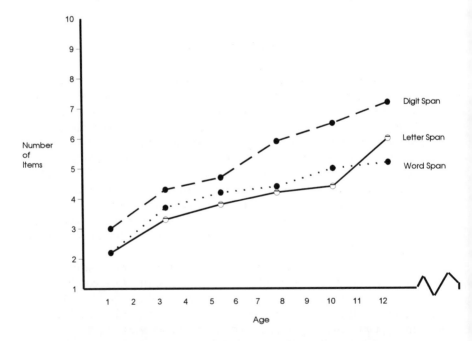

FIG. 2.1. Developmental differences in digit span, letter span, and word span. From Dempster (1981). Copyright 1981 by the American Psychological Association. Adapted with permission.

Rehearsal. Age increases in digit span have been hypothesized to be due to developmental increases in spontaneous use of rehearsal. This hypothesis was assessed by analyzing developmental memory span data for primacy effects—that is, high memory for items placed early in the list of digits to be remembered compared to items placed later. The assumption was that use of rehearsal provides greater encoding opportunities for material presented early in a list compared to later material, and, hence, greater memory of first compared to later material would suggest the operation of rehearsal (e.g., Atkinson & Shiffrin, 1968; Waugh & Norman, 1965). Although researchers were able to find primacy effects in children's digit-span data, they generally did not obtain developmental differences in the presence of primacy effects (e.g., Harris & Burke, 1972; Huttenlocher & Burke, 1976). Thus, this research tactic failed to yield support for the position that developmental improvements in memory span performance are due to developmental shifts in the use of rehearsal.

More recent analyses have been slightly more supportive of the conclusion that rehearsal during learning lists of digits is more common at the end of the grade-school years than among younger children. For example, when Hitch, Halliday, Schaafstal, and Heffernan (1991) had 5-year-olds label pictures in a memory span task, their performances improved, suggesting that they did not verbally label items to be remembered as they were presented. In contrast, when 11-year-olds labeled, their short-term memory performances worsened, suggesting to Hitch et al. (1991) that labeling (i.e., saying the name of each picture on the list aloud once) was interfering with covert multiple-repetition rehearsal processes. Phonologically similar items (e.g., rat, cat, mat, hat, etc.) are particularly difficult to rehearse relative to items that are not phonologically similar. Hitch et al. (1991) observed that when their participants prepared for short-term recall of item lists silently, the phonological-similarity effect was much more pronounced for 11-year-olds than 5-year-olds, consistent with the hypothesis that the older children rehearsed and the younger children did not. In contrast, when the children in the study were required to label the items to be remembered, there was a striking phonological similarity effect at both age levels. In summary, there is mixed evidence that increases in rehearsal with increasing age can account for developmental differences in memory span.

Chunking. Miller (1956) introduced the "magic" number 7 (± 2) as the maximum number of chunks of verbal information that could be held in short-term memory at any given instant. The magic in this approach was that although capacity in terms of chunks was invariant, individual differences in short-term memory capacity (e.g., Simon, 1974) could be explained in terms of different-size chunks. Simon (1974) reviewed a number of tests of his hypothesis and concluded that "the psychological reality of the chunk has been fairly well demonstrated, and the chunk capacity of short-term memory has been shown to be in the range of five to seven. Fixation of information in long-term memory has been shown to take about 5 to 10 seconds per chunk" (p. 487). From this perspective, age differences in memory span are presumed to be due to larger and larger information sequences being encoded as chunks with increasing age, permitted by expanding and ever more accessible conceptual knowledge with development, knowledge that can be used to identify meaningful chunks of information in the list of items on the list to be remembered. With larger chunks, the amount of information that can be stored and processed simultaneously increases proportionately. Because the degree of chunking that is possible depends on the amount of prior knowledge possessed by a learner, chunking is a prior-knowledge-dependent strategy (Chi, 1978).

Dempster (1978) compared the short-term memory performances of 7-, 9-, and 12-year-old children who were presented various materials (numbers, consonants, words, nonsense syllables). Developmental differences were obtained when the materials were chunkable, but not when chunking was not possible given the material. Unfortunately, Burtis (1982) failed to obtain data that complemented Dempster's (1978) finding. Burtis presented 10- to 14-year-olds with easy-to-chunk, somewhat difficult-to-chunk, and difficult-to-chunk consonant sequences. Regardless of age, Burtis' subjects seemed to chunk all of these materials, undermining the conclusion that chunking alone could account for age-correlated increases in recall of consonants.

Although it is difficult to explain the discrepant findings in these two studies, in neither piece of research were students' prior familiarity with the consonant sequences determined directly. A study carried out by Chi (1978) did control this factor with more complex materials. She compared the abilities of chess experts and novices in memorizing chess board positions. Most fascinating from a developmental perspective, the children were the experts in this study and the adults the novices. Although the children performed more poorly than the adults on a digit-span task, the results were reversed for recall of the chess positions. Chunking was implicated in the postexperiment interviews, with child experts indicating that they viewed the whole chess board as the unit of learning. The children who knew a lot about chess were in a better position to create chunks than were the less knowledgeable adults.

Item Sequencing. Some researchers (e.g., Chi, 1977; Dempster, 1981; Huttenlocher & Burke, 1976) suggested that age differences in memory span may be due in part to the requirement that materials on memory span lists be reproduced in order. They believed that this ordering requirement would especially penalize very young subjects, because very young children are not familiar with the sequential ordering of ordinal numbers.

In support of this hypothesis, Chi (1977) reported 100% improvement in recall performance by 5-year-olds when the order of items was not considered. Case, Kurland, and Goldberg (1982) ignored ordering of information in their study of children's short-term memory and obtained higher "memory span" values than are obtained when correct serial ordering is required (cf. Flavell, Friedrichs, & Hoyt, 1970; Yussen & Levy, 1975). Findings from the Munich Longitudinal Study on the Genesis of Individual Differences (LOGIC; Schneider & Weinert, 1995; Weinert & Schneider, 1992) revealed that the ordering requirement particularly affects recall in children younger than 6 years of age: When children were first tested at the age of 4 years, free recall of the word lists developed by Case et al. (1982) was significantly better than serial recall of the same items. Format of recall (i.e., free vs. serial) no longer mattered when children were retested 2 and 4 years later, that is, at the ages of 6 and 8 years, respectively. Thus, although the data base is not extensive at this point, there is some support for the hypothesis that sequential ordering skill may be part of the cause of age differences in memory span.

Summary. Rehearsal, chunking, and sequencing strategies have all received some support as affecting the development of memory span. Even so, there are alternatives to strategies that also enjoy research support as developmental mediators of span improvements.

Speed of Information Processing

There is no doubt that speed of processing generally increases with age during childhood (e.g., Chi, 1977; Keating & Bobbitt, 1978; Spring & Capps, 1974). There are also clearly cut data indicating that speed of item identification is correlated with memory span performance (Case et al., 1982; Chi, 1977; Nicolson, 1981)

Case et al. (1982), in particular, tested whether there was a causal relationship between speed of activation and memory span performance. This was tested by constructing to-be-recalled lists that were composed of materials that were named at the same rate by children and adults. Case et al. (1982) reasoned that if memory span is dependent on speed of naming, then span differences between children and adults should be eliminated with materials that are processed at the same rate by both groups. On the other hand, if span increases are mediated by other factors, then memory span performance should be better for adults than children, even with materials processed at the same speed. Case et al. (1982), in fact, found that with speed of processing equated, children and adults had comparable memory spans. Nicolson (1981) reached a similar conclusion with a sample of 8- to 12-year-old children, reporting no age-related memory span differences when reading speed was equated across age levels.

Consistent with the hypothesis that speech rate is an important determinant of memory span, and that developmental differences in span reflect developmental differences in naming speed, Hulme, Thomson, Muir, and Lawrence (1984); Hulme and Tordoff (1989); Roodenrys, Hulme, and Brown (1993); and Kail and Park (1994) demonstrated relationships between increasing speech rate with development (i.e., ability to say items to be remembered quickly and hence to repeat them more in a given time) and memory span increases with development. For example, in these studies, when subjects had their speech rate slowed by putting longer words on the lists to be remembered (i.e., slowed when thought of as words per unit time), memory span declined as would be expected if speech rate was important in determining capacity. Other variables associated with speech rate, such as duration of words and the amount of pause time between words, also are associated with working memory span as expected (i.e., the slower, the smaller the span) and with development (i.e., shorter durations and pause times with increasing age associated with greater working memory span; Cowan, 1994; Cowan et al., 1994; Cowan, Wood, & Keller, 1995).

Analyses of population differences also support the conclusion that speech rate is an important determinant of short-term capacity: Chen and Stephenson (1988) provided an analysis accounting for digit-span differences between American and Chinese children in terms of naming speed: Chinese digits can be pronounced much more quickly than English digits; the digit spans of Chinese children were longer than the spans of English children. Chen and Stephenson's (1988) analysis ruled out alternative explanations of this cross-cultural difference, such as differences in practice and strategy use between the two cultures (see Geary, Bow-Thomas, Fan, & Siegler, 1993; Stigler, Lee, & Stevenson, 1986, for confirming evidence).

Another impressive illustration of the importance of naming speed for digit span comes from a study by Ellis and Henneley (1980). Ellis and Henneley recruited a sample of children whose first language was Welsh and whose second language was English and assessed their digit spans in both languages. Intraindividual comparisons revealed that significantly higher digit spans were obtained in English, the children's second language, than in Welsh. Although this finding may be surprising at first glance, it is in accord with the results of the Chinese–English comparisons described above in that larger digit spans were found for the language with number words that are more quickly articulated (i.e., English).

Finally, Raine, Hulme, Chadderton, and Bailey (1991) reported reduced verbal short-term memory in speech-disordered children (i.e., slower speaking children) relative to children with normal speech, even when other factors, such as IQ, were controlled. It thus seems likely that speed of item identification (e.g., recognizing a picture or a word) and speed of saying items (i.e., speech rate), or both in combination (Henry & Millar 1991; Kail, 1992a; Kail & Park, 1994; Roodenrys et al., 1993), are important determinants of memory span. Developmental differences in speed can at least partially explain development-correlated span differences. More about this possibility later in this chapter.

Kail's Analyses of Developmental Increases in Speed of Processing

The question of whether there really are structural increases in capacity—that is, more slots—with development rages on in the 1990s, with the alternative being that increases in chunking and speed with development permit more to be packed in each slot. The possibility that there really are developmental increases in fundamental processing capacity is enjoying a renaissance due to a series of analyses by Kail (1988a, 1991, 1992b, 1993).

Basically, Kail observed that with development, there are consistent increases in speed of processing. The increases in speed are so consistent that essentially the same mathematical function relates speed of processing to developmental level for a variety of tasks (e.g., speed of tapping, moving pegs on a pegboard, button release, a simple code-cracking task, mental addition, picture matching). Kail argued that this suggests a common pool of cognitive resources are used to perform the various tasks he has studied, and that pool of resources increases with development.

We are impressed that his basic result has proved so replicable. Kail's interpretation of his finding as indicative of increasing structural capacity with increasing age is an important hypothesis in the middle 1990s, one that requires additional evaluation, however, before it is accepted, with such evaluations challenging. Unfortunately, we are not sanguine that conventional psychological methodologies could resolve the issue of whether there really is an increase in biological capacity with development. More positively, a number of neurophysiological measures are now being refined for use in cognitive investigations, including positron emission tomographic measures of brain functioning, that potentially could be used to address such issues (Detterman, 1994; Pressley with McCormick, 1995, chapter 6).

THE IMPORTANCE OF SHORT-TERM (WORKING) MEMORY IN COGNITION

Short-term memory is the capacity in which conscious processing takes place. The more limited an individual's short-term memory, the more limited the processing that she or he can do.

Individual Differences in Mental Ability

Individual differences in intellectual ability are in fact correlated with differences in short-term and working memory capacities. For example, mentally retarded people perform more poorly on memory-capacity-demanding tasks than people of average intelligence (Hulme & MacKenzie, 1992). So do learning-disabled students relative to normally achieving students (Hulme & MacKenzie, 1992; Siegel & Ryan, 1989; Swanson, 1992, 1993; Swanson & Cooney, 1991). In contrast, gifted students perform better on tasks such as memory span relative to normally achieving students, especially when the task demands memory of materials from their areas of high competence (Dark & Benbow, 1990, 1991). Again, it is impossible to know whether such differences are due to structural differences or processing differences. For example, speed of processing increases going from gifted to normal to intellectually handicapped people (Jensen, 1981; McGarry-Roberts, Stelmack, & Campbell, 1992; Pressley with McCormick, 1995, chapter 18). Yes, these populations also differ in terms of strategies and conceptual knowledge (see Pressley with McCormick, 1995, chapter 18), and thus, there is no end of possibilities in accounting for performance differences on short-term memory demanding tasks between people differing in mental ability!

Performance of Complex Tasks

The performance of a number of complex tasks has proven to depend on short-term capacity. Individual differences in comprehension ability (Carpenter & Just, 1989), both at the sentence level (MacDonald, Just, & Carpenter, 1992) and with respect to longer texts (Daneman & Carpenter, 1989; Schneider & Näslund, 1992), are associated with differences in working memory for verbal material. So are other reading-related competencies, such as decoding skills in children who are learning to read (e.g., Gathercole & Baddeley, 1993, chapter 6; Liberman, Mann, Shankweiler, & Werfelman, 1982), vocabulary development (Gathercole, Willis, Emslie, & Baddeley, 1992), and spelling (Ormrod & Cochran, 1988; Schneider & Näslund, 1992, 1993). Children's abilities to plan drawings (Morra, Moizo, & Scopesi, 1988), reason about moral dilemmas (Stewart & Pascual-Leone, 1992), and reason about categorical relationships (Rabinowitz, Howe, & Lawrence, 1989) all correlate with working memory differences.

Finally, use of capacity-demanding memory strategies depends in part on functional capacity, with the execution of capacity-demanding strategies more certain with increasing age during childhood (e.g., Guttentag, 1989; Kee & Davies, 1988, 1990, 1991; Rabinowitz & Kee, 1994). For example, to test this possibility, Cariglia-Bull and Pressley (1990; Pressley, Cariglia-Bull, Deane, & Schneider, 1987) studied children's ability to execute a capacity-demanding imagery representational strategy for learning of sentences. Whether children benefitted from the imagery instruction (i.e., whether there was an imagery vs. control difference on a memory posttest) depended on children's short-term capacity, as reflected by individual differences in performance on classic memory span tasks (e.g., word span). That is, the imagery versus control difference in performance was only detected when short-term-memory span was relatively high. What should be apparent from the many relationships between capacity and complex performances is that any complete theory of thinking (of any sort) must include short-term capacity as a prominent determinant of successful complex processing (e.g., Kyllonen & Stephens, 1990). Any complete theory of cognitive development must not only describe and explain how capacity changes with development but how developmental changes in capacity interact with other aspects of cognition.

DEVELOPMENTAL IMPROVEMENTS IN EFFICIENT INHIBITION AND RESISTANCE TO INTERFERENCE

It has been known for a very long time that failures to inhibit prepotent responses can interfere with making of other responses. For example, young children often have more difficulties than older children in inhibiting impulsive motor responses that interfere with making of other motor responses (Luria, 1961). Analogously, impulsivity more often is observed in young children's perception and cognition than in older children's behaviors (e.g., in analysis of perceptually similar pictures to match identical pictures; see Meichenbaum, 1977, and Pressley, 1979, for reviews). Many observed that younger children are more distractable than older children; they are more susceptible to task interference from distractions (for a variety of analyses, see Hale & Lewis, 1979). A wide variety of developmental improvements in functioning have been explained by developmental increases in inhibition efficiency and resistance to interference (Bjorklund & Harnishfeger, 1995; Dempster, 1995; Harnishfeger, 1995): These include development improvements in speeded classification (e.g., Strutt, Anderson, & Weil, 1975); selective listening (e.g., Doyle, 1973); Stroop-task performance (e.g., speed of reading the word "blue" when printed in red, speed of reading the word "dog" superimposed on a picture of a cat; e.g., Tipper, Bourque, Anderson, & Brehaut, 1989); selective memory (i.e., memory of material to be learned over material to be ignored when both types of information are presented; Hagen & Kail, 1973); selective attention (e.g., Lane & Pearson, 1982), including selective attention to a context-appropriate meaning of a word with multiple meanings (e.g., Johnson, 1994; Swimney & Prather, 1989); conservation (e.g., Bruner, 1966; Gelman, 1969); and searching (Sophian, Larkin, & Kadane, 1985).

Most relevant here, arguments have been advanced that much of memory development is related to development of cognitive inhibition and resistance to interference. There are three closely related arguments being advanced: (a) Bjorklund and Harnishfeger (1990; Harnishfeger & Bjorklund, 1993) contended that with development, increases in inhibition of task-irrelevant cognitions free up proportionately more of working memory, so that with advancing age more of children's available capacity is devoted to processing of task-relevant information. In support of this position, Harnishfeger and Bjorklund (1993, 1994) analyzed intrusions during children's recall following list learning (i.e., recall of words not on the list). There were clear developmental reductions in such intrusions between the preschool years and Grade 6. (b) Dempster (1991, 1992, 1993, 1995) contended that resistance to interference and distraction improves with development, based on some of the lines of evidence reviewed in the last paragraph. (c) Brainerd and Reyna (1989, 1990a, 1990b, 1993, 1995; Reyna, 1995; Reyna & Brainerd, 1995) contended that developmental improvements in resistance to interference are important because in planning and making responses of all sorts, there are sources of interference. Thus, because verbal recall of a list of words must occur serially (i.e., people can only say one word at a time), the word being said interferes with memory of the other words, and memory of the words in waiting interferes with saying the item being recalled. Thus, for younger children who are very susceptible to interference, recall is really tough due to the interfering crosstalk in the system. Young children's situations are exacerbated because children tend to encode more literally and rely more on verbatim encodings than do older children, who are more likely to construct and rely on fuzzy codings (i.e., gist): Because verbatim traces are more susceptible to interference effects than fuzzy traces according to Brainerd and Reyna, younger children's memories are undermined more by interference than older children's memories. (More about fuzzy trace theory is discussed in the next two chapters.)

Bjorklund, Dempster, Brainerd, and Reyna all believe that much of memory development previously explained by developmental changes in other mechanisms, such as capacity, conceptual knowledge, strategies, and metacognition, actually reflects neuropsychological development related to development of inhibition and resistance to interference. Our view is that at present this claim is simply too strong based on the evidence to date, including the voluminous evidence reviewed in the chapters that follow, that there are other factors that are very important in memory development. Yes, there are developmental improvements in inhibition and resistance to interference. The challenge is to sort out how these improvements both contribute to and may in part be due to developmental changes in short-term capacity, knowledge, strategies, and metacognition.

SUMMARY

Several general conclusions emerge from the data considered in this chapter. As yet, the case is not strong that age-correlated performance increases in memory span should be interpreted as enlargement of some biologically determined capacity. Even if developmental increases in short-term capacity prove to be largely biological, it may have nothing to do with increases in neurological structure. For example, the case seems to be strong and getting stronger that the increasingly efficient execution of operations with development is due in part to developmental increases in processing speed. Such increases may be almost entirely a consequence of structural changes other than structural increases in the number of "memory slots." Also, there are developmental improvements in inhibition that might account some for increases in functional short-term capacity.

As the discussion in subsequent chapters turns to strategies, metacognition, and the knowledge base as determinants of developmental improvements in memory performance, it is important to remember that regardless of whether the actual short-term, explicit memory capacity of the child's biological endowment changes with increasing age, there is no doubt that functional capacity definitely increases with development. Much of the development that is documented in the rest of this book undoubtedly depends on the development of more efficient, basic processing (i.e., better and quicker use of the biologically determined short-term, explicit memory capacity that is available).

Chapter 3

The Knowledge Base

It has been recognized for some time that memory performance is highly dependent on the developing knowledge base. Flavell (1985) eloquently described the situation: "Thus, what the head knows has an enormous effect on what the head learns and remembers. But, of course, what the head knows changes enormously in the course of development, and these changes consequently make for changes in memory behavior" (p. 213).

Long-term knowledge contains information about how to do things (i.e., procedural knowledge) and conceptual facts about the world (declarative knowledge; e.g., Siegler, 1983). Although no exact equivalence exists between procedural knowledge and strategies, the most important types of procedural knowledge considered in this book are memory strategies, which are considered in detail in the next chapter. The concern in this chapter is more on the declarative knowledge base and how it affects memory directly.

THE REPRESENTATION
OF DECLARATIVE KNOWLEDGE

There has been a great deal of work in the last two decades on the nature of declarative knowledge in children. The many alternative conceptions that have been explored are covered in this section.

Concepts

A person's concept of something is his or her understanding of it, which often corresponds to a larger societal conception (Klausmeier, 1990). Concepts can be related hierarchically to other concepts in networks of connections (e.g., Collins & Loftus, 1975; Norman & Rumelhart,1975). Thus, all living things can be subdivided into animals and plants. Animals can be
32

further subdivided into reptiles, mammals, birds, insects and spiders, and so on, each with associated features (e.g., hair, vertebra, warm-bloodedness in mammals).

Classical Piagetian theory included the claim that preschool (preoperational) children experience great difficulties doing tasks that involve classification of hierarchical concepts. Thus, according to Piagetian theory, if a preschooler were given a set of 10 pictures of 7 elephants and 3 bears, he or she would have difficulty with questions such as, "Are there more elephants or animals?" Piagetians assumed that preschooler difficulties with such tasks reflect a lack of understanding of the hierarchical relationship between animals and specific animals (Inhelder & Piaget, 1964).

When children are carefully instructed about what is required in such tasks, however, there is considerable evidence that children can do them (Winer, 1980), at least for familiar classes (e.g., Smith, 1979; Steinberg & Anderson, 1975). One modification that makes a hierarchical classification task easier is to enumerate the objects presented in the problem for the preschooler. Thus, rather than presenting objects as "dogs and cats," with the task of deciding whether there are more "dogs" or "animals," present them as "six dogs and two cats," with the task of deciding whether there are more dogs or animals (Winer, 1974). Another modification is to make certain that the relationship of the concrete objects to both the subordinate and the superordinate categories is apparent. Thus, wooden blocks, painted half red, are more likely to be seen as both "red" blocks and "wooden" blocks than blocks fully painted red, a quality that presumably obscures their woodenness (Tatarsky, 1974). Such problems also are solved better when typical category items are used in the problems than when the problems are posed with atypical category items (e.g., Carson & Abrahamson, 1976; Lane & Hodkin, 1985).

In general, there is substantial evidence that even preschool children possess knowledge about the semantic hierarchical relations between some of the concepts they know. On the other hand, children's categorization and processing of categories is anything but adultlike:

1. There are many reports in the literature of children failing class inclusion problems when unfamiliar concepts are presented.
2. Preschoolers also have difficulties when instructions do not make task requirements obvious.
3. Children's preferred way of representing categorizable content often is not along category lines but with respect to thematic relations they can detect among objects. Thus, when given a group of objects that can be sorted along categorizable lines (e.g., tiger, elephant, monkey, giraffe, banana, orange, grapes, apple), preschoolers often sort along thematic lines (e.g., monkeys eat bananas, elephants and giraffes live in the same house at the zoo, a tiger could eat an apple, mommy puts

oranges and grapes in her fruit salad; e.g., Bruner, Olver, & Green-field, 1966). Such sortings suggest that schematic representations play a large role in children's early knowledge. (See the discussion of schemata later in this chapter.)

4. That children's categories do not always correspond to those of adults is also evident from their underextensions of concepts—using duck to refer only to one's pet duck—and their overextensions—using duck to refer to any bird larger than a robin (Bloom, 1973; Clark, 1973).

5. Children often sort into many more categories than adults do (Saltz, Soller, & Sigel, 1972).

6. Sophisticated studies of children's concepts have revealed striking qualitative differences between the concepts of preschoolers and those of older children and adults. For example, Carey (1985), in an investigation of children's biological knowledge, demonstrated that 10-year-olds' understanding of *animal* included relations between the processes of eating, breathing, growing, dying, and reproducing, whereas 4-year-olds did not understand the criticality of these functions in animals, although they could distinguish animals from nonanimals. Vosniadou and Brewer (1992) demonstrated that many children in Grades 1, 3, and 5 have conceptions of the Earth differing from adults' understanding. Some children viewed it as rectangular, others as a disk, some as a hollow sphere, and others as a flattened sphere.

In summary, although some of children's knowledge probably is in categorical hierarchies like those of adults, many concepts that children hold differ from those of adults. Moreover, children are less likely to rely on hierarchical categorical knowledge than are adults when they are performing tasks that could be mediated by hierarchical knowledge. How development of hierarchical categorical knowledge and its use occurs is not completely understood and is the target of much research (e.g., Markman, 1989). It is known that these developments are due in part to experience, however. For example, Vosniadou and Brewer (1992) observed that as children were exposed to adult conceptions of the Earth, their own conceptions of it changed.

Memory Schemata

Most U.S. 10-year-olds know what goes on at a birthday party. Description of that knowledge in terms of hierarchical concept models, however, would be clumsy and long-winded if it could be done at all. Memory schemata, however, can represent how a number of concepts co-occur in particular situations in orderly relation to one another.

Consider knowledge of birthday parties as Minsky (1975) did. There are certain objects that are always present and actions that always occur. (a) The attendees wear clothes. (b) They bring presents. (c) Games are played. (d) There are decorations. (e) There is a meal. (f) There is a cake. (g) There is ice cream. Items (a) through (g) specify the top level (i.e., the fixed level) of the birthday party frame. Associated with each of the parts of the fixed schema are constraints on how the frame can be filled out. For example, (a) the clothes are usually Sunday best, although simply good clothes sometimes are acceptable. Also, (b) the present must be something that the birthday child would like to receive. It is bought and wrapped in birthday gift wrap.

Nelson, Hudson, Fivush, Bauer, and their colleagues in particular have established that much of children's long-term knowledge of the world is schematic. Not surprisingly, the schemata that children possess are determined by recurring events in their lives. Thus, children have schemata representing events such as dinner (at home and at McDonald's), bedtime, making cookies, birthday parties, and going to a museum (Hudson & Nelson, 1983; Hudson & Shapiro, 1991; McCarthy & Nelson, 1981; Nelson, 1978; Nelson & Gruendel, 1981).

If a child is presented a brief story pertaining to one of his or her schemata, the child can answer inferential questions about the story—that is, he or she can answer questions that require knowledge about the situation described in the text that is over and above the information specified in the text. As an example, consider what happens when a child is questioned about the following short story: "Johnny and his mom and dad were going to McDonald's. Johnny's father told him he could have dessert if he ate all his dinner. They waited in line. They ate their hamburgers. And they had ice cream" (Hudson & Slackman, 1990, p. 378).

When presented the question, "Why did they stand in line?" the 4- to 7-year-olds in the Hudson and Slackman study had no difficulty responding, despite the fact that there was no mention in the story of why they had stood in line. The McDonald's schema—understood by many preschoolers in the United States—contains this information

That schemata can have powerful effects on children's comprehension and memory is evident when preschoolers are presented with stories that are not quite right in that they include information inconsistent with schemata stored by most children. What children do is to make inferences to "fix" the story to be consistent with their schemata (Hudson & Nelson, 1983).

Moreover, children are often willing to accept that some schema-relevant event occurred in a story even though it did not. In Hudson (1988), the 4- to 7-year-olds heard stories about going to McDonald's and grocery shopping. They were then given a recognition test and were asked to discriminate sentences they had heard before from those they had not heard. The most important finding was that the children were quite willing to accept script-relevant sentences that had not been presented in the story as if they had been presented. In short, children have schemata for familiar events that determine how new information is processed, interpreted, and retrieved.

Schemata in Very Young Children.   Children begin to develop schemata early in life (for a review, see Hudson, Fivush, & Kuebli, 1992). A study reported in Fivush (1987) was revealing on this point. Fivush presented 14- and 20-month-old children an array of objects, some of which were consistent with a kitchen schema (i.e., pan, plate, cup, spoon) and some of which were consistent with a bathroom schema (i.e., comb, toothbrush, toothpaste, soap). The children were instructed to play with the objects. The order of touching them was the main dependent variable, which was definitely not random. The majority of the children played with objects associated with only one of the two schemata. About 20% of the sample played with the items for one schema first and then played with the items associated with the other schema.

Bauer and Mandler (1989) presented simple sequences of events to children (e.g., taking a toy bear's shirt off, placing the bear in the tub, and washing the bear). The children were then required to reenact the events both immediately after they were presented and 2 weeks later. Schematically familiar events were better recalled than events not related to schemata possessed by the children. Bauer and Thal (1990) observed that when 2-year-olds recalled naturally orderable sequences that had been presented to them out of sequence, they tended to "correct" the ordering of the information. Data such as these and those reported by Fivush (1987) suggest that children's representations of the world are organized along schematic lines from a very early age and that these schematic relations are very similar to the schematic relations of older children and adults (Bauer & Fivush, 1992).

That said, it must be emphasized that older children have more extensive schematic knowledge, and schemata emerge from repeated experiences in a setting more quickly for older as compared to younger children (Farrar & Goodman, 1992; Fivush, Kuebli, & Clubb, 1992; Price & Goodman, 1990). In addition, many of the scripts possessed by 3- to 4-year-old children are very general, becoming increasingly specific and complete with development (e.g., Adams & Worden, 1986).

Negative Effects of Semantic Schemata on Memory.   Possessing familiar schemata can cause problems in remembering specific events consistent with the schemata. Nelson and Hudson (1988) reported an unpublished study in which they obtained no structural differences between 3- to 5-year-olds' general scripts about birthday parties and their reports about specific birthday parties. Nelson and Hudson argued that this represented a fusion process in memory, a blending of the specific episode with the general script. That this process is not limited to young children is suggested by data reported by Gehringer and Strube (1985). Their study included 10- to 11-year-old students, as well as samples of 18- to 20-year-old adults and 35- to 40-year-old adults. They found that all groups in their study distorted both biographical and autobiographical information to conform to stereotypical scripts, with few and unremarkable developmental differences in the structure of recall.

Schematic Knowledge of Academic Tasks.   Not surprisingly, students develop schemata for recurring intellectual tasks, students' schematic understanding of academic tasks being an arena of great interest to educational psychologists. Both students' knowledge of the schematic structure of stories and their understanding of the schematic structure of common mathematics problems have received attention from developmental and educational psychologists.

Stories have schematic structures that are familiar to readers (Kintsch & Greene, 1978). Mandler (e.g., 1978, 1987) and Stein (Stein & Glenn, 1979; Stein & Nezworski, 1978) have been particularly active in analyzing the structure of stories. According to Mandler's theory, a *story* consists of a setting and an event structure composed of episodes. Each episode has a beginning, which is an event initiating a *complex reaction*; a complex reaction, which is composed of an emotional or cognitive response and a state the protagonist wishes to achieve; a *goal path*, which involves a plan of action by the character and the consequences of setting the plan of action in motion; and an *ending*, which is a reaction.

There are at least four types of evidence that substantiate the existence and psychological importance of story grammar knowledge. First, when stories conform almost perfectly to ideal story grammar forms, developmental differences in recall are fewer than when stories deviate from the ideal structure. In fact, age differences in quantity of recall are striking when story elements are presented in other than canonical order (McClure, Mason, & Barnitz, 1979; Stein & Nezworski, 1978). In contrast, even preschool children are capable of recalling temporal sequences in ideally structured stories (Wimmer, 1980).

Second, stories that do not conform to the story grammar structure are difficult to remember (and are processed more slowly) compared to stories that do conform, with this finding holding for both children and adults (e.g., Kintsch, Mandel, & Kozminsky, 1977; Mandler, 1978; Mandler & Johnson, 1977; Nelson & Gruendel, 1981; Stein & Nezworski, 1978). This conclusion holds not only for text that is heard but also for stories presented on television (e.g., Collins, Wellman, Keniston, & Westby, 1978). Adults who process such stories, however, do seem more able than children to reorder and shuffle the information that they are presented to make the story consistent with story grammar conventions, at least when prompted to do so (e.g., Stein & Nezworski, 1978). Children have a great deal of difficulty reordering story elements in the service of memory (Buss, Yussen, Mathews, Miller, & Rembold, 1983).

Third, when story information is presented originally in an order other than one consistent with conventional story grammar, both children and adults tend to fix the story up at recall to make it consistent with story grammar (Mandler, 1978; Mandler & DeForest, 1979; Stein & Glenn, 1975, 1979). (This is reminiscent of Hudson & Nelson's, 1983, finding, discussed earlier, with respect to semantic schema.) Such structural similarity of story recall in normal children, learning-disabled children, and adults from different cultures (Bower, Black, & Turner, 1979; Nelson, 1978; Mandler, Scribner, Cole, & DeForest, 1980; Weaver & Dickinson, 1984) suggests that certain general structural schemata have universal meaning.

Last, the probability that an element will be recalled from a story varies with the role it plays in the story as defined by story grammar. Thus, major setting, initiating event, and consequence elements are more likely to be recalled than attempts, which are more likely to be recalled than internal responses and reactions (Mandler, 1984; Mandler & DeForest, 1979; Mandler & Johnson, 1977; Stein & Glenn, 1979).

An absolutely critical point is that the development of the story schema occurs in school because of school. Varnhagen, Morrison, and Everall (1994) tested kindergarten and first-grade children who were just old enough to make it into kindergarten or Grade 1, respectively, and other children who just missed entrance into these grades because of their birth dates. These children were tested in the fall and spring of the school year and in the fall of the following school year. This design permits separation of age and schooling effects. At testing, the students were asked to remember simple stories and produce stories as well. Both the recall and production data reflected increasing use of story schemata as a function of schooling independent of age, validating that knowledge and use of story grammar is affected by primary-level schooling.

Besides knowledge of story grammar, students also acquire other schematic knowledge as they proceed through school. Most of the mathematics problems presented in elementary and high school textbooks have typical structures. For instance, Mayer (1982) analyzed high school algebra texts and identified about 100 common problem types. Any Algebra 1 textbook will contain a problem like this one:

If a car travels 10 hours at 30 minutes per hour, how far will it go?

For many Algebra 1 graduates, this problem activates their schemata for "distance = rate × time" problems.

Consider some other examples of problems that are representatives of particular types of problems (all examples from Mayer, Larkin, & Kadane, 1984, pp. 246–247):

If a machine can produce 10 units per hour, how many units can be produced in an 8-hour day? (output = rate × time)

If pencils cost 5 cents apiece, how much will a dozen pencils cost? (total cost = unit cost × number of units)

How much will be earned if $1,000 is invested at 8% interest for 1 year? (interest = interest rate × principal)

Working through those problems has an effect on long-term schematic knowledge of problems. Students who have completed high-school math and science courses have developed schemata for the problem types in these courses. Students completing such courses can classify problems into types (e.g., Hinsley, Hayes, & Simon, 1977). Additionally, students use their problem-solving schemata as they identify what information is critical to process and what is not as part of problem solving (e.g., Hayes, Waterman, & Robinson, 1977; Mayer, 1982; Robinson & Hayes, 1978).

Concluding Comment About Memory Schemata. People have schematic representations about familiar activities and recurring events. These schemata abstract the relationships between different parts of these activities and events. The ability to form schemata and use them in thinking are fundamental human competencies, as suggested by that fact that some schematic representations are available even to very young children, and are used readily by them in many situations. Indeed, the evidence is quite strong that schematic processing in children is much more similar to than it is different from adult schematic processing (e.g., Fabricius, Hodge, & Quinan, 1993).

Case-Based Knowledge

Before there can be a schema, there must be individual cases that include information about concepts, procedures, and how the components of the case are related. There are important differences between memory for specific episodes and what is encoded in schemata.

For example, Fivush, Hudson, and Nelson (1984) studied kindergarten children's memories for a specific trip to a very special museum, one distinguished because it was a museum of archeology. Their memories of the trip to this special museum were contrasted to their general memories of what happens on trips to museums. Memories of the specific museum trip were tapped immediately after the trip occurred, 6 weeks following the trip, and 1 year later. One striking result was that memory of the specific museum trip did not include intrusions from the more general "museum-trip" script nor did events that occurred on the specific trip receive mention when the kindergarten students told about museum trips in general.

We agree with Fivush et al.'s (1984) conclusion that the clear separation of the memory for the specific trip and the general event schema suggests that memory for specific cases and schematic memory are two different types of encodings of information. (This is consistent with the more general theory of memory advanced by Tulving, 1972, that there are episodic memories and more general, semantic memories.) The potential for episodic, case knowledge to have long-term impact on thinking is also supported by these data in that memory of the specific case (especially the ability to recognize specific parts of the museum in a picture recognition task) was still quite good 1 year after the trip to the museum. Indeed, some specifics of the museum trip were remembered even 6 years after the trip occurred (Hudson & Fivush, 1991; see Wagenaar, 1986, for additional evidence that single events are remembered for at least 6 years).

Hudson (1990) provided another interesting study contrasting memory for a specific event, attendance at one session of a creative movement workshop, with more general memory of repeated sessions at the workshop. The participants in the study were nursery school and kindergarten children. Memory of details was better for the workshop immediately proceeding the test trial if only one workshop had been attended rather than four workshops. When four workshops had been attended, the children tended to recall the sequence of events during the workshop better than when only one workshop had been attended. That is, with repeated encounters of the workshop, some general knowledge of relationships between activities during the workshop had been built up, information critical to a schematic representation of such workshops. One cost of this improved memory for sequence with repeated visits to the workshop was that details from Workshops 1, 2, and 3 were misremembered as having occurred during Workshop 4. Once a schema is formed, memory of specific details declines, with an increase in the possibility of interference due to memory of specific happenings on occasions other than the one that is to be remembered in detail.

Verbal and Nonverbal Images

Paivio (e.g., 1971, 1986; especially Clark & Paivio, 1991) posited that knowledge is composed of complex associative networks of verbal and imaginable representations. The verbal system contains wordlike codes for objects and events and abstract ideas, codes that are only arbitrarily related to what they represent (e.g., the word *book* has no physical resemblance to an actual book). The imagery system contains nonverbal representations that retain some resemblance to the perceptions giving rise to them (e.g., an image of a book shares features with the perception of an actual book). These include visual images (e.g., of a bell), auditory images (e.g., the sound of a bell), actions (e.g., ringing motion), skeletal sensations related to emotion (e.g., racing heart), and other nonlinguistic representations. Thus, the imagery representation for a book has visual and tactual qualities associated with books. Verbal representations tend to be sequential, whereas the imagery system can encode a number of features simultaneously. Images can be dynamically transformed, as when you mentally walk around an image of the classroom in which your educational psychology course meets.

Shepard and his colleagues (e.g., Shepard & Metzler, 1971) conducted a particularly telling series of experiments that documented one role of imagery in thinking. They presented their adult subjects with a complex geometric figure and a second figure, which was either the same figure (but rotated 0 to 180 degrees) or a mirror image (also rotated some number of degrees). The task was to decide whether the original figure and the rotation were the "same" figure or "different." The most critical outcome was that the amount of time to recognize that the figure was the same was a linear function of the number of degrees of rotation required to make the figure parallel to the original figure. It was as if the participants were "flipping" the geometric figures in their heads, using some kind of spatial code.

Even 4-year-olds can do such mental flipping. Thus, it takes longer for a 4-year-old to decide that a capital R and an upside down R (i.e., flipped 180 degrees) are the same letter than it takes for the 4-year-old to decide that the R and an R on its side (i.e., flipped 90 degrees) are the same letter (e.g., Marmor, 1975). In general, older children and adults are faster and more adept at mental imagery rotation than younger children (e.g., Kosslyn, Margolis, Barrett, Goldknopf, & Daly, 1990).

Children's images are dynamic. Take a look at the pairs of drawings in each row of Fig. 3.1. Can you mentally combine the paired drawings to produce an object? Most adults can do so, for example, reporting the following images for each of the pairs in Fig. 3.1 (from top to bottom): a skipping rope, a piece of candy, a butterfly, a car, a pipe, a mushroom, a boat, an anchor, and an envelope. Now, suppose you are given the composite objects in the left-hand column of Fig. 3.2, with the request to subtract the portion of the drawing in the right-hand column. What object or objects are left? From top to bottom, adults often report the following: ice creams, fish, bow tie, cloud, pot, vase, bowl, sword, and cross. What is important here is that Brandimonte, Hitch, and Bishop (1992) found that both 6- and 10-year-olds also could combine and subtract picture components using mental imagery, although the 10-year-olds were more successful than the 6-year-olds. Children can juggle mental images in their minds.

Pictorial Effects on Dual Coding.   With children, without a doubt, the most frequent approach to stimulating dual coding is to present pictures along with verbal presentations (e.g., stories with pictures representing the meaning described in text; words and pictures of their referents). The evidence is simply overwhelming that when meaning-redundant pictures accompany verbal materials, learning is greater than when content to be learned is presented verbally only, a result generally interpreted as consistent with dual coding theory (Levie, 1987; Levin, Anglin, & Carney, 1987; Peeck, 1987; Pressley & Miller, 1987). Since those analyses, more evidence has been produced that pictures facilitate children's verbal memory (e.g., Miller & Pressley, 1989; Small, Lovett, & Scher, 1993; Tajika, Taniguchi, Yamamoto, & Mayer, 1988).

Motoric Effects on Dual Coding.   One other method for stimulating children's imagery is through motoric actions (e.g., Cohen, 1989; Piaget & Inhelder, 1971). For example, Wolff and Levin (1972; Wolff, Levin, & Lon-

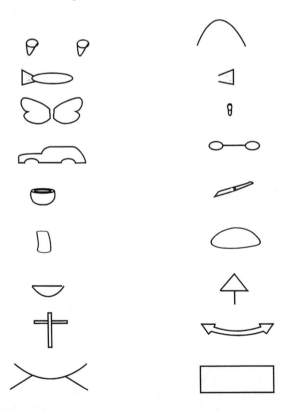

FIG. 3.1. Mental combining task. Slightly modified after Brandimonte, Hitch, and Bishop (1992). Copyright 1982 by Academic Press. Reprinted with permission.

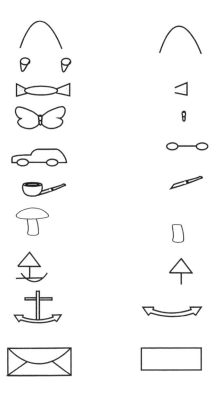

FIG. 3.2. Mental subtraction task. Slightly modified after Brandimonte, Hitch, and Bishop (1992). Copyright 1992 by Academic Press. Reprinted with permission.

gobardi, 1972) hypothesized that imagery instructions might be more effective in the early grade-school years if students were encouraged to act out the elaborative actions preschoolers and kindergarten children were attempting to imagine (e.g., act out with their hands a cow chasing a dog for the paired associate, cow–dog). In fact, imagery and motor instructions combined did increase associative learning at these developmental levels, with Wolff, Levin, and their colleagues concluding that the motoric actions stimulated the development of imagery.

Consistent with Wolff and Levin's thinking, when preschoolers are asked to remember actions, their memory often is better if they carry out the actions rather than simply verbally rehearse the names of the actions (e.g., Heindel & Kose, 1990). The dual-coding explanation of this effect is that hearing the list stimulates a verbal coding; hearing the list and acting it out stimulates verbal and motoric dual coding (Cohen, 1989).

Concluding Comments About Dual Coding.   The case in favor of dual-coding operations (e.g., pictures and words, motor actions and words) as a means of increasing memory is strong. Expect a great deal of future research relevant to dual coding theory, stimulated especially by Kosslyn's (1994) impressive integration of imagery research to date with contemporary directions and themes in neuroscience.

Fuzzy Traces

Brainerd and Reyna (1990b, 1993, 1995) believed that memory representations are on a continuum from literal and verbatim to fuzzy, skeletal, and gistlike. There are multiple memory traces for any event that a person experiences, some of which may be more literal, some of which are very fuzzy, and some of which are somewhere in between. The multiple representations can and often do exist relatively independently of one another.

People extract gist and verbatim information from input they receive, although there is in general a bias more to extract gist than verbatim information and rely on gist in thinking rather than verbatim information. There is increasingly greater encoding of and reliance on gist information relative to verbatim information as development proceeds (i.e., older children encode and rely on gist more than do younger children). The developmental increase in reliance on gist is sensible and adaptive according to Brainerd and Reyna's theory, because fuzzy traces are more easily accessed and used and are less susceptible to interference and forgetting than verbatim traces.

There is some evidence for the developmental shift from reliance on verbatim information to reliance on gist. In one study, Brainerd and Gordon (1994) gave simple numerical problems to preschool and second-grade children. For example, in one problem, children were told that, "Farmer Brown owns many animals. He owns 3 dogs, 5 sheep, 7 chickens, 9 horses, and 11 cows." They were then asked a series of questions, some requiring verbatim knowledge (e.g., "How many chickens does Farmer Brown own, 7 or 5?") and others requiring only gist (e.g., "Which of Farmer Brown's animals are the most, cows or horses?"). Preschoolers performed best on the verbatim questions, whereas second graders did better on the questions requiring knowledge of gist. Although the performance on verbatim questions was equivalent for the kindergarten and second-grade children, the second-grade children outperformed the kindergarten children on the gist questions.

Reyna and Brainerd (1995) interpreted a variety of data from studies of discrimination learning to face recognition to causal inference as reflecting a developmental preference by younger children for verbatim information relative to older children's preference for gist. The advantages for the developing child relying increasingly on fuzzy traces rather than verbatim traces are great according to fuzzy trace theory. Even so, there still is less support for fuzzy trace theory than for most of the other representational theories summarized in this section and less of a broad base of support for the theory.

Concluding Comments

There is evidence that a variety of different types of representations function in thinking. That is, the mind has a variety of types of representations that participate fluidly in interaction with one another as part of skilled thinking. The various representational theories each seem to explain some memory and cognitive phenomena better than other positions. And of course, these representations are not mutually exclusive. For example, there seems to be a lot of imagery in schematic thinking (Sadoski, Paivio, & Goetz, 1991). There seem to be both fuzzier and more verbatim images (Kosslyn, 1994).

PRIOR KNOWLEDGE MEDIATION
OF MEMORY AND LEARNING

Older children know more than younger children in most domains. Age differences in content knowledge can affect memory in three main ways (Bjorklund, 1987). First, it can make specific information more accessible because it is more richly represented and therefore more vivid (Chechile & Richman, 1982; Ghatala, 1984; Lindberg, 1980). Second, a well-developed knowledge base facilitates recall by activating associations among sets of items in long-term memory in a rather effortless, automatic way. The older child's more elaborate semantic knowledge has more associations and stronger associations among items or concepts. Items are more easily accessed because they can be triggered by more stimuli (e.g., Bjorklund & Bjorklund, 1985; Bjorklund & Zeman, 1982). Third, well-developed content knowledge can support use of strategies and metacognitive processes, which in turn help recall (Bjorklund, 1987, 1988; Bjorklund & Harnishfeger, 1990; Frankel & Rollins, 1985; Hasselhorn, 1995; Rabinowitz, 1984; Rabinowitz & Chi, 1987; Schneider, 1986). In support of this third point, a number of studies have shown that children (and adults) more readily acquire and generalize strategies to new sets of materials when more familiar (as opposed to less familiar) stimuli are used (Best, 1993; Bjorklund & Buchanen, 1989; Rabinowitz, Freeman, & Cohen, 1992).

Impact of Expertise

Numerous studies have been conducted on expert–novice differences in various domains such as chess, science, sports, or medicine (for reviews see Ericsson, Krampe, & Tesch-Röemer, 1993; Ericsson & Smith; 1991). Most developmental studies using the expert–novice paradigm focused on the impact of content knowledge on memory. From a developmental perspective, the major advantage of the expert–novice paradigm is that knowledge and chronological age are not necessarily confounded. That is, there are child novices and experts in a variety of domains as well as adult novices and experts in the same domains.

One of the first important findings in the developmental expert–novice literature on knowledge effects on memory was that children learn more when studying "new" information related to their area of expertise than when they study content from an unfamiliar domain. For instance, the second graders in a study by Pearson, Hansen, and Gordon (1979) could be categorized as snake experts or novices. Questions on a short text about snakes dealt with information explicitly presented in text as well as with facts that were only implied in text but could be deduced based on prior knowledge. As expected, the experts answered the questions much better than the novices. The relatively greater superiority of experts on text-implicit questions was considered due to the operation of snake-content schema possessed by the experts but not the novices.

A second dramatic demonstration of the effects of the knowledge base on children's learning was provided by Chi and Koeske (1983). A 5-year-old dinosaur expert was asked to retain two lists of dinosaur names of equal length, one list consisting of familiar names and the other of relatively unfamiliar names. Immediate recall was much better for the list of familiar names. The same pattern of results was found in a posttest about a year later, which Chi and Koeske (1983) interpreted to mean that a direct relationship does indeed exist between the degree of prior knowledge and the ability to memorize.

Other studies contrasting experts and novices have provided additional impressive demonstrations of factual knowledge effects on memory performance. As expected, superior memory performance by experts is almost always limited to areas of expertise, however (Chase & Simon, 1973; Chi, Feltovich, & Glaser, 1980; Chiesi, Spilich, & Voss, 1979). In particular, Chi (1978, 1981, 1985) produced striking developmental data consistent with this conclusion.

Chi (1978) recruited experienced and inexperienced chess players and gave them the task of recalling various chess positions presented to them briefly. The most interesting aspect of this research was that subjects' knowledge correlated negatively with age: The children (average age = 10 yrs) were the experts and the adults were the novices. Although the children performed significantly worse on traditional memory span tests than the adults did, they averaged much better on the chess-related memory tasks. They were able to remember more chess positions correctly, needed fewer trials to reach the learning criteria, and predicted their performance more accurately.

One article in particular (Chi, 1978) has stimulated follow-up studies. With respect to chess expertise, Schneider, Gruber, Gold, and Opwis (1993), summarized in Fig. 3.3, were able to demonstrate that the more a memory task could be mediated by knowledge of chess, the greater the advantage for child and adult chess experts relative to novices. That is, the expert advantage was greatest for memory of meaningful chess positions, next for random presentations of chess pieces on a board, and nonexistent for memory of board positions for another game not related to chess. As in Chi (1978), the expert advantage was also nonexistent for a short-term memory task not involving memory of chess pieces (i.e., digit span). Similar to findings by Roth (1983), no performance differences between adult and child experts were found. Taken together, the chess studies provided evidence that rich content knowledge enables a child to perform like an adult expert and better than an adult novice, showing the disappearance or even reversal of usual developmental trends.

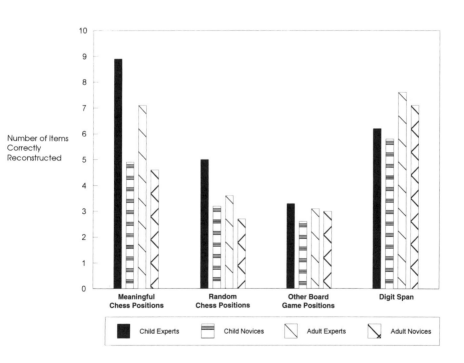

FIG. 3.3. Recall of chess positions, recall of other board
game positions, and digit span.

Prior Knowledge Versus General Intelligence

Schneider, Körkel, Weinert, and their colleagues (e.g., Schneider, Körkel, & Weinert, 1990) provided some of the most detailed research to date on the power of domain-specific knowledge relative to another intellectual factor often considered to be a potent determinant of performance—general intelligence. Schneider, Körkel, and Weinert (1989) and Schneider and Körkel (1989) measured both the soccer expertise and the general intelligence of their participants, in what were studies of text comprehension and memory. The data were absolutely striking. At every age level (between 8 and 12 years of age) and on every measure of comprehension and memory, soccer expertise was associated with high performance compared to the lower performance of soccer novices. Most critically, general intellectual aptitude was not a strong determinant of performance (i.e., overall there was a slight tendency for subjects with high general aptitude to do better than low aptitude subjects, although this was a very small effect, especially compared to the huge effect of soccer expertise).

These results were complemented by Recht and Leslie (1988), who reported that junior high students with high prior knowledge about baseball learned more from reading a passage about baseball than students with low prior knowledge of baseball. In their study, weaker readers with high prior knowledge learned more than otherwise stronger readers who were low in prior knowledge. We emphasize that Schneider, Bjorklund, and their colleagues never dismissed general aptitude as an important determinant of performance much of the time. For example, Schneider and Bjorklund (1992) reported that in list-learning situations, both general intelligence and prior knowledge have effects on recall: In that study soccer expertise predicted recall of lists composed of soccer terms but not recall of nonsoccer lists; intelligence predicted recall of both soccer and nonsoccer lists. Schneider, Bjorklund, and Maier-Brückner (1996) also confirmed main effects of expertise and aptitude, with expertise reducing but not eliminating the relationship of IQ to memory tasks involving deliberate strategies.

Prior Knowledge Versus Interest

One possible explanation of expert–novice differences is that they are actually combinations of greater knowledge and greater interest in the content in question. Experts are both knowledgable and interested in their area of expertise, and there is a literature substantiating that children learn more content when material is interesting to them (Asher, Hymel, & Wigfield, 1978; Belloni & Jongsma, 1978; Bernstein, 1955; Estes & Vaughan, 1973; Stevens, 1980). The small amount of research that does exist in fact suggests that children's interest and knowledge probably both contribute to comprehension and learning of text (Baldwin, Peleg-Bruckner, & McClintock,

1985), and, thus, our suspicion is that work on interest will prove complementary rather than antagonistic to the theoretical position that the knowledge base is an important determinant of memory.

Prior Knowledge Versus Strategy Effects

Many times, older children's recall of information is more organized than younger children's recall, as discussed in considerable detail in chapter 4. One interpretation (e.g., Moely, 1977) of increasingly organized recall with development is that older students are more likely to use strategies intentionally, either to reorganize the input at study, and hence make content to be learned more memorable or to do so at testing to organize their recall. An alternative interpretation (Lange, 1973, 1978) is that the performance and organization increases with development represent nothing more than an expanding and ever more interconnected knowledge base, a more certainly accessible knowledge base with development (see especially Rabinowitz & McAuley, 1990).

Bjorklund (e.g., 1985, 1987) explored this latter possibility in some detail. For instance, Bjorklund and Zeman (1982, 1983) presented 7-, 9-, and 11-year-old children with two structurally similar memory tasks. The subjects were supposed to remember the names of their classmates (class recall task) and memorize and recall a list of taxonomically classifiable items. Subjects of all ages could remember the names of their classmates equally well. Students clustered their recall using seating arrangements, reading groups, and sex, with such clustering comparable at each of the age levels. Because a postrecall interview did not provide much evidence that the children's behavior in the class recall task reflected conscious memory strategies, Bjorklund and Zeman (1982, 1983; also Bjorklund, 1985, 1987) concluded that children's clustering and performance on the class recall task was mostly due to the automatic activation of associative relations (i.e., relations based on seating, reading group, and gender).

In a follow-up study, Bjorklund and Bjorklund (1985) induced subjects to use a specific retrieval strategy (i.e., use seating arrangement to mediate recall). Organizational measures (clustering) were affected by use of this strategy (in fact, organization was maximized). Consistent with other observations that young children can learn some retrieval strategies to a high level of competence with little effort (e.g., an alphabetic retrieval strategy in Chi, 1985), even young children could follow the new retrieval instructions and produced clustering values comparable to those of the older subjects. Nonetheless, there was no improvement in level of recall as a function of use of the strategy. Bjorklund and Bjorklund (1985) argued that this result was consistent with their position that the employment of intentional memory strategies has only a minimal effect on performance in this type of task.

Even so, our view is that much of Bjorklund's research has not been (and could not be) definitive in determining whether increases in memory are due to increasing use of strategies or an expanding knowledge base: Unfortunately, in recall of clusterable lists, there is no pattern of outcomes that would definitely implicate either strategies or automatic use of knowledge-mediated associations and reorganizations, a point Bjorklund acknowledged (Bjorklund & Buchanen, 1989, p. 453). When recall is low, it is always possible that the poor performance reflects failure to use strategies or lack of a knowledge base. When recall is high, it could be due to intentional use of categorization and clustering as a strategy, automatic mediation by the knowledge base, or a combination of strategy and knowledge-base mediation. That is, with increasing knowledge, it may be easier to apply a categorization strategy—the associations between list items and the category label would be stronger and the associations between list members would be stronger and more diverse—and thus, use of the categorization strategy might be more likely (Guttentag, 1984; Guttentag, Ornstein, & Siemens, 1987). Children are more likely to use procedures that are easier to apply rather than procedures that are more difficult to use. That is, the increasing knowledge base increases motivation to use categorization/clustering strategies by reducing the amount of effort required to apply them to lists, a possibility supported by the outcomes in a number of studies (Alexander & Schwanenflugel, 1994; Best, 1993; Best & Ornstein, 1986; Bjorklund, 1988; Bjorklund & Buchanen, 1989; Bjorklund, Schneider, Cassel, & Ashley, 1994; Hasselhorn, 1992; Pritchard, 1990; Rabinowitz, 1988; Rabinowitz et al., 1992). Effective learning is a function of knowledge and strategies. Strategies and other knowledge articulate and interrelate in cognition rather than compete.

Concluding Comments About Prior Knowledge Mediation of Memory

Prior knowledge is certainly a powerful determinant of memory and learning. Knowledge theorists have been interested in determining if knowledge per se is an important determinant of memory relative to other variables. It certainly is a more important determinant of memory than developmental level as indexed by age. Whether it is as clearly separable from general intelligence, interest, and strategy use are somewhat more ambiguous. Our position is that excellent memory involves all of these factors—knowledge, strategies, biologically determined intelligence and capacities, and motivation associated with interest. There is theoretical value in separating these factors, but there is also theoretical value in understanding how they articulate. We hope that the frustrations in separating the effects of these variables will lead to research that illuminates interactions and coordinations between them. Mind is not a horse race among knowledge, strategies, capacity, and motivation but rather a product of a team of horses working together.

WHEN PRIOR KNOWLEDGE DOES NOT AUTOMATICALLY IMPROVE MEMORY AND PERFORMANCE

There is little doubt that prior knowledge affects memory, as we reviewed. Even so, prior knowledge does not automatically participate in cognition in every situation that it could. This point is important to emphasize, for there have been a number of occasions when prior knowledge effects have been less dramatic than they were expected to be.

Limits on Prior Knowledge-Mediated Inferences

Studies of inferential memory by Paris and his colleagues (Paris, 1975, 1978; Paris & Lindauer, 1977, 1982; see also Trabasso & Nicholas, 1980) hypothesized that prior knowledge can affect children's memory. Children in Paris' experiments (e.g., Paris & Carter, 1973; Paris & Lindauer, 1976; Paris & Upton, 1976; Schmidt, Paris, & Stober, 1979) were presented sentences that were followed by memory tests. For example, in a study reported by Paris and Lindauer (1976), 7-, 9-, and 11-year-olds were presented isolated sentences in which instruments either were implied or explicitly stated (e.g., "The workman dug a hole," or, "The workman dug a hole with a shovel"; Experiment 1). At testing, the instruments were provided as cues and participants were required to recall the sentences. For example, *shovel* was the test cue for the workman sentence.

The most important finding was that, with younger children, explicitly stated instruments were more effective retrieval cues than implied instruments; with older children, instruments were equally effective cues for recall of both instrument-explicit and instrument-implicit sentences. Paris and Lindauer concluded that the failure of implied instruments, relative to explicit instruments, to serve as retrieval cues for their younger participants was because the 7-year-olds did not make instrumental inferences at encoding (i.e., online); they also reasoned that implied instruments were as effective test cues as explicit instruments for the older children because they had inferred the instruments at encoding. That is, implied instruments were part of the mental representations of the instrument-implicit sentences for the older but not the younger participants, according to Paris and Lindauer.

Doubts about Paris and Lindauer's (1976, 1977) conclusion that older children make instrumental inferences online arose in light of subsequent empirical analyses of adult retrieval of instrument-reference sentences when given instruments as test cues. Corbett and Dosher (1978) demonstrated, for instance, that even when a low-probability instrument for an action was explicitly stated in a sentence, a high-probability instrument was an effective retrieval cue. The high-probability instrument permitted correct guessing of the sentence verb given its associated instrument, even if the instrument was not present in the original sentence. Moreover, once the verb was recalled, the object of the sentence sometimes followed, in part, because it was also associated with the verb and instrument (e.g., *hole* for *shovel* and *dug*). That is, providing an instrument as a retrieval cue provided a great start at recalling the entire sentence, stimulating offline inferential processing via associative mechanisms. Corbett and Dosher's (1978) analysis, combined with findings that older children more automatically and completely use available retrieval cues (e.g., Kobasigawa, 1977), undermined confidence in Paris and Lindauer's (1976) conclusion that their older subjects made instrumental inferences online. Other analyses of adult learning and memory of instrumental-implicit sentences were also inconsistent with Paris and Lindauer's (1976) analyses and consistent with the possibility that the effects observed by Paris and Lindauer were retrieval rather than encoding effects (e.g., Dosher & Corbett, 1982; McKoon & Ratcliff, 1992; Singer, 1979a, 1979b)

Van Meter and Pressley (1994) re-examined whether spontaneous encoding of instruments occurs when 10- to 14-year- olds read instrument-implicit sentences. Children's online instrumental encoding was tested here using a procedure based on recognition memory priming of instrument words given some of the letters from the words (i.e., a word fragment). The participants in the study either read instrument-implicit sentences or instrument-explicit sentences (e.g., *Her friend swept the floor with a broom*). Half of the participants who were presented instrument-implicit sentences were induced to think of the implied instruments as they the read sentences; the remaining participants simply read the instrument-implicit sentences. At testing, word fragments were presented corresponding to the subjects (e.g., F_ _ _ _ D) and instruments of the sentences (e.g., B _ _ _ M). Following Whitney and Williams-Whitney's (1990) reasoning, Van Meter and Pressley (1994) expected that successful completion of word fragments would be more likely if the children thought about the subjects and instruments when they processed the sentences presented to them. Thinking about a word while processing sentences, either because the word was explicitly presented in the sentences or inferred while the sentence was presented, should prime the subject's recognition of it when fragments of the word are presented on the posttest. In the absence of such priming through prior processing, word fragment completion depends on a participant's ability to locate lexical entries in long-term memory that satisfy the letter constraints specified by the fragment as well as the semantic constraints specified in the directions given to participants at testing.

Thus, Van Meter and Pressley (1994) reasoned that if spontaneous coding of instruments occurs online as certainly and completely as children can make inferences, such as when they are instructed to do so, fragment completion rates should be equally high in implicit-sentence-only and implicit-instrument/induced-to-generate-instruments conditions. Instrument fragment completion in both of these conditions also would be expected to be greater than in the no-exposure control condition. To the extent that online instrumental encoding was not as certain and complete as possible in the implicit sentence-only condition, it would be expected that the instrument fragment completion rate in that condition would be less than in the implicit-instrument/induced-to-generate condition. If no online inferencing occurred in the implicit-sentence-only condition, the instrument fragment completion rate in that condition would be expected not to differ from the chance level of performance (i.e., performance in the no-exposure control condition).

Without instruction to infer the implied instruments, the instrument fragment completion rates never exceeded the guessing rate nor did it approach the level of instrument fragment completion when children were induced to infer instruments and when they read instrument-explicit sentences. In contrast, equivalent recognition of sentence subjects occurred in all of the conditions in which the participants read sentences, so that differences in instrument fragment completion really reflected differences in memory of the instrument. Based on the pattern of outcomes they observed, Van Meter and Pressley (1994) concluded that children's spontaneous generation of instruments was anything but certain by the late elementary- and middle-school grades.

There is little doubt that meaning making during processing of words, sentences, and longer text involves interactions between externally presented information and prior knowledge. In particular, based on prior knowledge, people often construct inferences that go beyond the information they are presented. The point here is that when they do so is situationally constrained, rather than a simple function of development as Paris and his colleagues believed in the 1970s. For example, Casteel (1993) demonstrated that children in Grades 3, 5, and 8 and adults were more likely to generate inferences when they were necessary to understand a text than when they were not. Another situational variable that makes a difference, especially with weaker child readers, is explicit instruction over a number of weeks about how to combine different pieces of information in text to construct higher order meaning (Yuill & Oakhill, 1991).

Limits of Recently Acquired Prior Knowledge on Subsequent Learning

In Brown, Smiley, Day, Townsend, and Lawton (1977, Experiment 2), prior knowledge was developed in children. Some of the second-, fourth-, and sixth-grade participants received information about a topic a week before they were presented a text passage that could be interpreted in light of this information. The memory of even the youngest subjects in the study was affected by this prior-knowledge-building manipulation. Particularly relevant here, the children made many constructive errors in recalling the text passage, making inferences that were consistent with the prior knowledge they had acquired the week before. The presence of relevant prior knowledge clearly affected the children's learning of related but "new" material.

Even so, more recent research has made clear that development of prior knowledge does not lead to certain prior-knowledge-mediated learning and performance. The criterion task in DeMarie-Dreblow (1991) was recall of a list of birds. Before presentation of this list, children (Grades 2–5) in a prior-knowledge-building condition received a great deal of instruction intended to increase their "prior" knowledge about some of the birds that appeared on the subsequently presented list. This was accomplished via videotapes and experimenter explanations about attributes characterizing birds (e.g., type of feet, diet, nesting, migration patterns). This instruction, in fact, did increase subjects' knowledge of the birds taught.

What this knowledge did not do, however, was promote subsequent learning of lists of birds. That is, recall was not increased by the knowledge manipulation. The experimenter monitored whether subjects overtly rehearsed during list presentation, moved the presentation cards around (e.g., to form and use categories), or self-tested. Use of these strategies also was not affected by the knowledge manipulation.

Suggesting that the knowledge manipulation may have been too difficult for young children, DeMarie-Dreblow (1991) replicated the most important features of her study with adults, producing the same results: The knowledge-instruction manipulation increased knowledge but did not affect list learning.

On the face of it, DeMarie-Dreblow's (1991) study might be seen as damaging to the theoretical position that high prior knowledge mediates memory, either through automatic associations to the knowledge base or by enabling the use of strategies (e.g., use of categorizing strategies is only possible if subjects know or can devise categories that differentiate content to be learned). Fortunately, for knowledge theorists, there are alternative interpretations of the data. In order for knowledge related to listed items to make an impact on list learning, that knowledge may need to be learned to a very high degree, sufficient so that associations with the prior knowledge occur automatically rather than with conscious effort. When knowledge has just been acquired, as was the case in DeMarie-Dreblow's study, it may have been that the connections between the newly established knowledge and the birds' names was not so automatic.

Limited Accessing of Prior Knowledge When Trying to Learn New Content

People often do not relate new information that they are intentionally trying to learn to their prior knowledge. Thus, there has been interest in the development of strategies to encourage access and use of prior knowledge during intentional learning. Elaborative interrogation is one strategy for doing so. Studies of elaborative interrogation have involved learning of facts, sometimes embedded in extended texts (see chapter 4, this volume). A main assumption in studies of elaborative interrogation was that people often do not relate content to be learned to their prior knowledge to the extent that they could. The hypothesis was that if people were led to think more fully about facts to be learned, they would activate substantial prior knowledge. Thus, when presented new facts to learn, such as, "The first museum in Canada was in Ontario," subjects in elaborative interrogation conditions have been asked *why*-questions—They have been asked to explain why each fact made sense.

There have now been many demonstrations that elaborative interrogation facilitates factual learning more when children or adults have relevant background knowledge than when they do not, providing confirmation both that people do not activate prior knowledge as much as they might when processing facts to be learned and that for *why*-questioning to work, relevant prior knowledge is critical (Symons & Greene, 1993; Willoughby, Wood, & Khan, 1994; Woloshyn, Wood, & Willoughby, 1994; Wood, Willoughby, Bolger, Younger, & Kaspar, 1993). Extensive prior knowledge used in conjunction with the *why*-questioning strategy, which encourages the activation of prior knowledge related to the to-be-learned factual association, is a winning combination if the goal is to maximize learning. But that is not the whole story, for prior knowledge activation strategies are potentially disastrous if prior knowledge is errant. This situation is discussed in the next subsection.

Limited Effects of Prior Knowledge Activation Strategies

One strategy that is often recommended in the reading literature (e.g., Tierney & Cunningham, 1984) boils down to activating the background knowledge that one has (e.g., as an aid to comprehension and memory of text). When people possess background knowledge that is consistent with the content of the text, there is plenty of reason to expect that prior knowledge activation should increase learning, for at a minimum the reader is thinking "deeply" about the topic of the upcoming text (cf. Rickards, 1976; Rickards & Divesta, 1974; Watts & Anderson, 1971). Not surprisingly, people do remember more that they read if they possess and have activated relevant knowledge (e.g., Anderson & Pearson, 1984; Arnold & Brooks, 1976; Bransford & Johnson, 1972; Brown et al., 1977; Levin & Pressley, 1981; Pearson, Hansen, & Gordon, 1979; Tierney & Cunningham, 1984).

But what if the person does not possess relevant prior knowledge, and in fact, has misconceptions about the topic covered in the text. Positive effects following activation of incorrect prior knowledge is predicted by the theoretical view that information conflicting with prior knowledge and expectations is especially noticeable and noted, and thus, should be especially memorable (e.g., Graesser & Nakamura, 1982; Mandler, 1984; O'Brien & Myers, 1985; Peeck, van den Bosch, & Kreupeling, 1982; Schank, 1982). On the other hand, there is also the possibility of negative effects when a flawed knowledge base is activated. Interference, inferences, and intrusions from flawed prior knowledge can follow (e.g., Anderson & Pearson, 1984; Brown et al., 1977; Lipson, 1982; Pichert & Anderson, 1977; Smith, Readence, & Alvermann, 1984).

A study by Alvermann, Smith, and Readence (1985) illustrates the potential negative impact of activation of errant prior knowledge on children's comprehension and learning from text. Sixth-grade children either activated or did not activate prior knowledge about a passage before reading it. Thus, prior-knowledge-activation subjects who subsequently read a passage about light and heat from the sun (a passage containing information that clashed with prior knowledge typically possessed by sixth-grade students) were first asked to write down all that they knew about the topic. After writing the essay, the subjects read the text. Following completion of reading, subjects were first asked to write down everything that they could remember from the passage and then were given 10 multiple-choice questions, some of which were explicitly designed to contain foils consistent with misconceptions about light and heat from the sun possessed by sixth-grade students (determined by pilot testing). Procedures in the nonactivation condition were identical to those in the activation condition, except that there was no essay writing before reading.

The outcomes were rather striking in Alvermann et al. (1985). Free recall of the text was better when children did not activate the prior knowledge. Specifically, there was significantly less recall of text ideas that were incompatible with sixth-grade children's prior knowledge, and a trend toward less recall of the remainder of the passage (our reanalyses). In addition, multiple-choice questions that included misconception foils were less likely to be answered correctly in the prior-knowledge-activation condition. When contrasted to the positive effects produced by congruent prior knowledge in other studies, Alvermann et al.'s (1985) data make clear that prior knowledge activation is a double-edged sword. Activation of misconceptions can significantly interfere with learning of objectively more correct perspectives.

But it does not have to be that way. When errant prior knowledge is activated in the service of understanding why alternative information is more valid than errant prior knowledge, such activation can be part of the process of increasing learning. Woloshyn, Paivio, and Pressley (1994) presented students in Grades 6 and 7 with scientific facts, some of which were consistent with the prior knowledge of students in Grades 6 and 7 and some of which were much less likely to be consistent with their prior knowledge (i.e., based on a preliminary norming study). The students were given four consistent and four inconsistent facts for each of four topics—the solar system, plants, animals, and the circulatory system. For example, a prior-knowledge-consistent fact about the solar system was, "Although some people think that the size of a star is always the same, the size changes." A prior-knowledge-inconsistent fact about the solar system was, "In space, the sun's heat cannot even roast a potato."

The participants in Woloshyn et al. (1994) either attempted to learn the facts presented to them using elaborative interrogation, asking themselves why the fact as presented made sense, or read the fact over and over for the entire time it was presented. The positive effects of elaborative interrogation were consistent across a number of measures—recall and recognition, immediate and delayed (i.e., up to 6 months!). It seems that with children, how inconsistent prior knowledge affects learning depends on how it is activated and related to the to-be-learned information. We suspect that there will be more research on the acquisition of new information when the learner possesses inconsistent prior knowledge, for it is apparent that both children and adults often have misconceptions related to content they are expected to learn, such as much science content (e.g., Anderson, 1987).

Concluding Comments About Limits on the Benefits of Prior Knowledge

Available prior knowledge is not always accessed when it could be used. Sometimes this is a negative, as when activated prior knowledge can increase learning. Sometimes this is a positive, as when learners fail to think about prior misconceptions that clash with ideas they are now trying to learn. Many times in research on prior knowledge, interaction effects, typically between strategies and prior knowledge, and situational effects have been detected. Knowledge effects are not simply a matter of having knowledge or not having it, with the emphasis in this section that prior knowledge use is often not an automatic part of cognition.

CONCLUDING COMMENTS

Taken as a whole, the results in this chapter provide impressive evidence that a child's knowledge base can have a great effect on memory and performance, even though prior knowledge is not always used automatically.

There are many challenges that remain in elucidating knowledge-based effects, however. For instance, as the knowledge base develops, there are more concepts (even though they may be fuzzier, if Brainerd and Reyna were correct) and stronger interconnections between concepts, and thus, long-term memory should be more accessible with increasing age. With increased accessibility, both automatic and strategic processes should be facilitated, with the developmental dynamics of such increasing facility in processing not understood well at this point.

Conscious and systematic search of long-term memory for possible knowledge that could mediate memory is an important learning strategy (e.g., elaborative interrogation). That knowledge access often depends on strategy highlights that it is wrong to think of effective thinking as due either to knowledge or strategies. Thinking often involves articulation of knowledge and strategies but not always, for many of the effects reviewed in this chapter probably were mediated rather directly by the knowledge base, with conscious use of strategies playing a minor role. This subject is really much more complicated than it has been construed in the past, when theorists claimed that effective learning and memory was due either to strategies or knowledge alone.

Chapter 4

Strategies

The pioneering work of Flavell (e.g., 1970) and his associates especially stimulated research on information processing in children. They particularly focused on conscious and intentional memory activities, studying two potential difficulties in particularly great detail. One possibility was that young children do not produce strategies that can effectively promote learning (i.e., they have a production deficiency). Alternatively, children might produce strategies when learning, but the strategies would fail to facilitate performance as they do for older children and adults (i.e., the children would have a mediational deficiency; Reese, 1962).

The usefulness of the distinction between production and mediation deficiencies was apparent in Keeney, Cannizzo, and Flavell (1967). First, it was determined that some Grade 1 children used a verbal rehearsal strategy during list learning, whereas other Grade 1 children failed to do so. Memory was clearly better for the children who produced the rehearsal strategy. When the production-deficient children were taught the rehearsal strategy, their memory improved dramatically, however. Thus, the children who failed to use the strategy spontaneously had a production deficiency but not a mediation deficiency.

Moely, Olson, Halwes, and Flavell (1969) also demonstrated a production deficiency in grade-school children. In this case, kindergarten, first-, and third-grade children failed to use a sorting–clustering strategy when learning lists of potentially categorizable pictures. Again, it proved possible to teach the strategy to these children. As in Keeney et al., there were consistent correlations between use of the sorting–clustering strategy and memory performance.

The conclusion that was reached following these early experiments was that memory could primarily be understood as a transition from nonstrategic to strategic behavior. Age of "spontaneous" strategy use seemed to vary (e.g., rehearsal strategies appeared developmentally earlier than sorting–clustering strategies). It was profitable, however, to instruct children who did not use strategies on their own to execute them. However, it was apparent even in these early studies that continued use of strategies was not an automatic byproduct of instruction.

These findings stimulated a great deal of follow-up work. The developmental psychology of memory that followed was dominated by studies assessing the use and significance of strategies, the role of the knowledge base in memory and strategy use, and the relationship of strategy use to knowledge of memory (i.e., metamemory). Brown (1975) laid out five generalizations about memory development research, relying on dichotomous distinctions that seemed to characterize the work:

1. Although there were experiments on both intentional and incidental learning, research on intentional learning predominated.
2. Although memory development was sometimes studied as a means to an end following Soviet suggestions (e.g., Smirnov & Zinchenko, 1969), more often it was studied as an end in itself.
3. Most studies were of exact recall, although there were investigations of inexact recall (e.g., gist recall of text), involving constructive errors that reflected the learner's knowledge base.
4. The effects of strategies that produced "deep" compared to "shallow" comprehension were assessed (e.g., Craik & Lockhart, 1972), although this problem did not command the attention that it did in the adult literature.
5. Although the difference between memory for particular episodes versus semantic memory (memory of definitions, concepts, relationships that is not tied to memory of particular exemplars of the concepts or relationships) was recognized, following Tulving's (e.g., 1972) lead, most of the developmental work on memory strategies focused on episodic memory.

Since Flavell's seminal work, there has been an enormous amount of research on children's use of memory strategies. It is certainly not possible to review all of this work. The tactic that we take in this chapter is to review several important directions in strategic research, ones that went far in defining the study of memory strategies for the past 30 years.

STRATEGIC BEHAVIORS IN VERY YOUNG CHILDREN

We know much more about strategy use by school-age children than of that by preschoolers. In part this is because the early U.S. work (e.g., Hagen & Kingsley, 1968; Keeney et al., 1967) and Soviet research (e.g., Yendovitskaya, 1971) provided little evidence that intentional, strategic memorizing occurred before 6 years of age. In fact, it is fairly easy to produce data consistent with the conclusion by using the "modal memory" study model

(Brown & DeLoache, 1978; DeLoache, 1980). That approach involves presenting a sample of very young children with a memory task that is composed of unfamiliar materials that are presented in an unfamiliar context. In general, researchers have used the nonstrategic behavior produced by preschoolers in such situations as a baseline against which the progress of older subjects has been demonstrated. Recall in preschoolers has been studied with retrieval-of-hidden objects, memory-for-events, and memory-for-objects paradigms (Daehler & Greco, 1985). The main issue addressed in these studies was whether, and at which age, conscious, intentional memory activities are observable in very young children.

Retrieval of Hidden Objects

Two different research strategies have been used to study memory for location in small children. The first is composed of "naturalistic" studies, which are based on daily observations that are recorded in diaries or observation protocols. In general, these studies provided evidence of strategic behavior early in life. For example, when Ashmead and Perlmutter (1980) analyzed entries in mothers' diaries, they found evidence of development between 7 and 11 months of age. The younger children were observed remembering the locations of objects that had relatively fixed positions (e.g., telephone, closet). Older subjects were better able to recall objects with changing positions. Nelson and Ross (1980) also used the diary method and determined that toddlers (who just turned 2) employed more intentional memory activities for recall of events than for the location of meaningful objects. The older children were able to recall both objects and events accurately after a relatively long period of time (i.e., up to 3 months).

The second method of studying retrieval with young children is the "delayed reaction," or "hide-and-seek," task (DeLoache, 1984). In its simplest form, the child first observes an object being hidden. After a period of time that is filled with other activities, the child is requested to locate the hidden object. Using this approach, Perlmutter and her associates provided demonstrations that 2- to 3-year-olds make use of retrieval cues under certain conditions.

For instance, Blair, Perlmutter, and Myers (1978) showed children colored pictures one at a time. Then the picture was hidden in one of nine drawers in a small filing cabinet. In the retrieval-cue conditions, another picture of another object was attached to the front of the relevant drawer. In the control condition, no picture was attached to the front of the drawer. The children then looked away from the filing cabinets for 25 seconds before attempting to retrieve the hidden picture. Provision of a retrieval cue aided the search of the 27- to 45-month-old participants in the study. Perlmutter et al. (1981) obtained comparable results in a similar paradigm and concluded that even 2-year-olds can use picture cues to encode location and search for objects.

One of the most impressive studies of preschoolers' use of retrieval cues was conducted by Ritter, Kaprove, Fitch, and Flavell (1973), who demonstrated that younger preschool children's (i.e., 3-year-olds') effective use of retrieval cues occurred only when the task was very simple. They observed substantial development of retrieval cue use during the preschool years. In Ritter et al. (1973) the test material consisted of six pictures of people (e.g., a soccer player) and six small toys (e.g., a soccer ball)—each person was functionally related to one of the toys. The 3- to 5-year-old subjects watched as each person entered one of six houses and put his or her toy in a box with the toy in the box visible at all times. In contrast, the people were placed out of sight in the house. The child's task was to show a "twin" of each person (six pictures identical to the six people pictures that were hidden) the way to their partner. After this task, all materials were removed except for a single set of people pictures that were placed face down in front of the child. The children were then asked to recall the names of the toys. The children were free to use the picture retrieval cues if they chose to do so. The majority of children at each age level made use of the visible toys as retrieval cues during the first task, with no striking age differences. The second task yielded a clear developmental pattern, however. Approximately 20% of the 3-year-olds turned over the pictures of the people and used them as retrieval cues. In contrast, about 75% of the 5-year-olds used this device. Geis and Lange (1976) and Schneider and Sodian (1988) generated results complementary to Ritter et al. (1973).

It is one thing to use retrieval cues that are provided. It is quite another for children to prepare for retrieval themselves. Ritter (1978) conducted a now classic study that is relevant to this point. The task was to prepare to find a piece of candy hidden in one cup on a turntable containing six cups. Paper clips and gold stars that could potentially be used to mark the relevant cup were placed near the turntable. The children were aware of the memory requirement and of the fact that they would have to close their eyes as the turntable was spun. Each child was then given an opportunity to retrieve the candy.

After placing the candy in the cup but before spinning the turntable, the experimenter asked each child, "Is there something you can do to help you find the candy right away?"Using the paper clips or gold stars to mark the appropriate cup was defined as spontaneous preparation for retrieval. If a child failed to mark the cup following this nondirective question, graded prompts were provided to induce preparation for later retrieval. The least explicit of these consisted of the experimenter pointing to the clips and stars and saying, "Can these help you to find the candy right away?" A slightly more explicit prompt consisted of the experimenter pointing to the clips and stars and commenting, "Can you use these over here to help you find the candy right away?" More explicit still was the experimenter putting a marker on the cup and asking, "Will this help you find the candy right away?" and "Do you want to leave the marker there or put it some other place?"

Although Grade 3 subjects placed the retrieval cues spontaneously without prompting to do so, all preschoolers required prompting, with 3-year-olds needing more than 5-year-olds. Although all Grade 3 participants and 90% of the older preschoolers (4½ to 5½ years old) used the retrieval cues at testing to find the candies, approximately one third of the younger preschoolers (3 to 4½ years old) failed to prepare retrieval cues given even the most explicit prompting. Others (Beal & Fleisig, 1987; Sodian & Schneider, 1990; Whittaker, McShane, & Dunn, 1985) have produced data generally confirming the pattern of outcomes reported by Ritter (1978).

In interpreting the retrieval results presented thus far, we point out that looking for coins under a cup (as well as most of the other laboratory tasks used in these investigations) is not a particularly common behavior for children, and it might be expected that greater strategic activity would be obtained with more naturalistically valid search tasks. A study by De-Loache, Cassidy, and Brown (1985) is particularly interesting in this regard, offering evidence that precursors of strategic behavior in location tasks are observable in children between 18 and 24 months of age. The most important data were collected between the hiding of a Big Bird doll by an experimenter (e.g., under a pillow in the living room where the study took place) and the time when the children were asked to retrieve the toy from the hiding place. Although the children were occupied with very attractive toys during this interval, they frequently interrupted their activities to look at the hiding place, to point at it, or to repeat the name of the hidden object. A follow-up study provided data making clear that these were actually memory-related activities. In that study, when Big Bird was placed in the environment, but not hidden (e.g., put on top of a pillow in sight of the child) so that no remembering was required to retrieve the doll, few orienting behaviors occurred.

The DeLoache et al. (1985) data support the hypothesis that children as young as 2 years of age can use rudimentary memory strategies. These strategic behaviors were only observed in tasks with very simple structures, however. With harder tasks, intentional preparation for retrieval is not observed until later. Consider a study by Wellman, Ritter, and Flavell (1975). The goal in that study was to remember where an object was hidden—under one of three identical cups—from the time an experimenter left the room until her return. Three-year-olds but not 2-year-olds exhibited what appeared to be consciously intentional memory behaviors including watching and touching the correct cup. In fact, 3-year-olds seem to be strategic across various types of hide-and-seek games and location tasks (e.g., Haake, Somerville, & Wellman, 1980; Wellman & Somerville, 1982; Wellman, Somerville, & Haake, 1979).

Memory for Future Events

As was reviewed in chapters 1 and 3 (this volume), young children often remember events without intending to do so by developing schemata for familiar events. In contrast, Somerville, Wellman, and Cultice (1983) studied children's prospective memory for everyday activities in an effort to find deliberate memory behavior by preschoolers. Parents cooperated in this study of 2- to 4-year-olds. The parents instructed their children to carry out a particular activity at a specified future time. The event to be remembered was either one that was highly interesting and appealing to the child (e.g., getting candy) or one that would be of little interest to the child. The child either had to remember the event for a short period of time or for a long time. There was better memory at all age levels in the study for the interesting event and when the time interval was short, with the interest variable having a greater impact on performance. There were no significant effects in Somerville et al. that involved the age factor, suggesting that even 2-year-olds are capable of intentional memory, at least when given an interesting event to remember. (See Renninger & Wozniak, 1985, for complementary evidence documenting that interesting stimuli can prompt deliberate memory behaviors in young children.)

Memory for Lists of Objects, Pictures, and Words

Intentional memory strategies in young children can be inferred when encoding behaviors occur following instructions that indicate a future memory requirement, and the same behaviors do not occur following instructions that do not indicate that a memory test will occur (i.e., following intentional but not incidental learning instructions; Wellman, 1977a). One of the earliest studies with an intentional versus incidental instructional manipulation was reported by Appel et al. (1972). They observed no differences in the behaviors of preschoolers who were provided intentional versus incidental learning instructions (a result generally comparable to some of the Soviet data discussed in chapter 2, this volume). Appel et al.'s (1972) initial study of the differentiation hypothesis stimulated a number of follow-up studies (e.g., Galbraith, Olsen, Duerden, & Harris, 1982; Yussen, Gagné, Gargiulo, & Kunen, 1974; Yussen, Kunen, & Buss, 1975). In contrast to Appel et al. (1972), there was clear differentiation between intentional and incidental learning situations throughout childhood in most of these follow-up investigations, most critically, even with preschoolers.

    Baker-Ward, Ornstein, and Holden (1984) offered especially convincing evidence that preschoolers consciously memorize. Children in that experiment were presented either memory-neutral (play) or memory-relevant instructions. The subjects in the two play conditions were given no indication that they would have to recall information later. Children in the memory condition were informed that they could play with the toys awhile, but they should also do all that they could to remember a specified subsample of the toys (i.e., the items to be remembered). Subjects in the memory condition played significantly less than subjects in the play condition. Children in the memory condition were more likely than play subjects to name the objects to be remembered or to look at them intensely. These differences in the frequency of memory-related behaviors as a function of experimental condition were found at all age levels and increased with age. These memory-related behaviors affected the recall only of the 6-year-olds in the study, however. Baker-Ward et al. (1984) speculated that this might be because the newly learned strategies were not routinized to the point that they could actually be useful to subjects.

That there is not a strong relationship between the strategies preschoolers use during list learning and their subsequent recall was confirmed by Lange, MacKinnon, and Nida (1989). They presented 3- and 4-year-old children with lists of items to learn and observed the strategies used by the children to learn them. In general, the correlations between use of strategies and recall were low. For instance, the highest was for visual inspection of the items to be learned and it was only $r = .27$, a very modest relationship at best. Even when data were aggregated over strategies so that children were coded for any use of strategies compared to no use of them, the correlation between being a strategy user and recall was modest, $r = .41$. At least all of these correlations were in the right direction, with strategy use associated with at least slightly increased memory performance, although it is not always so.

Some researchers reported that preschoolers can elect strategies that actually impair their performances relative to how much they would remember if they were not intentionally trying to remember the material. Newman (1990) used a task and design very similar to the one in Baker-Ward et al.'s (1984) study. Moreover, the 4-year-olds in Newman's study evidenced the same strategies when asked to remember that Baker-Ward et al.'s (1984) subjects had. The difference was that the preschoolers in Newman's study in the memory condition remembered less on the subsequent test than preschoolers in the play condition. What was going on in the play condition? The children were creating verbal stories and constructing interactions between the toys. Taking unrelated objects and placing them in a meaningful context, such as a story that sensibly relates them or a picture that integrates them, facilitates memory (e.g., such stories and pictures are elaborations; Levin, 1976; Rohwer, 1973). Children who were asked to remember the items applied rote procedures, such as rehearsing the items and repeatedly looking at them, procedures that are known to be less efficient in learning lists than other procedures (Levin, 1976; Rohwer, 1973). Sometimes preschoolers elect to use strategies that actually impair their performance. See Rogoff and Mistry (1985) for additional evidence that young children often overgeneralize rote learning procedures that lead them to neglect meaningful connections in to-be-learned materials that can increase learning if only they are processed meaningfully, rather than by rote rehearsal. (Later in this chapter, we return to discussion of occasions when children use strategies without memorial benefits, when children manifest utilization deficiencies.)

Summary

Many strategic behaviors have been identified in preschoolers, behaviors that indicate self-directed, goal-oriented actions. These behaviors are especially obvious when children are studied in familiar surroundings and with familiar tasks (characteristic of many of the studies considered in this section). Even though preschoolers have some strategic skills, the ones they possess are extremely limited in scope of application. Overall, recent studies on preschoolers' memory have shown effective strategies, no strategies, and "faulty strategies" (i.e., strategic behaviors that do not help remembering; see Wellman, 1988) in young children. In the current trend to demonstrate the early emergence of memory strategies, we should not overlook the obvious fact that older school-age children are able to show their memory skills in a wider range of situations than preschoolers, including laboratory tasks. In the sections that follow, we examine these skills in more detail.

DEVELOPMENT OF AN ENCODING STRATEGY: REHEARSAL

Rehearsal has been studied very intensely by developmental psychologists, beginning with Flavell, Beach, and Chinsky (1966). They studied list learning by 5-, 7-, and 10-year-olds. The children wore space helmets while they prepared for serial recall of picture lists. The helmets were constructed so that the experimenter could see the child's mouth and thus determine if the child was verbally rehearsing the materials as they were presented. Only a very few 5-year-olds displayed multiple-item rehearsal strategies; in contrast, most of the oldest participants cumulatively rehearsed the list items.

Direct measurement of rehearsal was complemented in Flavell et al. (1966) and in other studies by less direct indicators of cumulative rehearsal. The most important of these was analysis of recall by serial position in the list. When especially good recall occurred for items early in the list (primacy effect), rehearsal processes were assumed (Belmont & Butterfield, 1977; Hagen & Stanovich, 1977). Primacy effects were generally not found when preschoolers and younger school children were left to their own devices to learn material. It is, however, relatively easy to evoke primacy in these nonproducers by training them to use rehearsal strategies (Gruenenfelder

& Borkowski, 1975; Hagen & Kingsley, 1968; Hagen, Hargrave, & Ross, 1973; Keeney et al., 1967; Kingsley & Hagen, 1969). Clear primacy during uninstructed learning can be observed from about 8 to 10 years of age.

In addition to correlations between primacy effects, use of rehearsal, and age, researchers who were interested in rehearsal were able to confirm a causal link between rehearsal and primacy through experimental manipulations. For instance, primacy effects are reduced among older but not among younger children when rehearsal opportunities are limited by time constraints (Allik & Siegel, 1976; Hagen & Kail, 1973).

Other measures of input activity also supported the conclusion that rehearsal develops. For example, one of the most important of these involved analyses of subjects' pauses while they studied (Ashcraft & Kellas, 1974; Belmont & Butterfield, 1969, 1971). Although 13-year-olds in Belmont and Butterfield's study displayed progressively longer pause times with the presentation of each new item on a serial list, pause times were more uniform as a function of list position with younger children (i.e., 9-year-olds). It was inferred from these results that the older subjects used an active, cumulative rehearsal strategy but that the younger subjects probably did little more than verbally label individual items as they were presented.

Ornstein, Naus, and Liberty (1975) made a detailed study of qualitative differences in the rehearsal of third, sixth, and eighth graders. The subjects were instructed to rehearse serial list items out loud, with 5 seconds provided between the presentation of each item. The typical age effects for serial recall were obtained. Older subjects both recalled more items and exhibited a primacy effect. In contrast, there were no age differences in the total amount of rehearsal nor was the correlation between amount of rehearsal and recall very large. Qualitative analyses of the rehearsal sets, however, were much more informative, with a rehearsal set defined as the number of items rehearsed together. Third graders tended to rehearse single items (rote repetition). The older subjects, however, put more items together in each rehearsal set. Ornstein et al. (1975) argued that older subjects' active rehearsal accounted for both their greater recall and the primacy effect that was obtained in their data.

Naus, Ornstein, and Aivano (1977) provided clear evidence that the difference in rehearsal set size between third graders and older children reflected a production deficiency. When they trained third graders to use three-item rehearsal sets, third graders displayed the primacy effect typical of older children. In addition, their recall was approximately at the level of Grade 6 children (also Ornstein, Naus, & Stone, 1977). A more thorough analysis of the third-grade students' rehearsal revealed more rigidity in the younger subjects than in older children, however, with younger children tending to form a single three-item set following each item and repeating it until the next item was presented. Older children tended to vary their three-item sets more.

When all of the relevant data are considered, it seems that the essential difference between the memorization processes of younger compared to older children are qualitative rather than quantitative. With development, passive one-word memorization strategies are replaced by cumulative rehearsal strategies, with the number of different items in a rehearsal set eventually reaching three or four (Ornstein & Naus, 1978). These cross-sectional results were complemented by longitudinal analyses in which the same trends in the development of rehearsal were noted (Guttentag et al., 1987; Kunzinger, 1985). All of the relevant data suggest that developmental increases in active, cumulative rehearsal play a crucial role in the explanation of age differences in free and serial recall tasks.

Possible Explanations of Young Children's Failures to Use Rehearsal Strategies

Studies of the content of older children's rehearsal sets reveals that better retention occurs when items are produced in groups that include both recently encountered items and items from earlier list positions (Cuvo, 1974, 1975; i.e., when rehearsal is cumulative). An interesting observation by Cuvo (1974) was that older school children and college students were more likely to include items that they liked in cumulative rehearsal sets. They focused on these items and that seemed to result in them being rehearsed more. Thus, one possible explanation of cumulative rehearsal is that *motivation* plays a role.

Kunzinger and Witryol (1984) believed that motivational stimulation of items would also affect younger children who normally prefer passive rehearsal strategies. They believed that the younger children might be motivated to pay more attention to the items that they were interested in. Motivation was manipulated by assigning a monetary value to items on the list, with some worth 1¢ and others worth 10¢. The second graders in the study were told that they would receive the amount of money associated with the items that were recalled later. In the control group, 5¢ was associated with each item. There were important differences in recall between the experimental and control conditions. The size of the rehearsal sets was doubled in the experimental condition to an average of more than two highly valued items. There was also a clear primacy effect in the experimental condition. The differential motivation condition thus produced effects that are compatible with those of direct training procedures (Ornstein et al., 1977).

A second hypothesis is that specific prior knowledge can activate memory strategies (Bjorklund, 1985, 1987; Chi, 1978, 1985; Naus & Ornstein, 1983; Ornstein & Naus, 1985; Schneider, 1993). Older children's cumulative rehearsal may be tied to the development of semantic memory, with older children having more concepts and interconceptual associations to trigger use of strategies. Tarkin, Myers, and Ornstein (reported in Ornstein & Naus, 1985) tested this hypothesis directly, examining the influence of the knowledge base on the rehearsal activities of young children. Eight-year-olds were presented word lists that varied in their meaningfulness and familiarity to children (even the least meaningful words, however, were known by all children). The children displayed age-typical rehearsal (i.e., fewer than two items per rehearsal set) for nonmeaningful items. In contrast, the learning sets for meaningful items contained more than three items. Memorization behavior with meaningful materials was comparable to the behavior of 11- to 12-year-olds with normal word lists (Ornstein & Naus, 1985). Highly meaningful stimulus materials make rehearsal processes and retrieval easier in that the learner profits from associations between the individual items that are activated automatically. Ornstein and Naus (1985) also demonstrated in a second example (the comparison of adult football experts and novices) that especially meaningful material increases the size of rehearsal sets. The familiarity of material seems to be an important determinant of use of more efficient and effective rehearsal procedures.

Guttentag (1984, 1985) proposed that young children do not employ cumulative rehearsal strategies spontaneously because the *mental effort* required to do so strains their functional capacity. Guttentag studied this hypothesis with a dual-task procedure (see the earlier discussions in chapters 3 and 4, this volume). In addition to rehearsing to-be-recalled items overtly, subjects simultaneously performed key tapping. The subjects were informed that rehearsing was the more important task, although they should try to do both at once. Mental effort was operationalized as the interference on key tapping produced by cumulative rehearsal. Interference was measured as the difference between normal tapping during a baseline period when simultaneous rehearsal was not required and tapping during rehearsal.

In Guttentag's first experiment, second, third, and sixth graders were instructed to employ the overt cumulative rehearsal strategy and to perform the motor task simultaneously. Even the youngest subjects were able to do this with no age differences in performance. There were, however, significant differences in the degree of interference experienced. Motoric performance was clearly disrupted more when younger children rehearsed compared to when older children did so. There were no age differences in interference when children were instructed to rehearse passively, however (Experiment 2). Based on these data, Guttentag (1984, 1985) argued that age differences in spontaneous use of cumulative rehearsal strategies may in part be due to the enormous effort required of young children in order to employ complex strategies. See Bjorklund and Harnishfeger (1987) and Kee and Davies (1988, 1991) for similar findings concerning the role of mental effort in the use of categorization strategies and elaboration strategies, respectively.

A study conducted by Ornstein, Medlin, Stone, and Naus (1985) is interesting because not only does it confirm the interference detected by

Guttentag, but it also provides a more exact analysis of the components of cumulative rehearsal that pose special difficulties for younger grade-school children (i.e., those that cause the mental effort). Ornstein et al. (1985) demonstrated that the efficiency of cumulative rehearsal improved considerably when second graders were provided additional visual cues as they rehearsed, that is, when previously presented items continued to be visible (thus, reducing the pressure on working memory to hold previously presented material in consciousness). It was clear in this study that cumulative rehearsal was easier for second graders given the visual cues: With the visual cues, they cumulatively rehearsed almost five items per set in response to the cumulative rehearsal instruction compared to about three items per set given the cumulative rehearsal instruction without pictorial support. Guttentag et al. (1987) used a similar manipulation and produced complementary data with children in Grades 3, 4, and 6.

Summary

Rehearsal is an "ill-defined group of memory strategies" (Brown, Bransford, Ferrara, & Campione, 1983; Flavell, 1985, p. 218). Thus, 5- and 6-year-olds often respond with single verbal labels in response to each item on a serial list. Slightly older children repeat the labels several times while an item is in view. The majority of 10-year-olds use cumulative rehearsal to learn serial lists. Although not considered in this section, more complex rehearsal tactics are evidenced by even older subjects. For instance, many university-age subjects use cumulative rehearsal for early list items followed by a fast-finish approach to final list items (e.g., Barclay, 1979).

Our understanding of rehearsal strategies was made possible by use of observational methods, especially when overt rehearsal was required of subjects. These analyses revealed that quantitative increases in rehearsal played little role in explaining recall data. In contrast, use of cumulative rehearsal has strikingly positive effects on recall.

Instructional experiments made clear than even children in first grade can carry out cumulative rehearsal strategies when taught to do so, even though very few Grade 1 children use cumulative rehearsal spontaneously. Procedures and materials can sometimes be modified, however, so that children who are normally production deficient with respect to cumulative rehearsal will employ more active rehearsal strategies. This occurs when there is high motivation for learning and when particularly meaningful or familiar material is employed. An important difficulty for younger children seems to be the mental effort required to carry out cumulative rehearsal. This is probably due to inefficient use of strategy components, such as maintaining previously presented items in short-term memory so that they can be included in rehearsal sets.

DEVELOPMENT OF ANOTHER ENCODING
STRATEGY: ORGANIZATION

Bousfield's (1953) research on subjective organization during learning
was pioneering work on subject-controlled memorizing activities (Murphy, 1979; Murphy & Puff, 1982; Pellegrino & Hubert, 1982). Bousfield's
methods permitted many inferences about processes that mediate learning and recall. In general, subjects were presented a list of words or
pictures in a random order in preparation for free recall. Organization
of the materials at output was presumed to reflect processes that occurred during study. For example, if a word could be categorized according to semantic categories and recall was organized following these
categories, it would be inferred that the learner engaged in intervening
organizational processes. In many cases, however, subjects were presented lists that did not contain items that went together in any consen-
sually meaningful way. Nonetheless, when subjects attempt to recall
such lists several times, it is often the case that there are trial-to-trial
regularities in recall (i.e., subjective organization).

Development of organizational strategies was studied with picture and
word lists, usually ones containing items that could be categorized. The
items were often selected using age-appropriate norms (e.g., Bjorklund,
Thompson, & Ornstein, 1983; Posnansky, 1978b), with common items from
familiar categories (e.g., animals, furniture, professions). Depending on the
age of the subjects, 3 to 12 categories were used, each containing three to
five items (Murphy & Puff, 1982). Subjective organization was most often
measured in developmental studies using the adjusted ratio clustering
(ARC) measure (Roenker, Thompson, & Brown, 1971) and the ratio of
repetition measure (RR; Bousfield & Bousfield, 1966). For both of these
measures, values close to 1 represent almost perfect organization and zero
indicates random responding.

Bousfield, Esterson, and Whitmarsh's (1958) study on conceptual and
perceptual clustering stimulated a flood of developmental work assessing
factors that affect organization. Many of the early developmental studies
on semantic grouping during free recall reported greater output clustering
with increasing age. The inference was that older children organized input
more in preparation for recall (e.g., Cole, Frankel, & Sharp, 1971; Moely et
al., 1969; Neimark, Slotnick, & Ulrich, 1971). A frequently cited result is
Moely et al.'s (1969) finding that only the 10- to 11-year-old children in that
study organized at a level that was significantly greater than chance (index
of organization = .6). This finding suggested that organizational strategies
develop somewhat later than the rehearsal strategies reviewed in the last
section. This makes sense because the discovery or creation of semantic
relations between items seems like a more complex and demanding process
than rehearsal.

Nonetheless, even young children's recall contains a lot of organization when lists containing highly associated items are learned (Haynes & Kulhavy, 1976; Myers & Perlmutter, 1978; Rossi & Wittrock, 1971; Sodian, Schneider, & Perlmutter, 1986). Lange (1973, 1978) argued, based on this result, that the output cluster values are less an indicator of conscious strategic operations than the interitem associations in the materials to be learned. A high degree of output organization for highly associated items probably occurs because recall of any particular item more or less automatically triggers recall of closely associated words. No consciously controlled strategic encoding processes are necessary for this mechanism to work.

Bjorklund (1985) also argued strongly that most of the age changes in the organization of children recall are not strategic but rather due to developmental changes in the structure and content of children's knowledge. One of Bjorklund's (1985) main assumptions was that with increasing age, the interitem relationships in semantic memory become more elaborate and could be activated relatively automatically. With increases in efficiency of knowledge access, older children can deal with material to be learned at a more abstract level (i.e., taxonomically).

Neither the strategic explanation nor the automatic knowledge-base mediation positions were entirely correct. A study by Schneider (1986) summarizes well the development of children's use of organizational strategies. Second- and fourth-grade children were given a recall task, with categorizable pictures serving as the stimulus materials. The pictures were movable and thus, could be sorted into piles. Subjects were permitted to do anything that they wanted to learn these items. Four different types of lists were used in the study. One list contained items that were highly related to the category (Battig & Montague, 1969), with high interassociations (Marshall & Cofer, 1970; Palermo, Flamer, & Jenkins, 1964) between some of the items on the list (hereafter, the High Related–High Associated list). Thus, the animals on this list included dog, cat, mouse, horse, cow, and pig. The second list was composed of items highly related to the category, but with low interitem associations (High Related–Low Associated). The animals on this list included tiger, elephant, cow, pig, bear, and dog. The third list was composed of items that were weakly related to the category, although there were some high interitem associations (Low Related–High Associated). Animals on that list were goat, deer, buffalo, hippopotamus, monkey, and lamb. The Low Related–Low Associated list included the animals beaver, rat, alligator, camel, squirrel, and giraffe.

In general, the fourth graders in the study employed much more categorical sorting during study than did the second graders. Not surprisingly, the fourth graders also clustered more at recall and recalled more than the second graders. In addition, there was a main effect on clustering for interitem associativity at recall, with highly associated lists producing more clustering. Most importantly, there was a striking age by list associativity interaction in the clustering data, such that low associativity especially penalized younger compared to older subjects. In fact, the clustering of high and low associated lists was approximately equal for the older subjects in the study. Although the main effect for associativity and the age by associativity interaction were not significant in the recall data, there were strong trends in the recall data mirroring the clustering data. In general, there were significant correlations between clustering at study, clustering at recall, and recall.

What emerges from Schneider's study is a portrait of second graders who use organizational strategies much less frequently than fourth graders. On the other hand, younger children's use of the clustering strategy can be evoked when the categories contain highly associated items. Both intentional strategic and automatic knowledge-base mediational factors are important in memory development.

One of the most interesting aspects of the Schneider (1986) data was that the children who used sorting behaviors were also the ones who engaged in other strategic activities like rehearsal and self-testing. One possible conclusion suggested by this outcome was that the children who sorted realized that sorting would positively affect memory.

This hypothesis was evaluated by Schneider (1986) by examining children's metacognition about strategies. If sorting behaviors at study are only a side effect of an increasingly elaborate knowledge base, then knowledge of taxonomic sorting as a strategy should show no substantial relationship to sorting during study. On the other hand, a correlation between strategy metamemory and sorting would be expected if children were engaging in intentional sorting in the service of a memory goal. Although there does not seem to be a correlation between strategy metamemory and sorting with 7- to 8-year-old children (Schneider, 1985, 1986; Weinert et al., 1984), there are consistently significant correlations (averaging between .3 and .4) among third and fourth graders (Andreassen & Waters, 1984; Hasselhorn, 1986, 1992; Schneider, 1985, 1986). This pattern of correlations is consistent with the hypothesis that intentional use of organizational strategies as mediators of sort–recall tasks develops during the grade-school years.

An additional important point that became obvious in Schneider's investigations was that it is very difficult to conclude a lack of strategy knowledge by a subject simply because the child fails to evidence sorting during study. Consider the study behaviors and comments of a second grader in Schneider (1986), a subject who made no obvious attempt to sort a list of low prototypical and low associated items: "They're all animals, clothes, furniture, and things to drive. Probably it helps if I put the animals and other things together that belong together. But these here? I don't know. Maybe it is just as good if I try to remember where each picture was located?"

This child clearly knew more about strategic use of categorization than indicated by input or output organization. What this case suggests is that effective use of categorization as a strategy depends on a well-developed knowledge base that includes remote associations and nonprototypical category members.

It does not seem to be very sensible to conclude that memory development boils down either to development of semantic knowledge or to development of intentionally deployed strategies. Realistic models of memory development during preschool and the grade-school years must consider the nonstrategic knowledge base, use of memory strategies, and metamemory (e.g., Ornstein, Baker-Ward, & Naus, 1988; Ornstein & Naus, 1985; Rabinowitz & Chi, 1987; Schneider, 1993).

As Ornstein and Naus (1985) summarized it, younger children's attempts at sort–recall tasks are stimulus-driven in that strong associative interitem relations between members of a list to be learned automatically induce some semantic encoding. During grade school, children experience enough memory tasks to discover strategic information, like the utility of exploiting categorical and associative relations between items (Ornstein et al., 1988). These observations fuel attempts to organize materials to be learned even when interitem associations are not salient (Best & Ornstein, 1986). That is, the benefits of automatic knowledge-based mediation lead to an insight that making associations and categorizations during study can affect recall that induces the child to attempt to use organization strategies in the future.

A recent longitudinal analysis has supported this portrait of the development of clustering/categorizing strategies (Schneider & Sodian, 1991; Schneider & Weinert, 1995; Sodian & Schneider, in press). A traditional sort–recall task was presented to a sample of about 200 children five times, when they were 4, 6, 8, 10, and 12 years of age. There were several interesting findings. First, analyses of the group means for sorting during study, clustering during recall, and recall performance confirmed gradual developmental increases in strategy use and recall performance, consistent with the outcome of most cross-sectional studies. Also in line with the results of most cross-sectional studies (e.g., Hasselhorn, 1990; Kee & Bell, 1981), the correlations between encoding strategies (sorting), retrieval strategies (clustering), and memory performance in the sort–recall task increased with age. Although intercorrelations among strategy and performance measures were low for the 4-year-olds ($r = .25$), they were of moderate size for the 6-year-olds and increased up to about .70 for the 10-year-olds (with a slight drop at age 12 that was due to ceiling effects in strategy use). That is, strategy use appears to become increasingly effective with age.

Summary

In general, the development of organizational strategies resembles the development of rehearsal strategies, although rehearsal is an earlier acquisition. Production deficiencies are obtained during sort–recall tasks with low prototypical and low associated materials well after cumulative rehearsal skills are used consistently and profitably.

We believe that the evidence considered as a whole suggests that both the increased knowledge base and the development of flexible and intentionally used organizational strategies contribute to developmental improvements in learning of categorizable lists. This is especially sensible because categorization strategies depend on a well-developed knowledge base for their efficient execution (i.e., one cannot categorize if one does not have knowledge of the relevant categories). Interactions between strategy use and the knowledge base are considered further in the next section.

ELABORATION STRATEGIES

Children are often presented factual knowledge that they are expected to acquire. Sometimes the facts are listed out; sometimes they are presented in text. Almost all research on learning of factual associations was conducted in the context of paired-associate learning. During study, both pair members are usually presented simultaneously. At testing, only the stimulus is presented with the subject required to recall the paired response. Success at this task is more likely if subjects somehow associate the stimulus and response terms meaningfully, if they elaborate the pairs (Rohwer, 1973). For instance, a verbal elaboration of the paired associate, *cat–apple*, could be, "The *cat* rolled the *apple* around." An imaginal elaboration might be an internal representation of a cat rolling the apple around, for example, an old yellow cat that one knew as a child playing with an apple that fell from the apple tree in the yard of the house that one grew up in.

One important elaborative strategy is the keyword method. It was devised by Atkinson and Raugh (1975) and originally adapted to child learning by Pressley (1977; Pressley & Levin, 1978). The keyword method is easily understood by considering a few examples. Suppose that as an English-speaking person you wish to remember that *der Spiegel* means mirror in German. The first thing to do is note a sound association between the German word and a familiar word in English. For instance, winners on game shows sometimes receive gift certificates for the Spiegel catalog. Then, form an image between this acoustically similar word (the keyword) and a mirror (the referent of the foreign item to be acquired). In this case, an image of someone holding a Spiegel catalog up to a mirror might do. Later, when *der Spiegel* is presented, the acoustic association to Spiegel catalog should come to mind, which would permit access to the interactive image that in turn permits retrieval of the meaning of *der Spiegel*.

Although there are some developmental constraints on the construction of elaborative mnemonics (covered later), in general, the evidence is quite consistent that if a learner is exposed to or can form an imaginal or verbal transformational elaboration, learning of paired associations of various types increases dramatically (e.g., Pressley, 1982; Rohwer, 1973). There is an enormous literature supporting the case that elaborative mnemonics, such as the keyword method and adaptations of it, can be engineered to facilitate learning of vocabulary definitions (e.g., Pressley, Levin, & Delaney, 1982), with this claim extending across a number of populations, including mentally handicapped children (e.g., Mastropieri, Scruggs, & Levin, 1987; Pressley et al., 1987; Turnure & Lane, 1987). Acquisition of basic social studies facts (e.g., countries and their capitals, states and their products, presidents and their accomplishments) can be facilitated by mnemonic elaborative techniques, as can memorization of many pieces of scientific information (e.g., chemical reactions, parts of the skeletal and nervous systems, and mathematical equations). See Levin (1981, 1983) and Higbee (1977, 1987), for examples.

A number of specific issues have been studied as part of elucidating the development of competent elaborative strategy use.

Uninstructed Use of Elaboration

There is greater use of elaborative strategies (without instruction to do so) with development. There are especially impressive increases in elaboration of paired associates and other factual materials from late childhood to late adolescence (Kemler & Jusczyk, 1975; Kennedy & Suzuki, 1977; Pressley & Levin, 1977a; Rohwer & Bean, 1973; Suzuki-Slakter, 1988; Waters, 1982).

Beuhring and Kee (1987a, 1987b) reported a set of results providing especially strong support for Rohwer and Bean's (1973) hypothesis. They included samples of 10- to 11-year-old children and 16- to 18-year-old adolescents. The subjects were presented two lists of 36 unrelated noun pairs. Each pair was shown one time for 15 seconds, and the subjects were told to learn it so they could recall the second pair member given the first. The subjects were also required to verbalize their thoughts while they studied. The researchers were extremely careful not to prompt the subjects about the types of strategies that could be used to learn the word pairs. It was explained explicitly that the purpose of the study was to find out what people really did to learn this material. There were several indicators that the subjects were faithful to the instructions, including high ratings of confidence that they had in fact reported all of the elaborations as they were occurring.

The verbalized strategies were classified into three categories: rehearsal, elaboration, and other associative strategies:

> Rehearsal was defined as the repetition of a noun pair with or without a conjunction (e.g., The CATTLE and the BAY) and Elaboration was defined as the description of a direct interaction between the members of a noun pair (e.g., The CATTLE swam in the BAY). Strategies that provided associations

other than a direct interaction were grouped together in a category of Other Associative Strategies (e.g., identifying an attribute the nouns shared in common such as color or shape; indicating that the pair members were owned by the same person; forming an interaction between the stimulus and a new, intermediate, response that would cue the actual response because of some preexisting association with it). (Beuhring & Kee, 1987b, pp. 260–261)

There was a dramatic decrease with increasing age in the mean number of rehearsals that were reported. There was concomitant increase in the number of elaborations and other associative strategies. Nearly all of the developmental increase in recall was accounted for by the developmental increase in elaborative strategy use.

Compared to other strategies reviewed earlier in this chapter, elaboration is a late development. It is also notable that elaboration was not universally applied by the end of the high school years in Beuhring and Kee (1987a, 1987b). Not all adolescents are elaborators in the absence of instruction to elaborate.

Elaboration When Instructed to Elaborate

Because of the enormous theoretical interest in the development of imagery skills during the 1970s and 1980s (e.g., Bruner, Olver, & Greenfield, 1966; Kosslyn, 1980; Piaget & Inhelder, 1971), the development of imaginable elaboration received much more attention than the development of verbal elaboration skills. Although there is evidence that even 4-year-olds can generate imagery mnemonics for paired associates when instructed to do so (e.g., Bender & Levin, 1976), a lot of prompting and environmental support is required (e.g., pairs are presented as toys rather than as words). Less prompting and support is required as subjects age, with development of imagery generation skill continuing until the end the of the elementary school years (e.g., Danner & Taylor, 1973; Kemler & Jusczyk, 1975; Pressley & Levin, 1977b, 1978).

It is unfortunate that more attention has not been given to children's verbal elaboration under instruction, because there is very convincing evidence that some verbal elaboration skills are developed far in advance of imagery elaboration. Even nursery school children's learning of paired associates can be improved easily by very brief instructions to them to construct meaningful sentences linking paired items (e.g., Levin, McCabe, & Bender, 1975; Milgram, 1967).

Transfer of Elaborative Strategies

Pressley and Dennis-Rounds (1980) were the first to propose that there might be striking changes during adolescence in the propensity to transfer elaborative strategies. Their hypothesis was stimulated in part by the

development of "spontaneous" elaborative strategy use during adolescence; Pressley and Dennis-Rounds hypothesized that much of the "spontaneous" strategy use by adolescents was probably transfer of elaborative
strategies that the teenagers had encountered in other contexts.

Pressley and Dennis-Rounds' (1980) subjects performed two associative
tasks. The first was learning of cities and their associated products, and the
second was the acquisition of Latin-definition linkages. There were three
conditions in the study that are relevant to the current discussion (this study
is taken up in greater detail in the next chapter). Subjects in two of these
three conditions were taught to use the mnemonic keyword method to
mediate city–product learning. Control subjects were left to their own
devices to learn the cities and their products. The critical manipulation with
respect to transfer occurred before the Latin words were presented. The
subjects who were given control instructions for city–product learning
were also given control instructions for Latin learning, as was one of the
two groups that were given keyword instruction for the city–product task
(hereafter, those in the no-transfer keyword instruction condition). Subjects
in the other keyword condition received additional keyword training before presentation of the Latin words (complete reinstruction condition).
They were taught explicitly how to apply the keyword method with Latin
words. Transfer would be apparent in this design if performance of no-
transfer instruction subjects exceeded the performance of control subjects
on the Latin task. The more performance in the no-transfer instruction
condition resembled performance in the complete reinstruction condition,
the greater the transfer.

There was no evidence of transfer among 10- to 13-year-old subjects: The
no-transfer instruction and control means were virtually identical. Consistent with the perspective that propensity to transfer increases during the
adolescent years, there was significant transfer among 16- to 19-years-olds.
That is, complete reinstruction in the keyword method was not necessary
to induce keyword method use on the Latin task. On the other hand,
performance in the no-transfer instruction condition was far below performance in the complete reinstruction condition at both age levels, indicating that spontaneous transfer was far from complete. Thus, although
these data support the case that transfer of elaborative strategy use increases during the adolescent years, it is apparent that transfer is far from
perfect during middle to late adolescence.

O'Sullivan and Pressley (1984) demonstrated that children can transfer
elaborative strategies they are learning, if the instruction they receive
provides metacognitive information about the utility of the strategy being
taught. Those investigators hypothesized that embellishing strategy instruction by adding information about when and where to use a trained
strategy (the keyword strategy) would increase children's generalized use
of the trained procedure. Students in Grades 5 and 6 were presented two
memory tasks during the experiment, both of which could be mediated

profitably with the trained procedure. The first task was learning the products manufactured in particular cities, and the second was acquisition of Latin word definitions. Control subjects learned both types of materials, but were provided no strategy instructions. In four other conditions, the subjects were taught to mediate the city–product task using the keyword procedure, with the conditions varying in the amount of "when" and "where" information about strategy use. No participants in the study were instructed to use the keyword strategy when the Latin task was presented—that is, the Latin task was a transfer task. In general, transfer of the keyword strategy from the city–product task to the Latin task was more likely given greater provision of when and where information during strategy instruction.

Knowledge-Base Effects

The first study of the development of knowledge-base effects on paired-associate elaboration was conducted by Pressley and Levin (1977b). They presented lists of paired associates to 7- and 8-year-olds and 10- to 12-year-olds. The pairs to be learned included ones that could be elaborated easily and quickly (based on an extensive pilot investigation) with readily available relationships in the knowledge base. For instance, the pair *needle–balloon* can be elaborated as a *needle popping a balloon,* and *towel–plate* can be elaborated as a *dish towel used to dry a plate.* The list also included pairs which were not so readily elaborated (e.g., *lamp–key, button–comb,* and *bird–watch).*

The subjects in Pressley and Levin (1977b) either were instructed to construct transformational images to learn the pairs (imagery condition), or they were permitted to study the pairs any way that they wanted (control condition). Half of the subjects were presented the pairs at a relatively rapid rate (i.e., 6 seconds), with the remaining subjects receiving the pairs at a slower rate (12 seconds). The main hypothesis in the study was that even if younger subjects could benefit from imagery instructions with pairs easy to relate and/or when the pairs were presented at a relatively slow rate, they might have greater difficulty using the strategy with pairs hard to relate and/or when the pairs were presented rapidly.

Consistent with expectations, the older children benefitted from the imagery-elaboration instruction for both easy and difficult pairs, regardless of the rate of presentation of the materials. Statistically significant facilitation due to imagery use was obtained with the younger children as well, except when the difficult pairs were presented at a rapid rate. Elaboration of difficult pairs required a search of the knowledge base that could not be completed in 6 seconds by the younger subjects. Older subjects could search the knowledge base at that faster rate.

Rohwer, Rabinowitz, and Dronkers (1982) provided additional data substantiating the dependence of mnemonic strategy use on the knowledge base and substantiating developmental shifts in the accessibility and use of the knowledge base in the service of elaborative strategy use as did Waters (1982) and Kee and Davies (1988, 1990, 1991; see Kee, 1995). It is clear from Rohwer et al. (1982), Waters (1982), Pressley and Levin (1977b), and Kee and Davies (1988, 1990, 1991) that knowledge-base factors are critical determinants of spontaneous use of elaboration strategies and use of elaboration strategies under instruction. Complete understanding of the development of elaborative competence requires consideration of non-strategic knowledge.

Summary

There is clear development of the use of elaborative strategies. Adolescents are more likely to use elaboration spontaneously than are children. Although older grade-school children can be taught many elaboration strategies, they do not transfer those strategies as readily as adolescents. The use of elaboration strategies depends greatly on the knowledge base, with developmental increases in knowledge permitting more flexible and complete elaboration.

DEVELOPMENT OF RETRIEVAL STRATEGIES

Sometimes it is possible to increase the probability of recall through strategic efforts at the time of testing—that is, when information that was studied must be retrieved. These strategies that can be used during recall to improve memory performance are known as *retrieval strategies*. In this section we consider in detail whether there are age differences in the use of retrieval strategies, and if so, whether development of retrieval skills improves memory performance.

Some anecdotal evidence from Schneider (1986) makes clear the importance of retrieval strategies for recall. Two fourth graders attracted some attention during the sort–recall task described earlier because both of them very purposely sorted the 24 pictures to be learned into the four categories represented on the list. These two subjects were not similar at all, however, in how they went about trying to recall the items on the test. One seemed to generate test answers in a random order, an observation supported by very low clustering in the recall data. This child's memory performance was slightly below average for Grade 4 subjects. In contrast, the commentary made by the other child implicated a more sophisticated retrieval strategy. He first recalled the four category names and thought about how six items had to be remembered for each one. He began recall with one category and shifted categories only after all six items were recalled. His memory test performance was perfect. Because the subjects did not differ in intelligence or memory span or in any other obvious way, it seems likely that the difference in their memory performances was due to their use of different approaches to retrieval. Kobasigawa (1977) analyzed in detail potential deficiencies in children's retrieval: (a) Children can fail to perceive that internal or external memory cues are potential memory aids, (b) they may lack strategies for locating target information in memory, and (c) they may not have enough experience with the problem to evaluate when the search process should be considered finished. Kobasigawa reached these conclusions largely from the results in his own program of research on the development of retrieval strategies, interpreted in the context of other research on retrieval.

Kobasigawa (1974) presented lists of categorizable items to 6- to 11-year-olds to learn for subsequent free recall. He also provided picture cards to the children during learning and recall. Each picture represented one of the categories on the test (i.e., a picture of a zoo for zoo animals). Six-year-olds generally did not use these retrieval cues at testing, but the cues were used more systematically by 8- to 11-year-olds. Developmental improvements in recall were interpreted by Kobasigawa (1974, 1977) to mean that there was a developmental difference in efficient use of retrieval cues.

There have been other analyses supportive of Kobasigawa's (1974, 1977) position that there is substantial development of retrieval strategies during the elementary years (Lange, 1973; Scribner & Cole, 1972). In some follow-up studies, researchers minimized age-correlated differences in encoding strategies, for example, by having the items sorted exactly according to their category membership during the learning phase. By holding what went on at encoding constant, the researchers reasoned that they could isolated the effects of retrieval processes better (Ceci & Howe, 1978; Ceci, Lea, & Howe, 1980; Williams & Goulet, 1975; Worden, 1974). Thus, Ceci and Howe (1978) employed lists to be learned that could be organized thematically or categorically and determined that their 4-, 7-, and 10-year-old subjects could organize the stimuli perfectly with respect to themes and categories. A cued-recall test given immediately following sorting employed category cues for half of the subjects at each age level and thematic cues for the remaining subjects. Cued recall varied little as a function of developmental level, suggesting that about the same number of items was available in memory for each of the age groups. Free recall was measured 1 day later. In contrast to the cued recall results, the free recall results were quite different. Older children spontaneously generated many of the category and thematic cues and used them flexibly to mediate free recall, but younger children did not do so. Not surprisingly, older children's recall was better than younger children's recall. Other researchers also succeeded in producing evidence of developmental increases in retrieval strategy use when encoding was held relatively constant (Hasselhorn, 1990; Keniston & Flavell, 1979; Salatas & Flavell, 1976).

We conclude that there are developmental differences in the efficient use of retrieval strategies. The attempts to isolate retrieval consistently succeeded in documenting clear trends in the development of efficient retrieval processes from 4 to 12 years of age.

UTILIZATION DEFICIENCIES

As we established earlier in this chapter, children sometimes have production deficiencies: There are memory strategies that they could use in a situation, and if they did, memory would improve. Sometimes, however, even though children can carry out a memory strategy, and perhaps even do so on their own without prompting or instruction to do so, they do not benefit from its application. Miller (1990, 1994) coined the term *utilization deficiency* to describe this situation, with her group doing the most work on utilization deficiencies (Miller & Seier, 1994).

Miller and her colleagues (Demarie-Dreblow & Miller, 1988; Miller, Haynes, DeMarie-Dreblow, & Woody-Ramsey, 1986; Miller, Seier, Barron, & Probert, 1994; Woody-Ramsey & Miller, 1988) conducted a series of studies in which a selective attention strategy can be executed. The children are presented a matrix of boxes with lids that can be lifted. Only some of these boxes contain objects, whose matrix location the children were to remember. The other boxes contain items for which the locations need not be remembered. The relevant boxes (i.e., whose locations were to be remembered) were marked with a cue; the irrelevant boxes were marked with a different cue. The basic finding representing a utilization deficiency is that children can be very selective in their examination of boxes during study time, lifting the relevant covers more than the irrelevant covers, with little positive effect on recall relative to when same-age children are not selective. Basically, the younger children are in the 5- to 11-year-old range, the more at risk they are for utilization deficiency in this paradigm. That is, the older the child, the more likely selectivity is associated with improved recall.

The most evidence of utilization deficiency has been produced with respect to learning of categorizable lists with organizational strategies (Bjorklund & Coyle, 1995; Bjorklund, Coyle, & Gaultney, 1992; Bjorklund et al., 1994). Thus, with free study, Bjorklund et al. (1992) observed children who clustered their recall without much benefit in recall level; in a sort–recall task, Bjorklund et al. (1994) observed elevated sorting and clustering in some situations that was not associated with higher recall than when sorting and clustering levels were lower, as did Alexander and Schwanenflugel (1994). Lange et al. (1990) failed to increase memory of 5- to 7-year-olds by teaching them to use an organization strategy. Even with directions and procedures designed to increase 4- and 5-year-olds' understanding of the benefits of using organizational strategies when studying categorizable lists, Lange and Pierce (1992) succeeded in producing only modest increases in recall as a function of use of an organizational strategy during study. Finally, the longitudinal findings by Sodian and Schneider (in press) on strategy effectiveness indicate a utilization deficiency in younger children as compared to older ones. Correlations between strategy use and recall increased dramatically over the age range under study, and performance gains in recall can be predicted from increases in strategy use in elementary school, but not during the preschool years. Nonetheless, there was less evidence of utilization deficiencies in this longitudinal work than in the previous cross-sectional studies.

The preferred explanation of this phenomenon is that when young children carry out unfamiliar strategies, it is very capacity demanding (Bjorklund & Coyle, 1995; Miller, 1994; Miller, Seier, Probert, & Aloise, 1991; Miller, Woody-Ramsey, & Aloise, 1991; Schneider & Bjorklund, in press). Recall from chapter 2, that young children's functional capacity also is less than that of older children. Thus, young children are doubly disadvantaged: Strategies take more effort, and young children have less capacity to devote to strategies. Moreover, the capacity demands are high both at original encoding and at retrieval.

Utilization deficiencies deserve additional study. Memory researchers have very much bought the Jenkin's (1974) conclusion that the head remembers what the head does, that use of strategies mediates memory. The work of Miller as well as that of Bjorklund and colleagues suggests that may be true only some of the time. Our guess is that more will be understood about the nature of memory and its development if developmental psychologists do a good job of documenting the prevalence of utilization deficiencies and explaining them when they occur.

CROSS-CULTURAL STUDIES
OF STRATEGY DEVELOPMENT

How typical or universal is the development of strategic competence? Because school is an institution where memory performances are expected and rewarded, there is the possibility that schooling affects the development of memory and memory strategies. Because amount of schooling and chronological age are completely confounded in Western culture, it is impossible to decide on the basis of Western data alone whether strategy development is a function of maturation, schooling, or age-correlated environmental experience other than schooling. There is an important role for cross-cultural experiments here.

The research strategy most frequently used in cross-cultural studies of memory consisted of measuring memory performance in U.S. and non-Western samples. Much of this work has been conducted with the Kpelle and Vai in Liberia, in Morocco, Mexico, and Guatemala, and with the aboriginals in Australia. We discuss briefly some of the most important of these studies.

Learning in Laboratory Tasks in Non-Western Cultures

Cole, Gay, Glick, and Sharp (1971) studied the development of free recall of lists of categorically related words, providing some of the most complete cross-cultural information on memory development. The well-known advantages of free recall consist of being able to assess both recall and the amount of clustering during recall (which can be taken as one indicator of the use of organizational strategies). Materials to be learned were carefully selected to ensure that the subjects (Kpelle from Liberia) would be quite familiar with them. Both lists of words and objects were used in these studies. For one series of experiments, three age groups were involved, 6- to 8-year-olds, 10- to 14-year-olds, and 18- to 50-year-olds. The two younger groups included approximately equal numbers of schooled and non-schooled subjects. None of the adults had attended school. A group of California children (in school, of course) served as the comparison group. The memory differences favoring the Americans over the Africans were enormous. The usual adult versus child differences in memory were obtained in the U.S. sample. In the Kpelle sample, however, the adults and children did not differ significantly. It was particularly noticeable in the African subjects that they did not improve much over trials. Finally, it was also apparent that the U.S. 11-year-olds and adults used categorical information to mediate recall. In contrast, low clustering was found for all ages within the Kpelle sample, suggesting that these subjects did not organize the material to be learned semantically. Taken as a whole, these results indicate that semantic organization strategies are not spontaneously employed by the Kpelle.

Wagner (1974) examined the degree to which intentional memory strategies were spontaneously employed in non-Western cultures. Wagner used a serial-memory task. It was assumed that the analysis of serial position curves would enable conclusions about intentional rehearsal processes (Atkinson & Shiffrin, 1968). The subjects was presented seven cards, each of which depicted two objects (an animal and a household object). The picture cards were only presented briefly and then turned over one by one. Following this, a test stimulus was presented containing one of the two items on one of the cards, with the child's task being to identify which of the seven cards turned over included this item.

Inferences about rehearsal strategies and structural memory characteristics were made by analyzing primacy and recency effects, respectively. Beginning at about 14 years of age, there were memory differences between the educated and noneducated samples that were primarily due to differences in the first few items in the list. That is, there was a primacy effect. Following Atkinson and Shiffrin's (1968) logic, Wagner (1974) assumed that the differential primacy effects reflected greater use of rehearsal in the educated compared to the noneducated sample. Wagner concluded from these results that memory strategies for serial recall are only employed spontaneously by subjects with schooling. The invariance of the recency effects across age groups and educational levels can, on the other hand, be interpreted to mean that structurally mediated parameters (i.e., short-term memory) should probably be considered universal.

Wagner (1978) pointed out an important problem with an earlier study (Wagner, 1974). The effects of education and urbanization were confounded in the earlier study. Whereas the subjects with school experience came from the capital of the Yucatan province in Mexico, the nonschooled subjects were recruited from the countryside. Thus, the between-group differences could have been due to educational or urban–rural differences. These two factors were separated by Wagner (1978).

Wagner's (1978) study included the serial task described previously. There were four age groups in the study (6- to 9-year-olds, 10- to 12-year-olds, 13- to 16-year-olds, and 17- to 22-year-olds). There were equal numbers of participants in each age group with subsamples of schooled and nonschooled subjects and subsamples of urban and rural subjects. Thus, it was possible to analyze age, educational, and urbanization effects separately. For the serial recall task, Wagner's (1974) results were replicated in his later (1978) study. In addition, however, both education and urbanization proved to be contributors to serial recall performance. The city versus country effect was especially apparent in the younger children. Younger city children remembered more regardless of schooling status. The educational effect was apparent among the older subjects, starting at about 13 years of age, with the effect of rural versus urban environment decreasing in importance with increasing age. The superiority of the schooled groups was reflected mainly in a primacy effect that was not apparent in the recall of the nonschooled subjects. This was interpreted by Wagner as additional evidence that rehearsal strategies are a byproduct of schooling.

More recent work by Wagner and Spratt (1987) reinforces the conclusion that culturally related experiences affect memory processing: For example, children in Morocco who experience Quranic primary schooling are exposed to a great deal of practice doing rote learning. That is, they memorize passages from the Quran. The most obvious way that the memory capacities of these children differ from same-age Moroccan children receiving modern schooling is in the superiority of their serial learning, which is memory for information in order. The Quranic students have developed strategies for doing the memory task demanded of them most frequently.

Cross-Cultural Laboratory Learning Studies Involving Western Populations

Not all Western countries are alike. Specifically pertinent here, parents in different Western cultures seem to provide different amounts of support for use of memory strategies. Carr, Kurtz, Schneider, Turner, and Borkowski (1989) performed an especially important study, demonstrating differences in parental encouragement of memory strategies, differences that were reflected in different approaches to memory by children as a function of culture.

In their study, German parents reported more instruction of memory strategies at home than did U.S. parents. When German children are tested on recall tasks, there are differences in how they go about these tasks relative to Americans. In particular, when German students are presented lists of items to learn, with the items selected from several different categories (e.g., furniture, animals, foods), they are more likely to make use of the categories in the list during study than are same-age U.S. children (see also Schneider, Borkowski, Kurtz, & Kerwin, 1986). When these results are combined with complementary outcomes produced by the same research group (see Deshmukh, Turner, Kurtz, & Borkowski, 1989; Kurtz, Borkowski, & Deshmukh, 1988; Kurtz, Carr, & Schneider, 1988; Kurtz, Schneider, Carr, Borkowski, & Rellinger, 1990) and the cross-cultural research summarized previously, the case builds that use of strategies by children is determined by experiential factors. In fact, in the case of German children, not only do their parents teach strategies more than U.S. parents, but so do their teachers (Kurtz et al., 1990). German children are surrounded by an interpersonal world urging them to be strategic, and this immersion affects their development.

Analytical cross-cultural research on memory also has contributed to understanding of Japanese–American differences in mathematics achievement. Yoshida, Fernandez, and Stigler (1993) presented Japanese and American children who were in Grades 4 and 6 with the same mathematics lesson. Whereas the Japanese students subsequently tended to recognize teacher statements centrally relevant to content from the lesson and not recognize irrelevant statements made by the teacher, U.S. students recognized both content relevant and irrelevant statements, consistent with the use of much better selective attention strategies by Japanese than U.S. students. This outcome is relevant here, because Japanese culture more fully immerses children in mathematics than does U.S. culture (e.g., Stevenson, 1992). (For convincing evidence that even good students in U.S. culture do not selectively attend to science content on the basis of its importance, see Reynolds, Shepard, Lapan, Kreek, & Goetz', 1990, study with Grade 10 students.)

Finally, the U.S. subculture of the deaf has provided an opportunity to test the hypothesis that strategy use is culturally and experientially driven.

Elementary-age deaf children are less likely to rehearse during list learning than hearing children of the same age. Bebko and McKinnon (1990) demonstrated that when years of language experience are considered, however, age differences in use of rehearsal during list learning disappear. Thus, a hearing 7-year-old has 7 years of language experience; so does an 11-year-old deaf child of deaf parents who began learning sign language at age 4. Deaf children with 7 years of language experience rehearse much like normal children with 7 years of language experience. In short, when researchers have found clever ways to control for extraneous factors, experience has proven a powerful predictor of strategy use. Kurtz (1990) provided an especially elegant summary that memory strategy use depends greatly on an individual's personal cultural history.

Memory of Text

Some of the best and most interesting cross-cultural research involves memory for text. In contrast to the results with laboratory tasks, most of the text research does not support the position that cultural background determines memory performance. On the contrary, universal schemata are operative during the encoding and recall of stories so that almost no differences in memory for text are observed as a function of culture or level of formal education.

For instance, in Mandler et al. (1980), children and adults from the Vai tribe of Liberia, with and without schooling, were presented with a total of five stories, four of which were Western in origin and one of which was from the Vai tribe. Significant differences were found between children and adults with regard to total recall of the stories. More importantly, however, there were no differences found in recall of familiar and unfamiliar types of stories (i.e., no tendency for cultural-specific results). Finally, a comparison of these results and those of earlier studies with U.S. grade-school children and college students (Mandler & Johnson, 1977) also provided clear evidence that the recall patterns of the stories (in terms of the structural elements of the stories that were recalled) remained relatively invariant in both cultures. Mandler et al. (1980) concluded from these results that the general schematic structure of stories was an important determinant of recall performance. The results supported the assumption that story schematic elements are important mediators of text learning and recall. (See chapter 3, this volume, for more on structural–schematic qualities of text as a determinant of memory.)

Further support for this conclusion was provided by Dube (1982) in a study of African and U.S. junior high school students and African adolescents without school experience. All groups were presented two stories of African origin and two of European origin. The African groups demonstrated better memory performance as a whole. Consistent with Mandler et al. (1980), Dube found no difference in memory of the European and African stories. The superior memory performance of the African subjects was interpreted by Dube as possibly being due to the African's greater experience with oral storytelling and retelling. Ross and Millsom (1970) obtained a comparable result in a comparison of adults from Ghana and New York. The Africans outperformed the Americans in story recall.

In drawing general conclusions about the cross-cultural text recall data, we would be remiss if we did not point out that there are some results that differ from the ones reviewed thus far. For instance, Kintsch and Greene (1978) found that U.S. students were much worse at recalling an Indian story than at recalling Grimms' fairy tales. Rogoff (1981) found that memory performance of young children varies with whether they have had formal education or not. Multiple regression analyses established that memory performances for two mythological stories was better predicted by number of years in school than by age or social background variables. When taken as a whole, however, the cross-cultural text studies provide clear evidence that recall of meaningful stories depends less on education than recall of unrelated materials used in laboratory studies. Because many stories in many cultures have structural–schematic properties, children throughout the world have opportunity to experience and learn these structures that can mediate learning and recall of text (e.g., Mandler, 1984). A comparable analysis can be applied to other ecologically meaningful tasks, ones for which there are few or small cross-cultural effects.

Ecologically Valid Memory Tasks

Kearins (1981, 1983) conducted some particularly good work on the effects of cultural familiarity effects on ecologically valid memory tasks. Kearins (1981) required subjects to look at an array of objects for about 30 seconds. Then, subjects were required to place the objects back into their array positions. Regardless of the types of objects in the arrays (i.e., modern items like bottles and knives or natural items like stones and leaves), aboriginal children were consistently better at remembering array locations. Kearins (1983) provided additional data supporting the criticality of stimulus familiarity, reporting differences favoring aboriginal children over Western children in verbal recall of wild animals. Kearins hypothesized that aboriginal children's interest in and knowledge about wild animals promoted their memory in this task. Kearins reported a variety of data suggesting that Anglo-Australian children were more likely to attempt verbal rehearsal strategies, whereas aboriginal children seemed to rely more on spatial–imaginal strategies. In summary, Kearins data clearly support the hypothesis that prior knowledge and culturally supported visual–spatial skills can more than compensate for verbal strategies.

Summary

Cross-cultural differences in children's memory seem to be very specific. It seems that use of rehearsal and organizational strategies during list learning is more common in Western cultures than in nonschooled societies. The development of the strategic skills that mediate strong performance on list-like tasks seem to be tied to schooling. Materials that possess similar meaningful structures that children experience universally (e.g., stories, scenes) are more likely to be remembered equally in schooled and nonschooled cultures than are materials that are not experienced universally.

We must caution, however, that the methodological problems involved in this cross-cultural research are enormous. For instance, the schooled and nonschooled children in a particular region may differ on many characteristics besides schooling—That is, there are obviously selection factors in determining who will go to school in these regions and who will not. Sometimes culturally specific personality characteristics undermine attempts to conduct comparisons. For instance, Rogoff and Mistry (1985) found that young Mayan children demonstrated poorer memory of stories than young U.S. children. As it turned out, the Mayan children were extremely uncomfortable in the experimental situation because they are usually not permitted to speak freely with adults. An anecdote like this suggests that other cross-cultural data may be tainted by social interaction effects not understood by Westerners.

CLOSING COMMENTS

Reseachers interested in memory development have spent a lot of time studying the development of encoding and retrieval, with some of the more important developments and issues taken up in this chapter. The development of encoding and retrieval strategies was probably attractive to memory development researchers at the end of the 1960s and beginning of the 1970s, in part because it seemed at that time that there were qualitative differences in strategy use as a function of age. At the end of the 1980s, strategy development appeared more continuous.

For instance, there was gradual development of rehearsal skills. Even preschoolers rehearsed the location of a hidden object by looking at the hiding place during a retention interval. Single-item repetition of words to be learned on lists was gradually replaced by increasingly complex cumulative rehearsal.

Early work on strategies was characterized by a narrowness of focus on strategies only, and then only in Western cultures. There is now a realization that use of encoding and retrieval strategies must be considered in interaction, and that use of these strategies depends on nonstrategic knowledge.

There is also an understanding that carrying out a strategy does not guarantee an effect on memory, with pursuit of utilization deficiencies being an important direction in the study of children's memory in the 1990s.

Some of the strategies that have commanded the greatest attention by workers in memory development seem to be ones that are most sensitive to schooling effects. That is, they do not develop universally, but rather are observed more in schooled societies than in nonschooled societies. In recent years, the work of researchers like Kurtz has done much to illuminate that the child's cultural environment does much to shape the child's memory behaviors. Culture affects both family life and the nature of schooling, with both of these impacting on development of children's cognitive competence.

Chapter 5

Metamemory

Metamemory, a term introduced by Flavell (1971), is knowledge about memory. Metamemory is important because of its role in regulating behaviors affecting memory, such as use of memory strategies. That is, knowing that a situation poses difficulties for memory can affect a person's memory behaviors in reaction to the situation. In general, there is both long-term knowledge of memory, which is reflected by factual knowledge of the variables affecting memory, and knowledge of the current state of one's memory (i.e., monitoring). Both types of metamemory have been studied extensively by developmental psychologists.

ASSESSMENT OF METAMEMORY

There are a variety of measures that have been used to capture what children know about memory.

Factual Knowledge About Memory

The best known metamemory interview study was Kreutzer, Leonard, and Flavell (1975). They interviewed children in kindergarten, Grades 1, 3, and 5 about memory, using 14 items containing one or more questions about memory storage and retrieval. These items assessed knowledge of person variables, task demands, and strategies. Many of the questions involved a decision between two options (e.g., whether to dial a telephone number immediately after hearing it or to get a drink of water before dialing). Other questions demanded more of the children. For instance, children's knowledge of retrieval strategies was tested by asking them to think of all the things they could do to try and find a jacket they had lost while in kindergarten.

Cavanaugh and Borkowski (1980) conducted the only complete replication of Kreutzer, Leonard, and Flavell's (1975) study. Other studies (e.g., Borkowski, Peck, Reid, & Kurtz, 1983; Brown, 1978; Kurtz & Borkowski, 1984; Schneider, 1986; Schneider et al., 1986; Weinert et al., 1984) tapped some of the items, with most of the followup data consistent with Kreutzer et al.'s (1975) original findings. It was established that the items used in the study were generally reliable (Kurtz, Reid, Borkowski, & Cavanaugh, 1982). In general, based on the interview data, researchers concluded that there were developmental improvements in understanding of variables affecting memory.

Nonetheless, it must be admitted that there is a long history of skepticism about the validity of self-reports and interview data (see Brown et al., 1983; Ericsson & Simon, 1980, 1984/1993). Many of the concerns are about the veridicality of verbal reports to actual cognitive processing. These problems are especially acute with children (Cavanaugh & Perlmutter, 1982). Young children's verbal skills are often inadequate for them to articulate their knowledge about memory (Cavanaugh & Perlmutter, 1982; Wellman, 1985).

Thus, Wellman (1977b, 1978) developed nonverbal techniques to explore metacognition in preschoolers, as did Yussen and Bird (1979). Justice (1985, 1986) followed with a procedure that involved presenting various memory strategies (looking, naming, rehearsal, and grouping) on a videotape. After watching the videotape and naming the four strategies (but without an opportunity to see the models attempting recall), the children made paired comparisons of the four strategies. For each pair, the children were asked to state which strategy was better for free recall of the items on a picture list. Investigators (Justice, 1985, 1986; Schneider, 1986; Schneider, Körkel, & Vogel, 1987) using this approach produced consistent data. Kindergarten and young elementary school children recognize differential effectiveness only when strategies produce dramatic differences in performance. Older elementary school children, however, can detect more subtle differences in strategy effectiveness.

Best and Ornstein (1986) developed a method of assessment based on peer tutoring. The method requires that older children (e.g., third or sixth graders) be asked to tutor a younger child (e.g., a first grader) about how to do a task (e.g., sort–recall) in order to maximize learning. The tutors' assignment was to describe to the younger children what they themselves would do when given a similar task. Tutors' instructions were taped and subjected to content analyses. The measure of metamemory was the extent to which the instructions included appropriate strategy instructions (e.g., appropriate use of organizational strategies for a sort–recall task).

In general, as is reviewed subsequently, children's factual knowledge of variables affecting memory increases with development. There are some differences as a function of method of assessment, but the developmental improvement in knowledge of memory facts is clear.

Memory Monitoring

In contrast to the work on long-term memory of facts about memory, Brown (e.g., 1978; Brown & DeLoache, 1978) focused on "here and now memory monitoring." Her frame of reference was the competent information processor, one possessing an efficient "executive" that regulated cognitive behaviors. This executive is aware of the system's capacity limits and strategies. The executive analyzes memory problems that the learner confronts and selects appropriate strategies. Very important, the executive monitors the success or failure of ongoing performance, deciding which strategies to continue and which to replace with potentially more effective and appropriate procedures.

In addition, the efficient executive monitors when one knows and when one does not know, an important requirement for competent learning (e.g., Holt, 1964). Brown took the perspective that such memory monitoring plays a large role in these executive actions, and that metacognitive effects on cognitive regulation are more important than other metacognitive functions. Brown recognized that children do not monitor well and often fail to make appropriate executive decisions. For instance, children often do not monitor comprehension problems when reading text (e.g., Baker & Brown, 1984; Garner, 1987; Körkel, 1987), and they fail to recognize when they do not have enough information to complete a task (e.g., Beal & Flavell, 1982; Flavell, Speer, Green, & August, 1981). A variety of overlapping conceptions of metamemory emphasizing monitoring followed Flavell and Brown's analyses (e.g., Kluwe & Schiebler, 1984; Nelson & Narens, 1980; Paris, Lipson, & Wixson, 1983; Pressley, Borkowski, et al., 1984; Pressley, Borkowski, & O'Sullivan, 1985; Pressley, Borkowski, et al., 1987; Pressley, Borkowski, & Schneider, 1989; Wellman, 1990). So did a great deal of research.

Performance predictions, as the name implies, are made prior to study of material to be remembered and involve estimation of how much will be learned. A form of performance prediction that has been used often in developmental research is prediction of one's own memory span (e.g., Flavell et al., 1970). Subjects are presented incrementally longer lists of materials to be learned (pictures, words, or figures), with the task to indicate whether she or he could still recall a list that long. The child's memory span is then tapped using the same lists. Comparison of the prediction value with actual memory span yields the metamemory indicator, which is usually interpreted as a byproduct of memory monitoring (i.e., children who have monitored their memory proficiently in the past should be more aware of their memory span than children who have not monitored at all or not monitored well in the past). Performance prediction accuracy can be measured for a variety of memory tasks, with recent applications to text learning (e.g., Körkel, 1987; Schneider et al., 1990; Schneider & Uhl, 1990).

In contrast to performance predictions, which are made before studying occurs, recall readiness assessments are made after material has been studied at least one time. One variation involves asking subjects to continue studying until their memory of material to be learned is perfect. For instance, Flavell et al. (1970) found that 5- to 6-year-old children are often too optimistic about their readiness for a test, with low levels of recall occurring after they claim that they are prepared for a test. Much more realistic assessments can be obtained from older children.

A number of developmental studies explored children's feeling of knowing (Brown & Lawton, 1977; Butterfield, Nelson, & Peck, 1988; Cultice, Somerville, & Wellman, 1983; Posnansky, 1978a, 1978b; Wellman, 1977a, 1979). Children were shown series of items and asked to name them. When a child could not recall the name of an object given its picture, she or he was asked to indicate whether the name would be recognized if the experimenter provided it. These ratings of feeling of knowing were then related to subsequent performance on a recognition test that included nonrecalled items. Like performance predictions and recall readiness estimates, feeling of knowing judgments were taken before the test of interest.

In contrast, other measures tap memory behaviors as they occur. Thus, verbal protocol techniques (e.g., Ericsson & Simon, 1980, 1984/1993) require subjects either to verbalize all thoughts that come to them while performing a task (i.e., think aloud) or to verbalize between trials.

Finally, children can be asked to judge their memory performance immediately after attempting a memory test (i.e., make postdictions; e.g., Berch & Evans, 1973; Bisanz, Vesonder, & Voss, 1978; Kelly, Scholnick, Travers, & Johnson, 1976; Masur, McIntyre, & Flavell, 1973). These judgments can involve estimating overall performance or estimating performance on an item-by-item basis.

DEVELOPMENT OF METAMEMORY

A lot of metamemory data was been produced in the last two decades, much of which was orderly and highly informative about children's knowledge about memory. We understand better both children's long-term, factual knowledge about memory and their abilities to monitor memory.

Children's Factual Knowledge of Memory

Many different types of factual knowledge have been tapped in studies of children's metamemory.

When Do Children Know the Relevant Mental Verbs? A basic type of metamemory is understanding mental verbs, such as *thinking, forgetting, or knowing*. Although Kreutzer et al. (1975) provided evidence that the youngest participants in their study (kindergarten children) could properly apply mental verbs, it has proven more difficult to determine preschoolers' knowledge of mental verbs. Their use of mental verbs is often incorrect (e.g., Misciones, Marvin, O'Brien, & Greenburg, 1978; Wellman & Johnson, 1979).

There are clear developmental improvements in understanding of mental verbs during the preschool years, however. For example, 4-year-olds understand that remembering and forgetting require having known at some time, whereas 3-year-olds do not (Lyon & Flavell, 1994); 4-year-olds understand that retention interval is a critical determinant of whether forgetting occurs (Lyon & Flavell, 1993). Knowledge of mental verbs is a long-term development, with children's understanding limited compared to adult understanding, including for verbs such as remembering versus understanding, recalling versus recognizing, planning, and comparing (e.g., Astington & Olsen, 1990; Booth & Hall, 1994; Lovett & Flavell, 1990; Schwanenflugel, Fabricius, & Alexander, 1994).

Knowledge of Person Variables. Knowledge about person variables includes knowledge about all variables or permanent personality attributes or states that can influence memory of information (Flavell & Wellman, 1977). Kreutzer et al. (1975) included only one item that tapped knowledge of person variables. They found that 9- and 11-year-olds could better conceptualize memory abilities in that they realized that memorization skills vary from person to person and from situation to situation. The 9- and 11-year-olds also knew that they did not have an equally good memory in all situations and that it was quite possible that their friends had a better memory than they did. In contrast, most of the kindergarten and first-grade subjects were convinced that they always remembered well and that they were better at remembering than their friends. In fact, 30% of the kindergarten children were convinced that they never forgot anything. This finding is consistent with other demonstrations that the memory-related self-concept of young children is unrealistic (e.g., Schneider, 1985; Schneider et al., 1986; Weinert et al., 1984). Five- and 6-year-olds generally tend to overestimate their performance.

In general, preschool children clearly have a great deal of difficulty in determining the importance of relatively stable personal characteristics (e.g., hair color, clothing, weight, age) that do and do not determine memory performance (Weinert & Schneider, 1987, 1995; Wellman, 1977b; Yussen & Bird, 1979). This is consistent with their limited knowledge of task variables affecting memory, which is taken up next.

Knowledge of Task Variables. There are a number of studies evaluating children's knowledge of task factors that affect memory. Wellman (1977b) provided the first hints that knowledge of task characteristics is available at the preschool level. The study included items related to a variety of factors that can affect memory, such as properties of materials (e.g., how much material there is to learn), circumstances of the learning situation (e.g., noise and length of study time), and external supports (e.g., help from friends or retrieval cues). The clearest results supporting competency in preschool children were obtained for the "number of items" and "noise" variables. Eighty-two percent of the children were convinced that 18 items are more difficult to remember than 3 items; 66 % of the subjects said that noise negatively influences memory performance. In contrast, only 37% of the subjects assumed that friends could be of help in retention, and only about 26% felt that the amount of total learning time would have an effect on memory performance.

Later studies (Weinert et al., 1984; Yussen & Bird, 1979) produced data suggesting that, if anything, Wellman (1977b) overestimated preschoolers' knowledge of task variables, probably because he eliminated subjects who could not answer simple control questions correctly. For instance, in both the Munich longitudinal study and in Yussen and Bird's (1979) research, only about 40% of the 4-year-old subjects could judge correctly the effect of the number of items on the difficulty of memory problems. The 4-year-old subjects in the Yussen and Bird study also made fewer correct responses for the noise and time variables compared to the preschoolers in Wellman's (1977b) research (11% vs. 55%).

More positively, by 6 years of age, children know a great deal about some task variables. Yussen and Bird (1979) reported that 6-year-olds' understanding of the significance of task characteristics is much more complete than the understanding of preschool children. About 78% of the first-grade 6-year-olds in their study knew that the number of items affected memory performance. Eighty-nine percent of the first-grade subjects indicated that noise negatively influences learning performance. Even the most difficult item (i.e., the relevancy of learning time for performance) was answered correctly by about half of the 6-year-olds.

Even so, it must be emphasized that other variables are poorly understood by children in the early elementary grades. For instance, 7-, 9-, and 10-year-old students in Moynahan (1978) were asked to judge which of two lists would be easier to learn, one composed of taxonomically organized items or one composed of conceptually unrelated words. Although both older groups recognized the advantages conferred by taxonomic structure, the 7-year-olds did not. This result was confirmed in follow-up studies (Schneider, 1986; Schneider, Körkel, & Vogel, 1987; Weinert et al., 1984). First-grade children also lack knowledge of retrieval factors and their effects on memory: The majority of first-grade children in Speer and Flavell (1979) did not recognize that recognition memory tasks are easier than recall tasks (the latter requiring more retrieval). Fifty-five percent and 65% of Kreutzer et al.'s kindergarten and first-grade subjects, respectively, knew that gist recall was easier than verbatim recall, compared to 100% of fifth-grade children who understood that verbatim recall was a more difficult retrieval task. Other studies (Borkowski et al., 1983; Kurtz & Borkowski, 1987; Kurtz, Schneider, Turner, & Carr, 1986; Myers & Paris, 1978) suggest that, if anything, Kreutzer et al. (1975) overestimated kindergarten and first-grade children's understanding of the relative ease of gist and verbatim recall. Although the majority of preschool and kindergarten children know that memory tasks are easier when retrieval cues are available, sophisticated understanding of retrieval cues and how they work develops during the grade-school years (Beal, 1985; Schneider & Sodian, 1988).

Knowledge About an Especially Important Task: Text and Its Structure. A good deal of effort has been expended determining children's knowledge of text structure. Brown and her colleagues (e.g., Brown & Smiley, 1977) conducted very visible research on this problem. Students were asked to rate the pieces of information in text as most important (top one fourth), slightly less important (second one fourth), less important still (third one fourth), and least important. Although seventh-grade students provided importance ratings that were roughly equivalent to the ratings provided by college-student adults, third-grade and fifth-grade children's ratings differed greatly from those of adults. One possible explanation of the apparently late development of text knowledge in this study is that the texts were fairly long and complicated as was the rating procedure.

Investigators who used shorter and less complicated texts as well as less complicated rating systems produced data suggesting greater knowledge of text structure by elementary school children. Unlike Brown's research, most of the follow-up studies used texts constructed on the basis of formal story grammars (Kintsch & van Dijk, 1978; Stein & Glenn, 1979; see chapter 3, this volume, for a brief discussion of story grammar). High metacognitive knowledge was assumed in these studies when children identified the more important elements in text to be the ones that are more central according to story grammar models.

For instance, Yussen, Mathews, Buss, and Kane (1980) showed that fifth graders could differentiate central information from less important information in text, but that second-grade children could not do so. Hoppe-Graff and Schöler (1980) obtained comparable results, as did Denhière and Le Ny (1980). Recent studies suggest, not surprisingly, that children are more proficient at differentiating important from less important information when reading text based on contents in which they possess expertise (Denhière, Cession, & Deschenes, 1986; Körkel, 1987).

Perhaps the most impressive demonstration of early knowledge of the relative importance of text elements was provided by Young and Schumacher (1983). Even 4- and 6-year-old children were sensitive to relative importance levels within simple picture stories. The importance ratings of preschool children correlated significantly with those of adults; the ratings of 6-year-olds were very similar to those of adults. Young and Schumacher's (1983) study is a clear example of the great effect that materials modifications can have on task difficulty. A finding such as this one prompts skepticism when researchers try to set an absolute age limit for certain abilities.

Knowledge About Strategies That Are Useful for Free Recall Tasks. Children's knowledge about organizational strategies that can be used to mediate free recall was tapped by a single item in Kreutzer et al. (1975). The subjects were shown nine picture cards (three from each of three categories), and they were told to imagine that these items had to be learned in a few minutes. They were also told that they could do anything they wished to acquire the items. There was a clear age trend. Only one kindergarten child use a categorization strategy, although many fifth-grade subjects did so. When partial category use was scored, 35% of the kindergarten children, 40% of the first-grade subjects, 70% of the third-grade participants, and 80% of the fifth-grade subjects evidenced rudimentary knowledge of organizational strategies.

Data on knowledge of categorization strategies has also been generated by comparing videotaped presentations of strategies pairwise. Sodian et al. (1986) presented lists containing items that could be categorized taxonomically or by color. The 4- and 6-year-olds made pairwise comparisons among taxonomic sorting, color sorting, random sorting, and looking strategies. The judgments of the 4- and 6-year-olds differed little, with only one significant difference between the two age groups. The taxonomic sorting strategy was judged much more positively by the older children. However, the 6-year-olds did not realize that the taxonomic sorting strategy was more potent than the color sorting approach.

The shift in knowledge about free recall strategies between kindergarteners and sixth-grade students was obvious in three studies using the paired-comparison method (Justice, 1985, 1986; Schneider, 1986). In general, preschoolers considered "looking at" as the best strategy, with taxonomic sorting, rehearsal, and naming trailing in popularity. (O'Sullivan, 1993, confirmed that preschoolers have great faith in the "looking at" strategy, even though it is ineffective in improving recall; so did Fabricius, Schwanenflugel, & Schick, 1995.) Kindergarten children were more likely to view the four strategies as equally effective. Second and fourth graders preferred grouping and rehearsal but did not differentiate between these two. By Grade 6 there is clear understanding that semantic grouping strategies are superior to rehearsal, naming, and looking.

Knowledge About Strategies That Are Useful for "Natural" Memory Tasks. Kreutzer et al. (1975) included one item to assess knowledge of strategies that could be used in preparation for future retrieval. Participants were asked to tell everything that they could do in order to be sure that they would remember to take their ice skates to school the next day. The answers could be placed into four main categories. The three external categories involved manipulation of the skates (e.g., putting them near the door), use of external memory cues (e g., notes), and relying on cues provided by other people (e. g., asking a parent to provide a reminder). The fourth category of answers involved internal processes that the child could carry out (e.g., rehearsal of the fact that the skates needed to be taken to school). There was a significant developmental increase in the number of strategies reported, although even kindergarten children were able to come up with at least one strategy each. All age groups reported more external than internal strategies. The strategies reported by third-grade and fifth-grade children seemed more clearcut and efficient than those provided by kindergarten and first-grade participants. In their replication work, Borkowski and his associates (Borkowski et al., 1983; Cavanaugh & Borkowski, 1980; Kurtz & Borkowski, 1984) obtained generally comparable data in response to the "skates" question.

A similar strategy question was included in the Munich Longitudinal Study (Weinert & Schneider, 1986, 1987, 1995). Four-year-olds were asked what they could do in order to remember to take their snack to preschool the next day. Children in this age group reported only external strategies, with 14% of the children suggesting a manipulation of the snack (e.g., put it near the door); 3% suggested construction of a note; and 3% said that they would ask someone else to help.

Kreutzer et al. (1975) also included an item to assess knowledge of retrieval strategies. The question was, "What would one do to find a jacket that had been lost in school?" The answers were classified by Kreutzer et al. (1975) in two main categories, *search* (search procedures carried out by the child) and *other* (strategies referring to solutions that involved other people). Subjects at all age levels suggested looking in places where the jacket would be likely to be found (e.g., the cloakroom) and asking people who would be likely to be helpful (e.g., the teacher). Every kindergarten child offered at least one solution, with first-grade children averaging two solutions. Suggestions to search systematically and elaborately were offered more often by older (fifth-grade students) compared to the younger participants. Follow-up research provided data that complements the Kreutzer et al. (1975) findings. Only about 25% of the 4-year-olds in the Munich Longitudinal Study generated retrieval strategies. Yussen and Levy (1977) reported that the number of reported strategies for retrieval of a lost object increased up until about 10 years of age; the number of strategies for finding an internal piece of information (how can one remember a birthday present that one thought to be a good idea but has forgotten in the meantime) increases well into adolescence according to the Yussen and Levy (1977) data.

Kreutzer et al.'s (1975) study also included problems that required subjects to make preparations to remember an upcoming event (i.e., the birthday party of a friend) and to retrieve information about an event that had already happened (i.e., to remember that Christmas when a particular present was received). The birthday party problem produced data that was similar to the data generated for the ice skates problem. Even the youngest children could come up with one or two strategies, with more and increasingly sophisticated strategies reported by the older children. In contrast, the memory of Christmas problem was extremely difficult. Kreutzer et al. (1975) reported that kindergarten children could hardly understand the task. First graders said that they would seek assistance from other people, as did third graders. Although fifth-grade subjects produced more strategies and more varied strategies, there was still room for improvement. Others (Cavanaugh & Borkowski, 1980; Kurtz & Borkowski, 1984) confirmed that very few adequate responses are generated for the memory of Christmas item until the end of the grade school years.

What emerges from the Kreutzer et al. (1975) data and the follow-up research is a portrait of developing knowledge of strategies from 4 years of age through the grade-school years and into adolescence. The development of knowledge about strategies during the grade-school years has been confirmed in other research aimed at elucidating children's understanding of strategies suitable for performing laboratory tasks.

Summary: Knowledge of Facts About Memory. Using sensitive methods that minimize demands on the child, it is possible to demonstrate some rudimentary knowledge of metamemorial facts in preschoolers (e.g., some understanding of mental verbs, knowledge of important versus less important elements in picture stories). Knowledge of facts about memory is more impressive in the primary-grade years, and much more complete by 11 or 12 years of age. Nonetheless, knowledge of memory is not complete by the end of childhood. For instance, understanding the relative importance of text elements continues to develop.

One of the most important findings produced by metamemory researchers is that there is increasing knowledge of strategies with increasing age. Although older grade-school children know most of the strategies covered by the metamemory measures reviewed in this section, there is increasing evidence that many adolescents (including college students) have little or no knowledge of some powerful and important memory strategies. There is also increasing knowledge about the characteristics of the strategies that children do know, including their relative potencies. This is absolutely critical metamemory for efficient thinking to take place.

Memory Monitoring

Performance Prediction Accuracy. If people have monitored their previous performances adequately, they should be able to predict future memory performances and be better able to do so than people who have not monitored in the past. That is the logic of accepting performance prediction accuracy as a measure of monitoring.

Although preschool children overpredict their memory performance consistently, elementary school children are much more accurate (e.g., Flavell et al., 1970; Kelly et al., 1976; Levin, Yussen, DeRose, & Pressley, 1977; Markman, 1973; Monroe & Lange, 1977; Worden & Sladewski-Awig, 1982). Whether elementary school children over- or underestimate performance seems to vary with the memory task. For instance, serial memory span is usually overestimated (e.g., Flavell et al., 1970), whereas recall of categorizable lists is underestimated (e.g., Worden & Sladewski-Awig, 1982). The latter result is probably not surprising given elementary school children's lack of awareness of the effects of categorizing on memory as discussed earlier.

Several studies tried to pinpoint preschoolers' difficulties in making performance predictions. One likely possibility is that many memory tasks are completely unfamiliar to preschoolers. Thus, preschool children make more realistic predictions when asked how far they can jump, which is a task that is familiar to them (Markman, 1973). Predictions are also more accurate when the memory task is conducted in a familiar context, such as a game (Justice & Bray, 1979) or in a simulated shopping situation (Wippich, 1980).

A particularly interesting question is whether predictions of overall performance improve in accuracy as experience with the memory task increases. There seems to be developmental improvement here. Subjects in Schneider (1986), Schneider et al. (1986), and Schneider and Uhl (1990) made a prediction before attempting a list-learning task. Then, after completing the list-learning task and test over the material on the list, the subjects were told that they would be doing another list-learning task and were asked to predict performance on this second list. Although first and second predictions do not differ in accuracy for second-grade and third-grade children, fourth-grade children's predictions did improve with practice. Pressley and Ghatala (1988) provided complementary data. In their study, first- and second-grade, fourth- and fifth-grade, and seventh- and eighth-grade subjects predicted performance on a vocabulary test, took the test, and then predicted performance on a future test of comparable difficulty. Although there was no evidence of prediction improvement from first to second prediction at the Grade 1 and 2 level, there was a strong trend toward improvement at the Grade 4 and 5 level and unambiguous improvement from first to second prediction at the Grade 7 and 8 level.

More negatively, prediction improvement may be limited to tasks involving fairly simple materials. When Schneider and Uhl's subjects went through the prediction–learning–testing–prediction–learning–testing cycle with prose materials, there were no improvements in prediction with practice. Schneider and Uhl (1990) speculated that accurate awareness of the amount recalled on a test of prose content may be less certain than accurate awareness for list items, and thus, test monitoring during prose study and testing might not be sufficient to permit improvements in predictions about future prose learning. (It was obvious in Pressley & Ghatala's, 1988, study with simpler materials that prior test monitoring and future test predictions were related.)

In addition to being able to predict overall performance better than preschoolers, grade-school children are also capable of predicting which items on a list are more likely to be remembered than other items (Kelly et al., 1976; Monroe & Lange, 1977; Worden & Sladewski-Awig, 1982). There are developmental shifts in accuracy of individual-item predictions, however. For example, Worden and Sladewski-Awig (1982) demonstrated that second-grade children were more liberal than six-grade children in their predictions. Thus, the younger rather than older children were more likely than the older children to predict memory of items that in fact were not remembered subsequently.

In summary, the most obvious improvement in performance prediction is the shift between preschool and the elementary school years from great overconfidence in future performance to more reasonable expectations. There are also more subtle improvements during the elementary school years, including increased use of awareness of past performance as a predictor of future performance and increased awareness of the relative recallability of particular pieces of information.

Monitoring When Information Is "On the Tip of the Tongue."
Wellman (1977a) studied the accuracy of children's feelings that they knew items, even when they could not recall them. He showed children pictures and asked them to name the object in each picture. For those objects that were not named, feeling-of-knowing judgments were elicited: The subjects were asked whether they knew the item well enough that they would recognize its name if they heard it. Then, a recognition test was given in which the name of the object was provided with the child required to select the item from a group of pictures. Feeling-of-knowing accuracy increased from kindergarten (youngest subjects in the study) to Grade 3 (oldest subjects in the study). Wellman (1977a) also noted that only the Grade 3 children registered the frustration that is typical of adults who have something on the tip of their tongue, but who cannot remember it (see Brown & Lawton, 1977, for similar developmental trends in a study of children with learning difficulties).

Cultice et al. (1983) presented 4- to 5-year-old children a simplified version of the task used by Wellman (1977a). The participants were asked to name children who were depicted on photos presented to them. The pictures included very familiar faces (i.e., children from their own preschool group), somewhat less familiar faces (i.e., children from another group in the preschool), and completely unfamiliar pictures. When the children could not name the person in the picture, they were quite capable of saying whether they would recognize the person when the name was provided. Thus, when feeling-of-knowing problems are simply structured and involve highly meaningful materials like faces, even preschoolers evidence the memory-monitoring competence tapped by the feeling-of-knowing task.

Knowledge of Test Readiness. Recall readiness assessments are made after material has been studied at least one time. In Flavell et al.'s (1970) study of memory span, kindergarten, first-grade, second-grade, and fourth-grade subjects provided recall readiness data. The subjects were asked to study the learning material long enough to be absolutely certain that they would be able to recall the entire list perfectly. There was clear developmental improvement in estimation of recall readiness. Kindergarten and first-grade children were usually unable to recall the entire list correctly, although they believed that they would be able to do so. Recall readiness estimates of second-grade and fourth-grade subjects were considerably more accurate.

Children are also less than expert in monitoring their preparation for a test over text. For instance, Ghatala, Levin, Foorman, and Pressley (1989) had fourth-grade children read a social studies article in preparation for a test on the article's content. In the condition of the study that tapped children's naturalistic regulation of study, the children were permitted to read the article as many times as they wished with the demand that they should not stop reading until they knew that they could achieve 100% performance on the completion test. A reward was promised if they in fact achieved mastery. The failure to monitor was clear. In three different replications, fourth-grade students overestimated how many items they would get right on the test and, therefore, understudied for the test.

Flavell et al. (1970) believed that the older children's more accurate assessments were due to their greater use of self-testing during study. Self-testing strategies were rarely observed in follow-up studies, however (e.g., Dufresne & Kobasigawa, 1989; Gettinger, 1989; Leal, Crays, & Moely, 1985). Apparently, most grade-school children do not spontaneously use task-relevant regulation strategies.

However, even very young children can be taught self-testing strategies that permit them to make reasonably accurate recall readiness judgments during list learning. For example, Brown and Barclay (1976) demonstrated that even children with learning disabilities (mental age = 8 years) could learn how to make more accurate recall readiness judgments.

Knowledge of Which Items Require Additional Study.   Masur et al. (1973) required first-grade, third-grade, and college students to learn a list of pictures and then free recall them. After the first study and first free recall trial, subjects were instructed to select half the pictures for additional study. Although third-grade and college students tended to select items not recalled correctly on the first trial, first-grade subjects did not seem to consider first-trial performance in making selection of items for additional processing. Similar findings were reported by Bisanz et al. (1978) for a paired-associate task. They found that fifth-grade and college students were more likely than first-grade or third-grade students to select items not learned on a first trial.

It is somewhat puzzling that young grade-school children do not choose to allocate more study to items that they have not yet mastered. It does not seem likely that it is because that they are unaware of which materials are not known. For instance, Pressley, Levin, Ghatala, and Ahmad (1987) and Pressley and Ghatala (1988) both showed that even first- and second-grade children are aware of which test items they are almost certainly answering correctly and which are probably being answered incorrectly, although there is developmental improvement in these discriminations during the grade-school years. When processing differentially learnable text, even second-grade children know which parts of text are easier to acquire than others (e.g., Danner, 1976).   Apparently, knowing which information is known already or easier to learn and which information is unlikely to have been mastered is not sufficient to result in appropriate self-regulation (i.e., studying the items that have yet to be learned).

Dufresne and Kobasigawa (1989; see Fig. 5.1) provided an exceptionally through analysis of potential relationships between awareness of knowledge state and cognitive self-regulation. They assessed spontaneous allocation of study time in first-, third-, fifth-, and seventh-grade children. Subjects were asked to study booklets containing either "easy" (highly related) or "hard" (unrelated) paired-associate items until they were sure they could remember all pairs perfectly. Whereas the first-grade and third-grade children spent about the same amount of time on easy pairs as they spent on hard pairs, subjects in the two older age groups devoted considerably more time to studying the hard items than the easy ones. These findings confirm the outcomes of previous studies in that cognitive self-regulation can be observed in older but not in younger school children (e.g., Bisanz et al., 1978). Dufresne and Kobasigawa (1989) noted that their younger subjects were able to distinguish between easy and hard item pairs. However, their monitoring skills were not translated into adequate control activities. Does this mean that children younger than 8 years of age

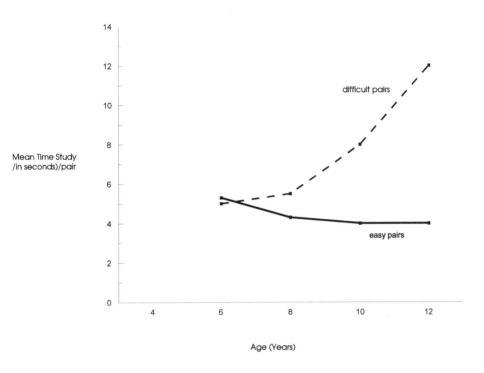

FIG. 5.1. Study time of difficult and easy pairs in Dufresne and Kobasigawa, 1989.
Constructed from data provided in the study.

are generally unable to self-regulate their learning behavior? A recent study
by Kobasigawa and Metcalf-Haggert (1993) indicates that even first-grade
children can allocate study time differentially when differences in item
difficulty are particularly salient. However, it is only in such specific
learning situations that young grade-school children are able to regulate
the use of study time in accordance with information on differential
learnability of item material.

There is no doubt that performance on study time apportionment tasks
strongly depends on the difficulty and complexity of the memory tasks
involved. For example, sophisticated selection of text material for additional study develops somewhat later than the grade-school years. An
optimal strategy for restudy of text is to concentrate not on the most
important ideas of the text (which will probably be recalled anyway) but
rather to concentrate on ideas of intermediate importance. One source of
difficulty for children is that they are not aware of the relative importance
of different parts of complicated text (Brown & Smiley, 1977; Kurtz &
Schneider, 1988), even though they can differentiate important from less
important information in short texts and simple, conventionally structured
stories (e.g., Denhière & Le Ny, 1980; Hoppe-Graff & Schöler, 1980; Yussen

et al., 1980). Brown, Smiley, and Lawton (1978) demonstrated that between fifth grade and college there is development in understanding of parts of text not mastered during a first study-test cycle. Consistent with the hypothesis that children would not make effective use of additional study opportunity, Brown and Smiley (1978) demonstrated that fifth-grade children's recall of text did not improve following 5 minutes of additional study. Seventh-grade, eighth-grade, and high school students did benefit from the additional study time, with the total pattern of data suggesting that knowledge of text parts that were not yet mastered may have directed restudy at those age levels.

"Testing" Effects on Awareness.   Pressley, Levin, and Ghatala (1984) determined that adults did not monitor the differential utility of strategies as they used them; they also determined that testing opportunities made more obvious the relative potency of strategies used by adults. That is, in their studies, when learners studied vocabulary using the keyword method for half the items and rote rehearsal for the remaining items, the learners did not realize that the keyword method was producing much better learning. When learners took a test on all of the vocabulary that were studied, the subjects became aware that they had learned more keyworded than rehearsed items.

   Pressley, Levin, and Ghatala's (1984) study also included 11- to 13-year-old children. There was a clear testing effect with children, although children were not as certain as adults to use the strategy utility information they obtained during testing when they selected between the two strategies in order to learn new vocabulary. Thus, Pressley, Ross, Levin, and Ghatala (1984) hypothesized that children may need prompting in order to use information about the usefulness of strategies that they derive from tests over material learned strategically. In general, this hypothesis was supported in the study. More positively, a variety of data support that children older than 5 monitor how much they learn with a strategy if they are given a test over the items studied with a strategy (Andreassen & Waters, 1989; Cunningham & Weaver, 1989; McGilly & Siegler, 1989). Consistent with Pressley, Ross, et al. (1984), however, there are other data documenting that although 4- to 8-year-olds monitor learning strategy effectiveness during test taking, they do not use the knowledge of strategy utility gained from testing to determine which strategies to use in the future (Fabricius & Cavalier, 1989; Ghatala, Levin, Pressley, & Goodwin, 1986; Ghatala, Levin, Pressley, & Lodico, 1985; Lodico, Ghatala, Levin, Pressley, & Bell, 1983; Rao & Moely, 1989). Test opportunities following strategy use increase knowledge of strategy effectiveness, although tests have a greater effect on learners' use of strategies the older the learner.

Summary: Monitoring. The only evidence of monitoring in pre-schoolers was produced in a simplified feeling-of-knowing task. Although there are clear increases in monitoring skills during the grade-school years, additional developments occur during adolescence. The data reviewed here are also consistent with the conclusion that effective monitoring occurs only in highly constrained situations during the early grade-school years and continues to develop well into adolescence.

METAMEMORY–MEMORY RELATIONSHIPS

One of the main motivations for research on metamemory has been the theoretical conviction that there are important relationships between knowing about memory and memory behaviors (e.g., Brown, 1978; Hagen, 1975). To determine if that was true, Schneider and Pressley (1997) evaluated 123 metamemory–memory correlation coefficients produced in various metamemory studies. The weighted average metamemory–memory correlation coefficient for these studies was .41. There is no doubt that there is a statistical association between metamemory and memory.

A typical feature of more recent studies is that they do not limit themselves to analyses of simple intercorrelations. In several studies (e.g., Kurtz et al., 1986; Schneider, 1986; Schneider et al., 1986; Weinert et al., 1984) multivariate regression analyses were used in order to determine the relative importance of metamemory components and other potential predictors (e.g., verbal intelligence, academic self-concept, attributional style) of semantic-organizational strategy use and/or memory performances in tasks that can be mediated by semantic categorization. From about third grade on, metamemory variables have emerged as significant predictors in these analyses (Kurtz et al., 1986; Schneider et al., 1986; Weinert et al., 1984). Metamemory often predicts memory even when other factors are controlled statistically (e.g., Borkowski et al., 1983; Kurtz et al., 1982).

Recent research on the relationships between metamemory and memory behaviors and performances increasingly have tended to use even more sophisticated approaches than regression, including path and causal models. The basic causal model for analysis of the relationship between metamemory and memory generally assumes that metamemory theoretically precedes memory behaviors and performances. Thus, a child's knowledge about his memory ought to influence strategic behavior, and the amount of strategic behavior should predict memory performance. There is convincing evidence of relationships between metamemory, strategic behaviors, and memory from these studies using causal modeling (Borkowski et al., 1983; Hasselhorn, 1986; Kurtz et al., 1982; Schlagmüller, Visé, Büttner, & Schneider, 1995; Schneider, Körkel, & Weinert, 1987; Weinert et al., 1984; Weinert, Schneider, & Knopf, 1988). Metamemory has proven to be consistently predictive of strategic behaviors in these multivariate analyses even when general factors like intelligence are taken into account. Even relatively young elementary school children possess knowledge about strategies that has a direct influence on strategic behaviors and consequently, subsequent memory.

In general, these analyses point to bidirectional relationships between metamemory and memory behaviors (Borkowski et al., 1990; Schneider, 1985). Metamemory can influence memory behavior, which in turn leads to enhanced metamemory. In comparison, the link between metamemory and memory is weaker than the link between metamemory and strategy use. Factors other than metacognitively directed strategy use can also influence memory (e.g., speed of information processing). We emphasize in presenting this conclusion, however, that it should not be considered a general statement about strategy functioning, since virtually all of the relevant causal model analyses have involved study of metamemory as a predictor of semantic-organizational strategies.

Perhaps that is an appropriate note with which to close this chapter on metamemory. Of the major memory constructs considered in this volume (i.e., memory capacity, knowledge, strategies), metamemory is the newest. Two decades of study have provided some knowledge about it but less complete and certain knowledge than exists about the other constructs highlighted in this volume. The relationships between metamemory, memory, and development have been powerful and orderly enough that we expect much additional research on metamemory in the years ahead.

Chapter 6

Concluding Observations

Our purpose in this chapter is to summarize briefly the most important conclusions that follow from what was reviewed here, as well as to comment on a few directions that might be profitably pursued in future research.

WHAT DEVELOPS?

What has emerged from the research to date is a model that explains memory development in terms of changes in basic memory capacities and mechanisms, declarative knowledge, use of memory strategies, and metamemory.

Basic Memory Capacities and Mechanisms

There is yet little agreement about the role of structural changes in memory capacity with development. There have been arguments that memory capacity was invariant over the life span (at least after 3 to 5 years of age), a theoretical argument that seemed inconsistent with robust correlations between age and children's performance on memory span tasks. How could this be? Case (1985; Case et al., 1982) argued that compared to younger children, older children can hold more information in short-term memory because they execute cognitive operations more efficiently than younger children. Older children have used these operations more—the more an operation has been used, the greater the automatic and efficient use of the operation. In addition, regardless of practice, it seems that there are developmental increases in the execution of cognitive operations (Dempster, 1981). They are carried out faster with development; irrelevant responses are inhibited more certainly; interference is less of a problem. Increases in knowledge with development permit more efficient chunking of information, which increases functional capacity. Because of increases in efficiency with development, execution of cognitive operations consumes less and less capacity with increasing age, and, thus, the functional operating space decreases. Thus, there is increasing capacity available for storage of input, even though the total amount of structurally determined capacity might not change with development. Siegler (1986) provided the following analogy between developmental changes in functional capacity and apparent changes in the capacity of a trunk of an automobile:

> The capacity of a car's trunk does not change as the owner acquires experience in packing luggage into it. Nonetheless, the amount of material that can be packed into the trunk does change. Whereas the trunk at first might hold two or three suitcases, it might eventually come to hold four or five. As each packing operation is executed more efficiently, trunk space is freed for additional operations. (p. 82)

Of course, there is an alternative possibility highlighted by Kail (e.g., 1992a). The developmental increases in efficiency are indicative of increasing actual capacity with development. That is, Kail has provided new evidence for the old thinking that actual capacity increases with age.

We doubt that conventional psychological methods are going to resolve the question of whether functional differences in capacity with development represent increases in operational efficiency or actual capacity (i.e., whether Case and like-minded developmentalists are right or Kail's perspective is more on target). More positively, cognitive neuroscience is making real progress in providing better understanding than ever about neurological capacity involved in determining short-term capacity.

Knowledge Base

What develops with respect to the knowledge base? First of all, it is clear in the 1990s that children's representations are very complex. From early in life, children encode schematically; this schematic representational competency is responsible for the strengths and weaknesses of children's autobiographical memory taken up in the introductory chapter. Children's schematic knowledge makes it easy for them to remember what occurred in a familiar scenario; schematic knowledge also accounts for constructive memory errors, with children often misremembering a particular event in ways that are consistent with their schematic knowledge related to the particular event (e.g., misremembering a visit to a particular museum by recalling things that happen at museums in general).

How both concepts are represented and operate in children's thinking is much better understood now than a decade ago. How episodic and case-based knowledge relates to semantic and schematic knowledge continues to be mapped out. The increased interest of developmental psychologists in representational issues has also inspired what is truly a developmental model of representation, fuzzy trace theory, which posits that children represent everything with a variety of traces simultaneously, some verbatim and some fuzzy. The younger the child, the more dominant the verbatim traces.

In the late 1970s and for much of the 1980s, some believed that most developmental improvements in memory reflected changes in the extent and accessibility of the nonstrategic knowledge base. Especially supportive of this position were empirical demonstrations that children's learning does not vary with age when materials to be learned are equally familiar and meaningful to children at different developmental levels (e.g., Chechile & Richman, 1982). Comparisons of child experts and adults novices were interpreted as striking support for the hypothesis that nonstrategic knowledge is a powerful determinant of performance. Chi's (1978) demonstration that 10-year-old chess experts could learn meaningful chess positions better than adult chess novices was especially well known.

In recent years, the strong knowledge-base hypothesis has yielded to the idea that cognitive development reflects multiple developments in basic capacities, knowledge, strategies, and metamemory and increasing articulation of these components. Thus, increasingly, there have been studies of components in interaction, for example, how use of some strategies depends on the knowledge base.

Strategies

The study of strategies like rehearsal and organizational grouping (i.e., for list learning) quickly made it clear that a relationship existed between age-correlated changes in memory strategies and performance changes. Many developmental psychologists in the 1970s believed that much of memory development could be explained as the development of increasingly flexible and more general memory strategies (e.g., Hagen, Jongeward, & Kail, 1975; Moely, 1977). Because most of the research supporting this hypothesis was generated with grade-school children, 5 to 11 years of age was considered to be an especially crucial period for memory development. These conclusions were premature, however, with a lot of evidence of strategy use during the preschool years and continuation of strategy development after childhood.

Metamemory

There was intensive study of metamemory during the last two decades. Both knowledge of facts about memory and children's memory monitoring were analyzed in detailed.

Memory facts can be divided into knowledge about persons, tasks, strategies, and the interactions between person, tasks, and strategies (Flavell, 1985; Wellman, 1983). The person category refers to whether children understand qualities of their own memories and those of other people. The task category consists of knowledge about what makes one task more difficult than another. The strategy category covers verbalizable knowledge about various encoding and retrieval strategies.

Early research on children's knowledge of memory facts (e.g., Kreutzer et al., 1975) created the impression that knowledge about memory develops quite early and is reasonably complete by Grade 3. More recent research has established that knowledge about persons, tasks, strategies, and the interactions of these variables continues to develop into adulthood.

Monitoring performance on a day-in, day-out basis increases understanding about the relative difficulties of memory tasks, thus, permitting predictions about future performance. That monitoring contributes to the knowledge of memory facts (e.g., that one memory task is more difficult than another) makes obvious that conceptual distinctions between various facets of metamemory (in this case, monitoring and knowledge of memory) are fuzzy indeed. Monitoring of performance in the present (which occurs in short-term memory) is distinctly different from knowledge about memory that is in long-term storage. For instance, monitoring yields online awareness of whether materials that are the current objects of study have been learned already or require additional study. Although children as young as 5 to 6 years of age have some rudimentary monitoring competence, monitoring develops throughout childhood and adolescence.

One of the most important research questions addressed by metamemory researchers was whether empirical support could be produced for theoretically specified connections between metamemory, strategic behaviors, and memory performances. In fact, there are significant relationships between knowledge, behaviors, and performances. The correlations found in the grade-school years were generally medium to high, increasing with increasing age of the children. The average correlation coefficient was .41.

Summary

Preschoolers have little knowledge of memory or variables affecting memory compared to the knowledge they will have when they are 10 and older. In fact, preschoolers possess some knowledge that is wildly inconsistent with reality (e.g., that they can learn enormous amounts of material in a short period of time). Only a few strategies are used during this preschool period, mostly ones that are deployed in familiar situations. There is little monitoring of performance. More positively, the nonstrategic knowledge base undergoes extensive development during this first five years, permitting memory of many schematic situations. Speed of information processing increases.

During grade school (i.e., 5 to 11 years of age), speed of information processing continues to increase. A number of memory strategies emerge and develop; the development of rehearsal and organizational strategies for list learning are documented in some detail in this book. Factual knowledge about memory increases during this period, and monitoring improves. The knowledge base continues to develop and greatly facilitates learning of content that is related to knowledge already possessed by children (e.g., children who know a lot about soccer can learn new information about soccer more easily than children who lack knowledge of soccer). It must be emphasized, however, that development of memory is far from complete by the end of the grade-school years.

Processing speed continues to increase during adolescence. More strategies are acquired during this interval (e.g., elaboration). Old strategies (e.g., rehearsal, organization) continue to develop and are used more flexibly. Monitoring continues to improve. Eighteen-year-olds know more about memory and cognition than do 12-year-olds. Nonetheless, most adults possess only fraction of the strategies, metamemory, and conceptual knowledge base that they could possess, so that we close by addressing the question of whether good information processing might be a fiction.

IS GOOD INFORMATION PROCESSING POSSIBLE?

Are there really good information processors, or was the portrait of good information processing in the first chapter a convenient fiction to justify the research reviewed in this volume? Unfortunately, there are no large-scale, process-sensitive direct observations of learning and memorization across a variety of ecologically valid domains to provide the answers to these questions, despite a great deal of interest in ecologically valid, self-regulated learning (e.g., Bandura, 1977, 1982; Meichenbaum, 1977; Pressley, Borkowski, & Schneider, 1987, 1989; Schunk & Zimmerman, 1994). More positively, there are data that permit the conclusion that some people regulate their learning better than other people do.

Good Information Processing in High Achieving Students

Interview studies about self-regulated learning in the real world have been conducted, and these suggest that some generally competent information processing occurs. One of the best of these was reported by Zimmerman and Pons (1986), who interviewed high school sophomores. Half of the participants were doing well in school and half were doing poorly. These students were probed about their studying in the classroom, at home, when doing writing assignments outside of class, when preparing for tests, and when they were unmotivated. Studying in these situations was tapped by having students respond to meaningful scenarios such as the following: "Most teachers give tests at the end of the marking periods, and these tests greatly determine report card grades. Do you have any particular method for preparing for this type of test in English or history?"(p. 617). These probes elicited rich responses from the students, with many general, goal-specific, and domain-specific strategies cited. For instance, students reported checking and recording what they did not know (i.e., a form of monitoring), organizing and transforming to-be-learned materials (e.g., making outlines), goal setting and planning ahead (e.g., formulating a 2-week study plan), seeking information (e.g., going to the library), taking notes, structuring their environments to be conducive to study, self-rewarding themselves for doing well, rehearsing, seeking social assistance (e.g., asking a knowledgeable friend for help), and reviewing texts and notes. The most striking finding in the study, however, was that the high- and low-achieving students differed greatly in their reported use of self-regulating strategies. The differences in strategy use between ability groups were most notable with respect to seeking information, monitoring, and organizing and transforming. Nonetheless, with the exception of checking their work, high-ability students reported more use of every strategy than did the lower ability participants.

Using a similar questionnaire, Zimmerman and Martinez-Pons (1988) tapped students' use of self-regulated strategies in six different contexts. The teachers of the students in the study also rated them for their self-regulated learning during class. There were strong associations between student self-descriptions, teacher ratings, and actual achievement in mathematics and English. In short, Zimmerman and Pons/Martinez-Pons' data in two studies suggest that some adolescents use strategies extensively and that there are substantial associations between achievement and reported strategy use.

Rohwer, Thomas, and their colleagues carried out one of the most extensive interview studies of classroom learning ever conducted. Students enrolled in junior high school, senior high school, and university social sciences classes served as subjects in the study. The courses that the students were taking were analyzed with respect to the demands that were placed on students and the supports that were provided to students to assist them in completing requirements. Study activities used by students were tapped with a questionnaire that included probes about how students selected important information to study, what they did to comprehend lecture and reading material, how they went about trying to memorize important content, and approaches they used to integrate material within or across informational sources.

An especially revealing set of analyses of these data was conducted by Christopoulos, Rohwer, and Thomas (1987; see also Thomas, 1988). They found that simple rehearsal and nonselective restudy decreased with increasing age level. With increasing age, there was more reporting of self-initiated extra processing of information that was anticipated to present comprehension or memory difficulties. There was also increasing self-initiated investigation, identification, and allocation of attention that was likely to be presented on a test. Selective notetaking increased with age, too. With increasing age, there also was increased elaboration, reorganization, contrasting, integration, and summarization of newly encountered information.

Christopoulos et al. (1987) also documented that with increasing age, however, courses place greater demands on students with diminishing supports, an argument that was bolstered by analyses of this large data set by Strage, Tyler, Rohwer, and Thomas (1987). Thus, Christopoulos et al. (1987) argued that much of the developmental increase in strategy use might be in reaction to changing environmental demands. Nonetheless, despite the pressures applied to university students by their class work, they often engage in less than optimally efficient processing, with some students using very good strategies and others relying predominantly on less efficient routines.

A follow-up of this study was conducted by Thomas et al. (1993) in Grade 12 biology classes. They found associations between student study activities and achievement, as measured by a researcher-administered measurement covering particular content covered in all of the biology classes. Consistent with the perspective throughout this book that strategy use depends on environmental variables, there was more reported strategy use in classes in which the instructors provided support to students in the form of feedback on tests and homework, more quizzes (see also Khalaf & Hanna, 1992), sample test questions for review, and review time in class. Challenging homework resulted in increased use of academic strategies.

The Zimmerman and Pons (1986) and Zimmerman and Martinez-Pons (1988) data and the data collected by Thomas and Rohwer and their colleagues are consistent with other reports of strategy use by adolescents, reports in which very direct measures of strategy use have been employed (Pressley, Levin, & Bryant, 1983). There are a number of sophisticated learning strategies that have been observed in some adolescents but not others. Individual differences in observed and reported use of strategies are almost always correlated with learning and achievement.

Consider three examples: (a) Barclay (1979) reported that a minority of high school students used "cumulative rehearsal and fast finish" to learn a serial list of single items (i.e., cumulatively rehearsing early items in a list combined with rapid processing of the final list items)—a strategy that positively affects performance compared to cumulative rehearsal, an approach more typical of high school students. (b) In studies of adolescent associative learning discussed earlier in this book (Beuhring & Kee, 1987a, 1987b; Kemler & Jusczyk, 1975; Pressley & Levin, 1977a; Suzuki-Slakter, 1988), only some adolescents used elaborative strategies (e.g., constructing interactive images or meaningful sentences containing the items to be associated). Invariably, those adolescents who elaborated learned more associations than did those who did not elaborate. (c) Brown and Smiley (1978) demonstrated that not all high school students use underlining and notetaking strategies when trying to learn text; students who do use these techniques learn more from text than students not employing these techniques. In short, by late adolescence there are students who are appropriately strategic in at least some demanding learning situations.

The research to date does not permit the conclusion, however, that anyone develops into a good information processor. It is not known whether there are people who are appropriately strategic across demanding situations. Would the same students who use the cumulative-rehearsal, fast-finish strategy for serial list learning be the ones who would use associative elaboration for pair learning and/or take notes during reading of text? It is not known whether there are people who consistently monitor when learning and thinking are going well and when they are going poorly, with strategies continued or changed contingent on performance successes and failures. The resolutions of these issues require intensive within-person investigations. It can be concluded based on the extant data, however, that even very capable adults (e.g., university students) often fail to behave like good information processors.

Development of Good Information Processing Through Instruction

One key to the development of good information processors might be instruction. There are important efforts to develop much better information processors using instruction, with researchers in special education especially active in this area of inquiry. Deshler and his associates at the University of Kansas (e.g., Deshler, Alley, Warner, & Schumaker, 1981; Deshler & Schumaker, 1988; Ellis & Lenz, 1987) particularly have lead these efforts, putting together a set of recommendations based on research results, experimenter and teacher intuitions, and theoretical convictions. In short, Deshler and his associates advocate extremely direct and explicit strategy instruction.

Their recommendations include fully explaining strategies, including each step of the procedures. In addition, Deshler espoused modeling of strategies by a variety of teachers in a variety of settings with conditions varied greatly over the course of instruction. The advantages of using the strategy should be fully explained, with students required to assess their own gains as a function of strategy use. The subjects need to rehearse the strategy explicitly and extensively. Students should be taught to use general monitoring and checking strategies in conjunction with other procedures. They should be taught to employ motivational procedures, like use of self-coping statements (e.g., "I can handle this") and use of self-reinforcement (e.g., "I'm doing well here"). These motivational components are included because of the belief by many children who experience learning difficulties that they really do not have the ability to carry out academic tasks (Ryan, Weed, & Short, 1986). Students should also be told explicitly to try to generalize strategies. They should be cued that trained strategies are relevant to future, real-world demands and that they should try to adapt the skills that they are learning to these new situations (cf. Hatano, 1982). Finally, the students have to be transited from the highly structured instructional environment to a world where the cues to use strategies are much less explicit and precise. Gradual loosening of control with the learner slowly assuming self-direction of his thinking is more likely to result in continued use of trained procedures than would an abrupt shift from a highly controlled instructional environment to unstructured settings (e.g., Schumaker, Deshler, & Ellis, 1986).

We believe that the many instructional recommendations made by Deshler and his associates make sense, and they are consistent with other suggestions that have been made following thorough analyses of the development of educationally relevant skills (e.g., Kendall & Braswell, 1985; Pressley, Goodchild et al., 1989).

Although much has been written about all the components and embellishments that should be included in good strategy training, there has been little evaluation of whether the en masse implementation of these recommendations really benefits performance as proposed. Perhaps even more disturbing, many of the components that are included in these packages of recommendations have not been tested in well-controlled experiments that permit the inference that the component is really critical to transfer; virtually none of the components have been subjected to extensive and exhaustive investigation. More such work is sorely needed, even though it is often very expensive. A detailed consideration of one such study by Moely and her colleagues (Leal et al., 1985) makes the time- and resource-intensive nature of this type of work obvious, but it also makes clear that such research is worth it.

Leal et al. (1985) wanted to determine if 8-year-olds could be taught the self-monitoring presumed to be so critical to good strategy use, including transfer of the monitoring skill to untrained problems. In particular, they studied whether children could be taught to test themselves to determine if additional study was necessary before they were ready for a criterion test. In two of the three conditions of the study, subjects were told that self-testing was useful for evaluating task performance. The subjects were required to practice self-testing with three practice items. The participants studied these items, looked away, tried to recall them, and then checked to determine that their recall was correct. The experimenter explained that if all items had not been recalled this would be an indication that not all of the items had been learned and additional study was necessary. The trained children were reminded at the beginning of each of 12 practice trials about the self-testing strategy and about how self-testing aids performance.

The two training conditions differed in that in one condition subjects performed all 12 practice trials on one task—free recall of lists of items for half of the subjects in this condition and serial recall of lists of items for the remaining participants in the condition. In the second training condition subjects practiced on both free and serial recall tasks, doing each for half of the practice trials. Leal et al. (1985) hypothesized that practicing self-monitoring with more than one task would promote generalization of the strategy relative to practice with one task, by increasing the child's awareness that the strategy could be applied to more than one situation. In particular, Leal et al. (1985) expected that general use of self-monitoring would be greatest with the two-task training, but some generalization would occur even with one-task training (e.g., Belmont, Butterfield, & Borkowski, 1978) relative to the third condition in the study, a control condition. Control children were also given 12 trials of practice, with half of the trials requiring serial recall and half requiring free recall. In contrast to the trained subjects, controls were never provided any information about how to study, although they were encouraged to do well and were given consistent praise for their efforts.

One week following the 12 training/control practice trials, subjects were administered tasks to determine if the self-monitoring strategy would be maintained in the absence of a verbal prompt to use the strategy. That is, subjects were given free and serial recall tasks. There was evidence of equal maintenance in the two trained conditions for both free and serial recall in that there was greater use of self-monitoring and greater recall in both of the trained conditions relative to the control condition. In addition, subjects were given three generalization tasks. In one, the children were required to learn the locations of stores on a blueprint of a shopping mall. In the second task, children were required to learn to spell sets of three six-letter nonsense words. The third task was a variation of paired-associate learning. There was evidence of 1-week generalization of self-monitoring in all three of these tasks in that more time was spent self-testing in the trained conditions than in the control condition. Again, however, there appeared to be equivalent generalization in the one- and two-task training conditions.

In short, Leal et al. (1985) failed to find any compelling difference between training with one task and training with two—a finding that seems to contradict recommendations by Deshler et al. (1981) and others that training with multiple tasks promotes durable use of strategies. As careful and thorough as Leal et al. (1985) were, however, it must be emphasized that their evaluation was limited to a comparison of training with one task versus two and to training of only self-testing. Much more careful work on transfer following practice on multiple tasks is required before a definitive conclusion would be justified. More well-controlled studies like Leal et al. (1985) are the most certain route to a definitive conclusion about the training with multiple tasks issue.

We recognize that we have recommended here two very different approaches to evaluation of strategy instruction—both evaluation of training packages and component analyses. The evaluation of packages and of components are complementary activities, not mutually exclusive or antagonistic ones. Both applied and basic research can and are contributing to the understanding of memory development, both natural development and development through instruction.

Summary

It seems likely that people can be educated to be better information processors, although we perceive that such education would not be easy to accomplish. We also do not know if training could ever be complete enough so that even some students would know and deploy appropriately a variety of strategies across a host of domains—or whether such general use of strategies could be developed to the point that there was highly automatized use of many different procedures. The only way to find out how much training can improve functioning is to do intensive, extensive, and long-term strategy training. The development of training packages is a move in the right direction; the training of teachers who are sensitive to the needs of process-oriented instruction is also desirable. The real challenge is to get all of these elements together and functioning for a long period of time with real students. Our point of view is that the many fine well-controlled laboratory studies aimed at specific aspects of memory (i.e., the studies that provided most of the data for this book) could and should be complemented by more ambitious field experiments aimed at improving memory and memory-strategy use as much as possible. It is time to start thinking big—to start thinking about realistic educational interventions that have the potential for broadly enhancing memory functioning in ways that directly improve ecologically valid intellectual performance of students for the rest of their lives.

The Pressley group has also been thinking big in their recent work. They have been conducting studies tapping simultaneous enhancement of repertoires of strategies, knowledge, metacognition, motivation, and functional capacity. The aim of this work was to understand the effects of teaching strategies designed to enhance ecologically valid learning. First, Pressley and his colleagues identified school settings in which effective strategy instruction was ongoing. In particular, some schools are now teaching students a variety of strategies for increasing memory of text; students are commonly taught to make images as they read, ask themselves questions about the content of text, summarize, and reread when confused. The Pressley group focused on schools in which teaching such packages of strategies seemed to produce exceptionally high achievement relative to what would be expected for the population. That is, consistent with much of the "effective schools" literature, they used an "outlier school" methodology (see Firestone, 1991).

At the heart of the instruction they observed were extensive direct explanations and modeling of strategies by adult teachers, with these teachers encouraging strategy application and adaptation over the course of the year. The students practiced use of strategies as part of reading in groups. Strategies are taught over long periods of time in these schools, permitting long-term practice in executing the strategies themselves (and hence increases in automaticity) and in identifying situations that call for the strategies (and hence in metacognition about the strategies). Teachers also provide some metacognitive information, especially emphasizing the advantages conferred by strategies. Students are explicitly taught to coordinate their extensive knowledge of the world with use of strategies. See Pressley, El-Dinary, et al. (1992) for detailed coverage of such instruction, which is substantially more flexible and multifaceted than predecessor strategies instruction.

Brown, Pressley, Van Meter, and Schuder (1996) recently conducted a quasi-experimental evaluation of such instruction. Lower achieving second-grade students in five classes received a year of strategy instruction as described in the last paragraph. Controls in five other classes received conventional instruction. Although the strategy-instructed and control subjects performed comparably during the first semester of the study on a variety of measures tapping memory for text material, by the end of the second semester, there were clear and large advantages for the strategy-instructed subjects over the controls.

Although the Brown et al. (1996) outcomes fuel enthusiasm for long-term strategy instruction that is rich in metamemory and motivational enhancement, rich strategy instruction is not common in schools (see Moely et al., 1992). If such instruction is ever to become more widespread, it is essential that the nature of such teaching not seem overwhelming to teachers. One way to increase understanding of such teaching is to increase understanding of the conceptual foundations of effective learning. We hope that this book advances that cause, making obvious that good thinking and learning is very complicated but that much of it can be understood in terms of capacity, conceptual knowledge, strategies, and metacognition.

This volume represents nothing more than a preliminary report. Memory development has been a fertile area of study since the end of the 19th century and seems a certain bet to be an interesting area of study well into the 21st century.

REFERENCES AND BIBLIOGRAPHY

Adams, L. T., & Worden, P. E. (1986). Script development and memory organization in preschool and elementary school children. *Discourse Processes, 9,* 149–166.

Alexander, J. M., & Schwanenflugel, P. J. (1994). Strategy regulation: The role of intelligence, metacognitive attribution, and knowledge base. *Developmental Psychology, 30,* 709–723.

Allik, J. P., & Siegel, A. W. (1976). The use of the cumulative rehearsal strategy: A developmental study. *Journal of Experimental Child Psychology, 21,* 316–327.

Alvermann, D. E., Smith, L. C., & Readence, J. E. (1985). Prior knowledge activation and the comprehension of compatible and incompatible texts. *Reading Research Quarterly, 20,* 420–436.

Anderson, C. W. (1987). Strategic teaching in science. In B. F. Jones, A. S. Palincsar, D. S. Ogle, & E. G. Carr (Eds.), *Strategic teaching and learning: Cognitive instruction in the content areas.* Alexandria, VA: Association for Supervision and Curriculum Development.

Anderson, R. C., & Pearson, P. D. (1984). A schema-theoretic view of basic processes in reading comprehension. In P. D. Pearson, M. Kamil, R. Barr, & P. Mosenthal (Eds.), *Handbook of reading research* (pp. 255–291). New York: Longman.

Andreassen, C., & Waters, H. S. (1984, April). *Organization during study: Relationships between meta-memory, strategy use, and performance.* Paper presented at the annual meeting of the American Educational Research Association, New Orleans, LA.

Andreassen, C., & Waters, H. S. (1989). Organization during study: Relationships between metamemory, strategy use, and performance. *Journal of Educational Psychology, 81,* 190–195.

Appel, F. L., Cooper, R. G., McCarrell, N., Sims-Knight, J., Yussen, S. R., & Flavell, J. H. (1972). The development of the distinction between perceiving and memorizing. *Child Development, 43,* 1365–1381.

Arnold, D. J., & Brooks, P. H. (1976). Influence of contextual organizing material on children's listening comprehension. *Journal of Educational Psychology, 68,* 711–716.

Ashcraft, M. A., & Kellas, G. (1974). Organization in normal and retarded children: Temporal aspects of storage and retrieval. *Journal of Experimental Psychology, 103,* 502–508.

Asher, S. R., Hymel, S., & Wigfield, A. (1978). Influence of topic interest on children's reading comprehension. *Journal of Reading Behavior, 10,* 35–47.

Ashmead, D. H., & Perlmutter, M. (1980). Infant memory in every day life. In M. Perlmutter (Ed.), *New directions for child development: Children's memory* (pp. 1–16). San Francisco: Jossey-Bass.

Astington, J. W., & Olsen, D. R. (1990). Metacognitive and metalinguistic language: Learning to talk about thought. *Applied Psychology: An International Review, 39,* 77–87.

Atkinson, R. C., & Raugh, M. R. (1975). An application of the mnemonic keyword method to the acquisition of a Russian vocabulary. *Journal of Experimental Psychology: Human Learning and Memory, 104,* 126–133.

Atkinson, R. C., & Shiffrin, R. M. (1968). Human memory: A proposed system and its control processes. In K. W. Spence & J. T. Spence (Eds.), *The psychology of learning and motivation* (Vol. 2, pp. 90–197). New York: Academic Press.

Baddeley, A. D., & Hitch, G. J. (1974). Working memory. In G. H. Bower (Ed.), *The psychology of learning and motivation* (Vol. 8). New York: Academic Press.

Baker, L., & Brown, A. L. (1984). Metacognitive skills and reading. In P. D. Pearson, M. Kamil, R. Barr, & P. Mosenthal (Eds.), *Handbook of reading research* (pp. 353–394). New York: Longman.

Baker-Ward, L., Gordon, B. N., Ornstein, P. A., Larus, D. M., & Clubb, P. A. (1993). Young children's long-term retention of a pediatric examination. *Child Development, 64,* 1519–1533.

Baker-Ward, L., Ornstein, P. A., & Holden, D. J. (1984). The expression of memorization in early childhood. *Journal of Experimental Child Psychology, 37,* 555–575.

Baldwin, R. S., Peleg-Bruckner, Z., & McClintock, A. H. (1985). Effects of topic interest and prior knowledge on reading comprehension. *Reading Research Quarterly, 20,* 497–504.

Bandura, A. (1977). Self-efficacy: Toward a unifying theory of behavioral change. *Psychological Review, 84,* 191–215.

Bandura, A. (1982). Self-efficacy mechanism in human agency. *American Psychologist, 37,* 122–147.

Barclay, C. R. (1979). The executive control of mnemonic activity. *Journal of Experimental Child Psychology, 27,* 262–276.

Baron, J. (1985). *Rationality and intelligence.* Cambridge, England: Cambridge University Press.

Battig, W. F., & Montague, W. E. (1969). Category norms for verbal items in 56 categories: A replication and extension of the Connecticut category norms. *Journal of Experimental Psychology Monographs, 80,* 3.

Bauer, P. J., & Fivush, R. (1992). Constructing event representations: Building on a foundation of variation and enabling relations. *Cognitive Development, 7,* 381–401.

Bauer, P. J., & Mandler, J. M. (1989). One thing follows another: Effects of temporal structure on 1- to 2-year-olds' recall of events. *Developmental Psychology, 25,* 197–206.

Bauer, P. J., & Mandler, J. M., (1992). Putting the horse before the cart: The use of temporal order in recall of events by one-year-old children. *Developmental Psychology, 28,* 441–452.

Bauer, P. J., & Thal, D. J. (1990). Scripts or scraps: Reconsidering the development of sequential understanding. *Journal of Experimental Child Psychology, 50,* 287–304.

Beal, C. R. (1985). Development of knowledge about the use of cues to aid prospective retrieval. *Child Development, 56,* 631–642.

Beal, C. R., & Flavell, J. H. (1982). The effect of increasing the salience of message ambiguities on kindergartner's evaluation of communicative success and message adequacy. *Developmental Psychology, 18,* 43–48.

Beal, C. R., & Fleisig, W. E. (1987, March). *Preschooler's preparation for retrieval in object relocation tasks.* Paper presented at the biennial meeting of the Society for Research in Child Development, Baltimore, MD.

Bebko, J., & McKinnon, E. E. (1990). The language experience of deaf children: The relation of spontaneous rehearsal in a memory task. *Child Development, 61,* 1744–1752.

Belloni, L. E., & Jongsma, E. A. (1978). The effects of interest on reading comprehension of low-achieving students. *Journal of Reading, 22,* 106–109.

Belmont, J. M., & Butterfield, E. C. (1969). The relations of short-term memory to development and intelligence. In L. P. Lipsitt & H. W. Reese (Eds.), *Advances in child development and behavior* (Vol. 4, pp. 30–83). New York: Academic Press.

Belmont, J. M., & Butterfield, E. C. (1971). What the development of short-term memory is. *Human Development, 14,* 236–248.

Belmont, J. M., & Butterfield, E. C. (1977). The instructional approach to developmental cognitive research. In R. V. Kail & J. W. Hagen (Eds.), *Perspectives on the development of memory and cognition* (pp. 437–481). Hillsdale, NJ: Lawrence Erlbaum Associates.

Belmont, J. M., Butterfield, E. C., & Borkowski, J. G. (1978). Training retarded people to generalize memorization methods across memory tasks. In M. M. Gruneberg, P. E. Morris, & R. M. Sykes (Eds.), *Practical aspects of memory* (pp. 418–425). London: Academic Press.

Bender, B. G., & Levin, J. R. (1976). Motor activity, anticipated motor activity, and young children's associative learning. *Child Development, 47,* 560–562.

Berch, D. B., & Evans, R. C. (1973). Decision processes in children's recognition memory. *Journal of Experimental Child Psychology, 16,* 148–164.

Bernstein, M. R. (1955). Relationship between interest and reading comprehension. *Journal of Educational Research, 49,* 283–288.

Best, D. L. (1993). Inducing children to generate mnemonic organizational strategies: An examination of long-term retention and materials. *Developmental Psychology, 29,* 324–336.

Best, D. L., & Ornstein, P. A. (1986). Children's generation and communication of mnemonic organizational strategies. *Developmental Psychology, 22,* 845–853.

Beuhring, T., & Kee, D. W. (1987a). Developmental relationships among metamemory, elaborative strategy use, and associative memory. *Journal of Experimental Child Psychology, 44,* 377–400.

Beuhring, T., & Kee, D. W. (1987b). Elaboration and associative memory development: The metamemory link. In M. A. McDaniel & M. Pressley (Eds.), *Imagery and related mnemonic processes: Theories and applications* (pp. 257–273). New York: Springer-Verlag.

Binet, H. (1909). *Les idees modernes sur les enfants* [Modern thinking about children]. Paris: Schleicher.

Binet, H., & Henri, V. (1894a). La memoire des mots [Memory of words]. *L'Année Psychologique, 1*, 1–23.

Binet, H., & Henri, V. (1894b). La memoire des phrases [Memory of phrases]. *L'Année Psychologique, 1*, 24–59.

Bisanz, G. L., Vesonder, G. T., & Voss, J. F. (1978). Knowledge of one's own responding and the relation of such knowledge to learning. *Journal of Experimental Child Psychology, 25*, 116–128.

Bjorklund, D. F. (1985). The role of conceptual knowledge in the development of organization in children's memory. In C. J. Brainerd & M. Pressley (Eds.), *Basic processes in memory development* (pp. 103–142). New York: Springer.

Bjorklund, D. F. (1987). How age changes in knowledge base contribute to the development of children's memory: An interpretive review. *Developmental Review, 7*, 93–130.

Bjorklund, D. F. (1988). Acquiring a mnemonic: Age and category knowledge effects. *Journal of Experimental Child Psychology, 45*, 71–87.

Bjorklund, D. F., & Bjorklund, B. R. (1985). Organization versus item effects of an elaborated knowledge base on children's memory. *Developmental Psychology, 21*, 1120–1131.

Bjorklund, D. F., & Buchanen, J. J. (1989). Developmental and knowledge base differences in the acquisition and extension of a memory strategy. *Journal of Experimental Child Psychology, 48*, 451–471.

Bjorklund, D. F., & Coyle, T. R. (1995). Utilization deficiencies in the development of memory strategies. In F. E. Weinert & W. Schneider (Eds.), *Memory performance and competencies: Issues in growth and development* (pp. 161–179). Mahwah, NJ: Lawrence Erlbaum Associates.

Bjorklund, D. F., Coyle, T. R., & Gaultney, J. F. (1992). Developmental differences in the acquisition and maintenance of an organizational strategy: Evidence for the utilization deficiency hypothesis. *Journal of Experimental Child Psychology, 54*, 434–448.

Bjorklund, D. F., & Harnishfeger, K. K. (1987). Developmental differences in the mental effort requirements for the use of an organizational strategy in free recall. *Journal of Experimental Child Psychology, 44*, 109–125.

Bjorklund, D. F., & Harnishfeger, K. K. (1990). The resources construct in cognitive development: Diverse sources of evidence and a theory of inefficient inhibition. *Developmental Review, 10*, 48–71.

Bjorklund, D. F., & Harnishfeger, K. K. (1995). The evolution of inhibition mechanisms and their role in human cognition and behavior. In F. N. Dempster & C. J. Brainerd (Eds.), *Interference and inhibition in cognition* (pp. 141–173). San Diego: Academic Press.

Bjorklund, D. F., Schneider, W., Cassel, W. S., & Ashley, E. (1994). Training and extension of a memory strategy: Evidence for utilization deficiencies in the acquisition of an organizational strategy in high- and low-IQ children. *Child Development, 65*, 951–965.

Bjorklund, D. F., Thompson, B. E., & Ornstein, P. A. (1983). Developmental trends in children's typicality judgements. *Behavior Research Methods & Instruments, 15*, 350–356.

Bjorklund, D. F., & Zeman, B. R. (1982). Children's organization and metamemory awareness in their recall of familiar information. *Child Development, 53*, 799–810.

Bjorklund, D. F., & Zeman, B. R. (1983). The development of organizational strategies in children's recall of familiar information: Using social organization to recall the names of classmates. *International Journal of Behavioral Development, 6*, 341–353.

Black, M. M., & Rollins, H. A. (1982). The effects of instructional variables on young children's organization and free recall. *Journal of Experimental Child Psychology, 33*, 1–19.

Blair, R., Perlmutter, M., & Myers, N. A. (1978). Effects of unlabeled and labeled picture cues on very young children's memory for location. *Bulletin of Psychonomic Society, 11*, 46–48.

Bloom, L. (1973). *One word at a time*. The Hague, Netherlands: Mouton.

Bolton, T. L. (1892). The growth of memory in school children. *American Journal of Psychology, 4*, 362–382.

Booth, J. R., & Hall, W. S. (1994). Role of the cognitive internal state lexicon in reading comprehension. *Journal of Educational Psychology, 86*, 413–422.

124   REFERENCES AND BIBLIOGRAPHY

Borkowski, J. G., Carr, M., Rellinger, E., & Pressley, M. (1990). Self-regulated cognition. Interdependence of metacognition, attributions, and self-esteem. In B. F. Jones & L. Idol (Eds.), *Dimensions of thinking and cognitive instruction*. Hillsdale, NJ: Lawrence Erlbaum Associates.
Borkowski, J. G., Levers, S., & Gruenenfelder, T. M. (1976). Transfer of mediational strategies in children: The role of activity and awareness during strategy acquisition. *Child Development, 47,* 779–786.
Borkowski, J. G., Peck, V. A., Reid, M. K., & Kurtz, B. E. (1983). Impulsivity and strategy transfer: Metamemory as mediator. *Child Development, 54,* 459–473.
Bourdon, B. (1894). Influence de l'age sur la memoire immediate [Effects of age on immediate memory]. *Revue Philosophique, 38,* 25–39.
Bousfield, A. K., & Bousfield, W. A. (1966). Measurement of clustering and of sequential constancies in repeated free recall. *Psychological Reports, 19,* 935–942.
Bousfield, W. A. (1953). The occurrence of clustering in the recall of randomly arranged associates. *Journal of Genetic Psychology, 49,* 229–240.
Bousfield, W. A., Esterson, J., & Whitmarsh, G. A. (1958). A study of developmental changes in conceptual and perceptual associative clustering. *The Journal of Genetic Psychology, 98,* 95–102.
Bower, G. H., Black, J. B., & Turner, T. J. (1979). Scripts in memory for text. *Cognitive Psychology, 11,* 177–220.
Brainerd, C. J., & Gordon, L. L. (1994). Development of verbatim and gist memory for numbers. *Developmental Psychology, 30,* 163–177.
Brainerd, C. J., & Reyna, V. F. (1989). Output-interference theory of dual-task deficits in memory development. *Journal of Experimental Child Psychology, 47,* 1–18.
Brainerd, C. J., & Reyna, V. F. (1990a). Can age X learnability interactions explain the development of forgetting? *Developmental Psychology, 26,* 194–204.
Brainerd, C. J., & Reyna, V. F. (1990b). Gist in the grist: Fuzzy-trace theory and the new intuitionism. *Developmental Review, 10,* 3–47.
Brainerd, C. J., & Reyna, V. F. (1993). Domains of fuzzy trace theory. In M. L. Howe & R. Pasnak (Eds.), *Emerging themes in cognitive development, Vol. I: Foundations* (pp. 50–93). New York: Springer-Verlag.
Brainerd, C. J., & Reyna, V. F. (1995). Autosuggestibility and memory development. *Cognitive Psychology, 28,* 65–101.
Brandimonte, M. A., Hitch, G. J., & Bishop, V. M. (1992). Manipulation of visual mental images in children and adults. *Journal of Experimental Child Psychology, 53,* 300–312.
Bransford, J. D., & Johnson, M. K. (1972). Contextual prerequisites for understanding: Some investigations of comprehension and recall. *Journal of Verbal Learning and Verbal Behavior, 11,* 717–726.
Braunshausen, N. (1914). *Die experimentelle Gedächtnisforschung - Ein Kapitel der experimentellen Pädagogik* [The experimental study of memory: A problem of experimental pedagogy]. Langensalza: Beyer & Mann.
Brewer, W. F. (1986). What is autobiographical memory? In D. C. Rubin (Ed.), *Autobiographical memory* (pp. 25–49). Cambridge, England: Cambridge University Press.
Brown, A. L. (1975). The development of memory: Knowing, knowing about knowing, and knowing how to know. In H. W. Reese (Ed.), *Advances in child development and behavior* (Vol. 10, pp. 103–152). New York: Academic Press.
Brown, A. L. (1978). Knowing when, where, and how to remember: A problem of metacognition. In R. Glaser (Ed.), *Advances in instructional psychology* (pp. 77–165). Hillsdale, NJ: Lawrence Erlbaum Associates.
Brown, A. L., & Barclay, C. R. (1976). The effects of training specific mnemonics on the metamnemonic efficiency of retarded children. *Child Development, 47,* 71–80.
Brown, A. L., Bransford, J. D., Ferrara, R. A., & Campione, J. C. (1983). Learning, remembering, and understanding. In J. H. Flavell & E. M. Markman (Eds.), *Handbook of child psychology* (Vol. 3, pp. 77–166). New York: Wiley.
Brown, A. L., & DeLoache, J. S. (1978). Skills, plans, and self-regulation. In R. S. Siegler (Ed.), *Children's thinking: What develops?* (pp. 3–36). Hillsdale, NJ: Lawrence Erlbaum Associates.
Brown, A. L., & Lawton, S. C. (1977). The feeling of knowing experience in educable retarded children. *Developmental Psychology, 13,* 364–370.

Brown, A. L., & Smiley, S. S. (1977). Rating the importance of structural units of prose passages: A problem of metacognitive development. *Child Development, 48*, 1–8.

Brown, A. L., & Smiley, S. S. (1978). The development of strategies for studying texts. *Child Development, 49*, 1076–1088.

Brown, A. L., Smiley, S. S., Day, J. D., Townsend, M. A. R., & Lawton, S. C. (1977). Intrusion of a thematic idea in children's comprehension and retention of stories. *Child Development, 48*, 1454–1466.

Brown, A. L., Smiley, S. S., & Lawton, S. C. (1978). The effects of experience on the selection of suitable retrieval cues for studying texts. *Child Development, 49*, 829–835.

Brown, R., Pressley, M., Van Meter, P., & Schuder, T. (1996). A quasi-experimental validation of transactional strategies instruction with previously low-achieving grade-2 readers. *Journal of Educational Psychology, 88*, 18–37.

Bruck, M., Ceci, S. J., Francoeur, E., & Renick, A. (1995). Anatomically detailed dolls do not facilitate preschoolers' reports of a pediatric examination involving genital touching. *Journal of Experimental Psychology: Applied, 1*, 95–109.

Bruner, J. S. (1966). On the conservation of liquids. In J. S. Bruner, R. R. Olver, & P. M. Greenfield et al. (Eds.), *Studies in cognitive growth* (pp. 183–207). New York: Wiley.

Bruner, J. S., Olver, R. R., & Greenfield, P. M. (Eds.). (1996). *Studies in cognitive growth.* New York: Wiley.

Brunswik, E., Goldscheider, L., & Pilek, E. (1932). Zur Systematik des Gedächtnisses [The systematic study of memory]. In E. Brunswik (Ed.), *Beihefte zur Zeitschrift für angewandte Psychologie, 64*, 1–158.

Burtis, P. J. (1982). Capacity increase and chunking in the development of short-term memory. *Journal of Experimental Child Psychology, 34*, 387–413.

Buss, R. R., Yussen, S. R., Mathews, S. R., Miller, G. E., & Rembold, K. L. (1983). Development of children's use of a story schema to retrieve information. *Developmental Psychology, 19*, 22–28.

Butterfield, E., Nelson, T., & Peck, J. (1988). Developmental aspects of the feeling of knowing. *Developmental Psychology, 24*, 654–663.

Campione, J. C., & Armbruster, B. B. (1985). Acquiring information from texts: An analysis of four approaches. In J. W. Segal, S. F. Chipman, & R. Glaser (Eds.), *Thinking and learning skills, Relating instruction to research* (Vol. 1, pp. 317–359). Hillsdale, NJ: Lawrence Erlbaum Associates.

Carey, S. (1978). A case study: Face recognition. In E. Walker (Ed.), *Exploration in the biology of language* (pp. 175–201). Cambridge, MA: MIT Press.

Carey, S. (1981). The development of face perception. In G. Davies, H. Ellis, & J. Shepherd (Eds.), *Perceiving and remembering faces* (pp. 9–38). London: Academic Press.

Carey, S. (1985). *Conceptual change in childhood.* Cambridge, MA: MIT Press.

Carey, S. (1992). Becoming a face expert. *Philosophical Transactions of the Royal Society of London: Series B, 335*, 95–103.

Carey, S., Diamond, R., & Woods, B. (1980). Development of face recognition: A maturational component? *Developmental Psychology, 16*, 257–269.

Cariglia-Bull, T., & Pressley, M. (1990). Short-term memory differences between children predict imagery effects when sentences are read. *Journal of Experimental Child Psychology, 49*, 384–398.

Carpenter, P. A., & Just, M. A. (1989). The role of working memory in language comprehension. In D. Klahr & K. Kotovsky (Eds.), *Complex information processing: The impact of Herbert A. Simon* (pp. 31– 68). Hillsdale, NJ: Lawrence Erlbaum Associates.

Carr, M., Kurtz, B. E., Schneider, W., Turner, L. A., & Borkowski, J. G. (1989). Strategy acquisition and transfer: Environmental influences on metacognitive development. *Developmental Psychology, 25*, 765–771.

Carson, M. T., & Abrahamson, A. (1976). Some members are more equal than others: The effect of semantic typicality on class-inclusion performance. *Child Development, 47*, 1186–1190.

Case, R. (1985). *Intellectual development: Birth to adulthood.* New York: Academic Press.

Case, R., Kurland, D. M., & Goldberg, J. (1982). Operational efficiency and the growth of short-term memory span. *Journal of Experimental Child Psychology, 33*, 386–404.

Cassel, W. S., & Bjorklund, D. F. (1995). Developmental patterns of eyewitness memory, forgetting, and suggestibility: An ecologically based short-term longitudinal study. *Law and Human Behavior, 19*, 507–532.

Cassel, W. S., Roebers, C. E. M., & Bjorklund, D. F. (1996). Developmental patterns of eyewitness responses to repeated and increasingly suggestive questions. *Journal of Experimental Child Psychology, 61,* 116–133.

Casteel, M. A. (1993). Effects of inference necessity and reading goal on children's inference generation. *Developmental Psychology, 29,* 346–357.

Cavanaugh, J. C., & Borkowski, J. G. (1979). The metamemory-memory "connection": Effects of strategy training and maintenance. *Journal of General Psychology, 101,* 161–174.

Cavanaugh, J. C., & Borkowski, J. G. (1980). Searching for metamemory- memory connections: A developmental study. *Developmental Psychology, 16,* 441–453.

Cavanaugh, J. C., & Perlmutter, M. (1982). Metamemory: A critical examination. *Child Development, 53,* 11–28.

Ceci, S. J. (1984). A developmental study of learning disabilities and memory. *Journal of Experimental Child Psychology, 38,* 352–371.

Ceci, S. J., & Bruck, M. (1993). The suggestibility of the child witness: A historical review and synthesis. *Psychological Bulletin, 113,* 403–439.

Ceci, S. J., & Bruck, M. (1995). *Jeopardy in the courtroom.* Washington, DC: American Psychological Association.

Ceci, S. J., & Howe, M. J. A. (1978). Age-related differences in free recall as a function of retrieval flexibility. *Journal of Experimental Child Psychology, 26,* 432–442.

Ceci, S. J., Lea, S. E. G., & Howe, M. J. A. (1980). Structural analysis of memory traces in children from 4 to 10 years of age. *Developmental Psychology, 16,* 203–212.

Chance, J. E., Turner, A. L., & Goldstein, A. (1982). Development of differential recognition for own and other race faces. *Journal of Psychology, 112,* 29–37.

Chase, W. G., & Simon, H. A. (1973). Perception in chess. *Cognitive Psychology, 4,* 55–81.

Chechile, R. A., & Richman, C. L. (1982). The interaction of semantic memory with storage and retrieval processes. *Developmental Review, 2,* 237–250.

Chen, C., & Stevenson, H. W. (1988). Cross-linguistic differences in digit span of preschool children. *Journal of Experimental Child Psychology, 46,* 150–158.

Chi, M. T. H. (1977). Age differences in memory span. *Journal of Experimental Child Psychology, 23,* 266–281.

Chi, M. T. H. (1978). Knowledge structures and memory development. In R. S. Siegler (Ed.), *Children's thinking: What develops?* (pp. 73–96). Hillsdale, NJ: Lawrence Erlbaum Associates.

Chi, M. T. H. (1981). Knowledge development and memory performances. In M. P. Friedman, J. P. Das, & N. O'Connor (Eds.), *Intelligence and learning* (pp. 221–229). New York: Plenum Press.

Chi, M. T. H. (1985). Interactive roles of knowledge and strategies in the development of organized sorting and recall. In S. F. Chipman, J. W. Segal, & R. Glaser (Eds.), *Thinking and learning skills. Research and open questions* (Vol. 2, pp. 457–483). Hillsdale, NJ: Lawrence Erlbaum Associates.

Chi, M. T. H., Feltovich, P. J., & Glaser, R. (1981). Categorization and representation of physics problems by experts and novices. *Cognitive Science, 5,* 121–152.

Chi, M. T. H., & Koeske, R. D. (1983). Network representation of a child's dinosaur knowledge. *Developmental Psychology, 19,* 29–39.

Chiesi, H. L., Spilich, G. J., & Voss, J. F. (1979). Acquisition of domain-related information in relation to high and low domain knowledge. *Journal of Verbal Learning and Verbal Behavior, 18,* 257–274.

Christopoulos, J. P., Rohwer, W. D., Jr., & Thomas, J. W. (1987). Grade level differences in students' study activities as a function of course characteristics. *Contemporary Educational Psychology, 12,* 303–323.

Clark, E. V. (1973). What's in a word? On the child's acquisition of semantics in his first language. In T. E. Moore (Ed.), *Cognitive development and the acquisition of language* (pp. 65–110). New York: Academic Press.

Clark, J. M., & Paivio, A. (1991). Dual coding theory and education. *Educational Psychology Review, 3,* 149–210.

Cohen, R. L. (1989). Memory for action events: The power of enactment. *Educational Psychology Review, 1,* 57–80.

Cole, M., Frankel, F., & Sharp, D. (1971). Development of free recall in children. *Developmental Psychology, 4,* 109–123.

Cole, M., Gay, J., Glick, J., & Sharp, D. (1971). *The cultural context of learning and thinking.* New York: Basic Books.

Collins, A. M., & Loftus, E. F. (1975). A spreading-activation theory of semantic processing. *Psychological Bulletin, 82,* 407–428.

Collins, W. A., Wellman, H., Keniston, A. H., & Westby, S. D. (1978). Age-related aspects of comprehension and inference from a televised dramatic narrative. *Child Development, 49,* 389–399.

Corbett, A. T., & Dosher, B. A. (1978). Instrument inferences in sentence encoding. *Journal of Verbal Learning and Verbal Behavior, 17,* 479–491.

Cowan, N. (1994). Mechanisms in verbal short-term memory. *Current Directions in Psychological Science, 3,* 185–189.

Cowan, N., Keller, T., Hulme, C., Roodenrys, S., McDougall, S., & Rack, J. (1994). Verbal memory span in children: Speech timing clues to the mechanisms underlying age and word length effects. *Journal of Memory & Language, 33,* 234–250.

Cowan, N., Wood, N., & Keller, T. (1995, April). *Why is speaking rate correlated with memory span?* Presented at the biennial meeting of the Society for Research in Child Development, Indianapolis.

Craik, F. I. M., & Lockhart, R. S. (1972). Levels of processing: A framework for memory research. *Journal of Verbal Learning and Verbal Behavior, 11,* 671–684.

Cross, J. F., Cross, J., & Daly, J. (1971). Sex, race, and beauty as factors in recognition of faces. *Perception and Psychophysics, 10,* 393–396.

Cultice, J. C., Somerville, S. C., & Wellman, H. M. (1983). Preschooler's memory monitoring: Feeling-of-knowing judgements. *Child Development, 54,* 1480–1486.

Cunningham, J. G., & Weaver, S. L. (1989). Young children's knowledge of their memory span: Effects of task and experience. *Journal of Experimental Child Psychology, 48,* 32–44.

Cuvo, A. J. (1974). Incentive level influence on overt rehearsal and free recall as a function of age. *Journal of Experimental Child Psychology, 18,* 167–181.

Cuvo, A. J. (1975). Developmental differences in rehearsal and free recall. *Journal of Experimental Child Psychology, 19,* 265–278.

Daehler, M. W., & Greco, C. (1985). Memory in very young children. In M. Pressley & C. J. Brainerd (Eds.), *Cognitive learning and memory in children. Progress in cognitive development research* (pp. 49–79). New York: Springer-Verlag.

Daneman, M., & Carpenter, P. A. (1989). Individual differences in integrating information between and within sentences. *Journal of Experimental Psychology: Learning, Memory, and Cognition, 9,* 561–583.

Danner, F. W. (1976). Children's understanding of intersentence organization in the recall of short descriptive passages. *Journal of Educational Psychology, 68,* 174–183.

Danner, F. W., & Taylor, A. M. (1973). Integrated pictures and relational imagery training in children's learning. *Journal of Experimental Child Psychology, 16,* 47–54.

Dark, V. J., & Benbow, C. P. (1990). Enhanced problem translation and short-term memory: Components of mathematical talent. *Journal of Educational Psychology, 82,* 420–429.

Dark, V. J., & Benbow, C. P. (1991). Differential enhancement of working memory with mathematical versus verbal precocity. *Journal of Educational Psychology, 83,* 48–60.

Davies, G. M. (1993). Children's memory for other people: An integrative review. In C. A. Nelson (Ed.), *Memory and affect in development: Minnesota symposium on child psychology* (Vol. 26, pp. 123–157). Hillsdale, NJ: Lawrence Erlbaum Associates.

Davies, G. M., Tarrant, A., & Flin, R. (1989). Close encounters of a witness kind: Children's memory for a simulated health inspection. *British Journal of Psychology, 80,* 415–429.

DeLoache, J. S. (1980). Naturalistic studies of memory for object location in very young children. In M. Perlmutter (Ed.), *New directions for child development: Children's memory* (pp. 17–32). San Francisco: Jossey-Bass.

DeLoache, J. S. (1984). "Oh where, oh where": Memory-based searching by very young children. In C. Sophian (Ed.), *Origins of cognitive skills* (pp. 57–80). Hillsdale, NJ: Lawrence Erlbaum Associates.

DeLoache, J. S., Cassidy, D. J., & Brown, A. L. (1985). Precursors of mnemonic strategies in very young children's memory. *Child Development, 56,* 125–137.

DeLoache, J. S., & Marlzoff, D. P. (1995). The use of dolls to interview young children: Issues of symbolic representation. *Journal of Experimental Child Psychology, 60,* 155–173.

DeMarie-Dreblow, D. (1991). Relation between knowledge and memory: A reminder that correlation does not imply causation. *Child Development, 62,* 484–498.

DeMarie-Dreblow, D., & Miller, P. H. (1988). The development of children's strategies for selective attention: Evidence for a transitional period. *Child Development, 59,* 1504–1513.

Dempster, F. N. (1978). Memory span and short-term memory capacity: A developmental study. *Journal of Experimental Child Psychology, 26,* 419–431.

Dempster, F. N. (1981). Memory span: Sources of individual and developmental differences. *Psychological Bulletin, 89,* 63–100.

Dempster, F. N. (1985). Short-term memory development in childhood and adolescence. In C. J. Brainerd & M. Pressley (Eds.), *Basic processes in memory development* (pp. 209–248). New York: Springer-Verlag.

Dempster, F. N. (1991). Inhibitory processes: A neglected dimension of intelligence. *Intelligence, 15,* 157–173.

Dempster, F. N. (1992). The rise and fall of the inhibitory mechanism: Toward a unified theory of cognitive development and aging. *Developmental Review, 12,* 45–75.

Dempster, F. N. (1993). Resistance to interference: Developmental changes in a basic processing mechanism. In M. L. Howe & R. Pasnak (Eds.), *Emerging themes in cognitive development: Vol. 1. Foundations* (pp. 3–27). New York: Springer-Verlag.

Dempster, F. N. (1995). Interference and inhibition in cognition: An historical perspective. In F. N. Dempster & C. J. Brainerd (Eds.), *Interference and inhibition in cognition* (pp. 3–26). San Diego: Academic Press.

Denhière, G., Cession, A., & Deschenes, A. J. (1986, March). *Learning from text: Effects of age and prior knowledge.* Paper presented at the annual meeting of the American Educational Research Association, San Francisco.

Denhière, G., & Le Ny, J. F. (1980). Relative importance of meaningful units in comprehension and recall of narratives by children and adults. *Poetics, 9,* 147–161.

Dent, H., & Stephenson, G. M. (1979). An experimental study of the effectiveness of different techniques of questioning child witnesses. *British Journal of Social and Clinical Psychology, 18,* 41–51.

Deshler, D. D., Alley, G. R., Warner, M. M., & Schumaker, J. B. (1981). Instructional practices for promoting skill acquisition and generalization in severely learning disabled adolescents. *Learning Disability Quarterly, 4,* 415–421.

Deshler, D. D., & Schumaker, J. B. (1988). An instructional model for teaching students how to learn. In J. L. Graden, J. E. Zins, & M. J. Curtis (Eds.), *Alternative educational delivery systems: Enhancing instructional options for all students* (pp. 391–411). Washington, DC: National Association of School Psychologists.

Deshmukh, K., Turner, L., Kurtz, B., & Borkowski, J. G. (1989, March). *Cognitive and metacognitive development in Maharashtrian children: The impact of schooling.* Paper presented at the annual meeting of the American Educational Research Association, San Francisco.

Detterman, D. K. (1994). Intelligence and the brain. In P. A. Vernon (Ed.), *The neuropsychology of individual differences* (pp. 35–57). San Diego: Academic Press.

Diamond, R., & Carey, S. (1977). Developmental changes in the representation of faces. *Journal of Experimental Child Psychology, 23,* 1–22.

Dosher, B. A., & Corbett, A. T. (1982). Instrument inferences and verb schemata. *Memory & Cognition, 10,* 531–539.

Doyle, A. B. (1973). Listening to distraction: A developmental study of selective attention. *Journal of Experimental Child Psychology, 15,* 100–115.

Dube, E. F. (1982). Literacy, cultural familiarity, and "intelligence" as determinants of story recall. In U. Neisser (Ed.), *Memory observed: Remembering in natural contexts* (pp. 274–292). San Francisco: Freeman.

Dudycha, G. J., & Dudycha, M. M. (1941). Childhood memories: A review of the literature. *Psychological Bulletin, 38,* 668–682.

Duffy, G. G., Roehler, L. R., Sivan, E., Rackliffe, G., Book, C., Meloth, M., Vavrus, L., Wesselman, R., Putnam, J., & Bassiri, D. (1987). The effects of explaining the reasoning associated with using reading strategies. *Reading Research Quarterly, 22,* 347–368.

Dufresne, A., & Kobasigawa, A. (1989). Children's spontaneous allocation of study time: Differential and sufficient aspects. *Journal of Experimental Child Psychology, 47,* 274–296.

Ebbinghaus, H. (1897). Über eine neue Methode zur Prüfung geistiger Fähigkeiten und ihre Anwendung bei Schulkindern [About a new method to test mental abilities and their application in school children]. *Zeitschrift für Psychologie und Physiologie der Sinnesorgane, 13*, 401–457.

Eisenberg, A. R. (1985). Learning to describe past experiences in coversation. *Discourse Processes, 8*, 177–204.

Ellis, E. S., & Lenz, B. K. (1987). *A component analysis of effective learning strategies for LD students.* Unpublished manuscript, University of South Carolina, College of Education.

Ellis, H. D. (1990). Developmental trends in face recognition. *The Psychologist, 3*, 114–119.

Ellis, H. D. (1992). The development of face processing skills. *Philosophical Transactions of the Royal Society of London, Series B, 335*, 105–111.

Ellis, H. D., & Flin, R. H. (1990). Encoding and storage effects in 7 year olds' and 10 year olds' memory for faces. *American Journal of Psychology, 94*, 27.

Ellis, N. C., & Henneley, R. A. (1980). A bilingual wordlength effect: Implications for intelligence testing and the relative ease of mental calculation in Welsh and English. *British Journal of Psychology, 71*, 43–52.

Engel, S. (1986). *Learning to reminisce: A developmental study of how young children talk about the past.* Unpublished doctoral dissertation, City University of New York, Graduate Center.

Ericsson, K. A., Krampe, R. T., & Tesch-Römer, C. (1993). The role of deliberate practice in the acquisition of expert performance. *Psychological Review, 100*, 363–406.

Ericsson, K. A., & Simon, H. A. (1980). Verbal reports as data. *Psychological Review, 87*, 215–251.

Ericsson, K. A., & Simon, H. A. (1993). *Protocol analysis: Verbal reports as data.* Cambridge, MA: MIT Press. (Original work published 1984)

Ericsson, K. A., & Smith, J. (Eds.). (1991). *Toward a general theory of expertise: Prospects and limits.* Cambridge, England: Cambridge University Press.

Estes, T. H., & Vaughan, J. L. (1973). Reading interest and comprehension: Implications. *The Reading Teacher, 27*, 149–153.

Fabricius, W. V., & Cavalier, L. (1989). The role of causal theories about memory in young children's memory strategy choice. *Child Development, 60*, 298–308.

Fabricius, W. V., Hodge, M. H., & Quinan, J. R. (1993). Processes of scene recognition in young children and adults. *Cognitive Development, 8*, 343–360.

Fabricius, W., Schwanenflugel, P., & Schick, K. (1995, April). *Conceptual change and theory of mind: Development of the concept of memory from kindergarten to adulthood.* Paper presented at the biennial meeting of the Society for Research in Child Development, Indianapolis.

Farrar, J., & Goodman, G. S. (1990). Developmental differences in the relation between scripts and episodic memory: Do they exist? In R. Fivush & J. Hudson (Eds.), *Knowing and remembering in young children* (pp. 30–64). New York: Cambridge University Press.

Farrar, M. J., & Goodman, G. S. (1992). Developmental changes in event memory. *Child Development, 63*, 173–187.

Feinman, S., & Entwisle, D. R. (1976). Children's ability to recognize other children's faces. *Child Development, 47*, 506–510.

Firestone, W. A. (1991). Educators, researchers, and the effective schools movement. In J. R. Bliss, W. A. Firestone, & C. E. Richards (Eds.), *Rethinking effective schools research and practice* (pp. 12–27). Englewood Cliffs, NJ: Prentice-Hall.

Fivush, R. (1987). Scripts and categories: Interrelationships in development. In U. Neisser (Ed.), *Concepts and conceptual development: Ecological and intellectual factors in categorization* (pp. 234–254). Cambridge, England: Cambridge University Press.

Fivush, R. (1994). Constructing narrative, emotion, and self in parent–child conversations about the past. In U. Neisser & R. Fivush (Eds.), *The remembering self: Construction and accuracy in the self-narrative* (pp. 136–157). Cambridge, England: Cambridge University Press.

Fivush, R., & Hamond, N. R. (1989). Time and again: Effects of repetition and retention interval on 2-year-olds' event recall. *Journal of Experimental Child Psychology, 47*, 259–273.

Fivush, R., & Hamond, N. (1990). Autobiographical memory across the preschool years: Toward reconceptualizing childhood amnesia. In R. Fivush & J. Hudson (Eds.), *Knowing and remembering in young children* (pp. 223–248). New York: Cambridge University Press.

Fivush, R., Hudson, J., Nelson, K. (1984). Children's long-term memory for a novel event: An exploratory study. *Merrill-Palmer Quarterly, 30*, 303–316.

Fivush, R., Kuebli, J., & Clubb, P. A. (1992). The structure of events and event representations: A developmental analysis. *Child Development, 63*, 188–201.

Flavell, J. H. (1970). Developmental studies of mediated memory. In H. W. Reese & L. P. Lipsitt (Eds.), *Advances in child development and behavior* (Vol. 5, pp. 181–211). New York: Academic Press.

Flavell, J. H. (1971). First discussant's comments: What is memory development the development of? *Human Development, 14*, 272–278.

Flavell, J. H. (1985). *Cognitive development* (2nd ed.). Englewood Cliffs, NJ: Prentice-Hall.

Flavell, J. H., Beach, D. H., & Chinsky, J. M. (1966). Spontaneous verbal rehearsal in a memory task as a function of age. *Child Development, 37*, 283–299.

Flavell, J. H., Friedrichs, A. G., & Hoyt, J. D. (1970). Developmental changes in memorization processes. *Cognitive Psychology, 1*, 324–340.

Flavell, J. H., Speer, J. R., Green, F. L., & August, D. L. (1981). The development of comprehension monitoring and knowledge about communication. *Monographs of the Society for Research in Child Development, 46*(5, Serial No. 192).

Flavell, J. H., & Wellman, H. M. (1977). Metamemory. In R. V. Kail & J. W. Hagen (Eds.), *Perspectives on the development of memory and cognition* (pp. 3–33). Hillsdale, NJ: Lawrence Erlbaum Associates.

Flin, R. H. (1980). Age effects for children's memory for unfamiliar faces. *Developmental Psychology, 16*, 373–374.

Frankel, M. T., & Rollins, H. A. (1985). Associative and categorical hypotheses of organization in the free recall of adults and children. *Journal of Experimental Child Psychology, 40*, 304–318.

Galbraith, R. C., Olsen, S. F., Duerden, D. S., & Harris, W. L. (1982). The differentiation hypothesis: Distinguishing between perceiving and memorizing. *American Journal of Psychology, 95*, 655–667.

Garner, R. (1987). *Metacognition and reading comprehension.* Norwood, NJ: Ablex.

Gathercole, S. E., & Baddeley, A. D. (1993). *Working memory and language.* Hillsdale, NJ: Lawrence Erlbaum Associates.

Gathercole, S. E., Willis, C., Emslie, H., & Baddeley, A. (1992). Phonological memory and vocabulary development during the early school years: A longitudinal study. *Developmental Psychology, 28*, 887–898.

Geary, D. C., Bow-Thomas, C. C., Fan, L., & Siegler, R. S. (1993). Even before formal instruction, Chinese children outperform American children in mental arithmetic. *Cognitive Development, 8*, 517–529.

Gehringer, M., & Strube, G. (1985). *Organization and recall of life events: What's special in autobiographical memory?* Unpublished manuscript. Max Planck Institute for Psychological Research, Munich.

Geis, M. F., & Lange, G. (1976). Children's cue utilization in a memory-for-location task. *Child Development, 47*, 759–766.

Gelman, R. (1969). Conservation acquisition: A problem of learning to attend to relevant attributes. *Journal of Experimental Child Psychology, 7*, 167–187.

Gettinger, M. (1989). Effects of maximizing time spent and minimizing time needed for learning on pupil achievement. *American Educational Research Journal, 26*, 73–91.

Ghatala, E. S. (1984). Developmental changes in incidental memory as a function of meaningfulness and encoding condition. *Developmental Psychology, 20*, 208–211.

Ghatala, E. S., Levin, J. R., Foorman, B. R., & Pressley, M. (1989). Improving children's regulation of their reading time. *Contemporary Educational Psychology, 14*, 49–66.

Ghatala, E. S., Levin, J. R., Pressley, M., & Goodwin, D. (1986). A componential analysis of the effects of derived and supplied strategy–utility information on children's strategy selection. *Journal of Experimental Child Psychology, 41*, 76–92.

Ghatala, E. S., Levin, J. R., Pressley, M., & Lodico, M. G. (1985). Training cognitive strategy monitoring in children. *American Educational Research Journal, 22*, 199–216.

Goldstein, A. G., & Mackenberg, E. J. (1966). Recognition of human faces from isolated facial features: A developmental study. *Psychonomic Science, 6*, 149–150.

Goodman, G. S., & Aman, C. (1990). Children's use of anatomically detailed dolls to recount a recent event. *Child Development, 61*, 1859–1871.

Goodman, G. S., Aman, C., & Hirschman, J. (1987). Child sexual and physical abuse: Children's testimony. In S. J. Ceci, M. P. Toglia, & D. F. Ross (Eds.), *Children's eyewitness memory* (pp. 1–23). New York: Springer- Verlag.

Goodman, G. S., & Clarke-Stewart, A. (1991). Suggestibility in children's testimony: Implications for child sexual abuse investigations. In J. L. Doris (Eds.), *The suggestibility of children's recollections* (pp. 92–105). Washington, DC: American Psychological Association.

Goodman, G. S., & Reed, R. S. (1986). Age differences in eyewitness testimony. *Law and Human Behavior, 10,* 317–332.

Goodman, G. S., Wilson, M. E., Hazan, C., & Reed, R. S. (1989, April). *Children's testimony nearly four years after an event.* Paper presented at the annual meeting of the Eastern Psychological Association, Boston, MA.

Gordon, B., Ornstein, P. A., Nida, R. E., Follmer, A., Crenshaw, M. C., & Albert, G. (1993). Does the use of dolls facilitate children's memory of visits to the doctor? *Applied Cognitive Psychology, 7,* 459–474.

Goulet, L. R. (1968). Verbal learning in children: Implications for developmental research. *Psychological Bulletin, 5,* 359–376.

Graesser, A. C., & Nakamura, G. V. (1982). The impact of a schema on comprehension and memory. In G. H. Bower (Ed.), *The psychology of learning and motivation: Advances in research and theory* (Vol. 16, pp. 60–109). New York: Academic Press.

Gruenenfelder, T. M., & Borkowski, J. G. (1975). Transfer of cumulative-rehearsal strategies in children's short-term memory. *Child Development, 46,* 1019–1024.

Guttentag, R. E. (1984). The mental effort requirement of cumulative rehearsal: A developmental study. *Journal of Experimental Child Psychology, 37,* 92–106.

Guttentag, R. E. (1985). Memory and aging: Implications for theories of memory development during childhood. *Developmental Review, 5,* 56–82.

Guttentag, R. E. (1989). Age differences in dual-task performance: Procedures, assumptions, and results. *Developmental Review, 9,* 146–170.

Guttentag, R. E., Ornstein, P. A., & Siemens, L. (1987). Children's spontaneous rehearsal: Transitions in strategy acquisition. *Cognitive Development, 2,* 307–326.

Haake, R. J., Somerville, S. C., & Wellman, H. M. (1980). Logical ability of young children in searching a large-scale environment. *Child Development, 51,* 1299–1302.

Hagen, J. W. (1975). Commentary. *Monographs of the Society for Research in Child Development, 4,* (Serial No. 159).

Hagen, J. W., Hargrave, S., & Ross, W. (1973). Prompting and rehearsal in short-term memory. *Child Development, 44,* 201–204.

Hagen, J. W., Jongeward, R. H., & Kail, R. V. (1975). Cognitive perspectives on the development of memory. In H. W. Reese (Ed.), *Advances in child development and behavior* (Vol. 10, pp. 57–101). New York: Academic Press.

Hagen, J. W., & Kail, R. V. (1973). Facilitation and distraction in short-term memory. *Child Development, 44,* 831–836.

Hagen, J. W., & Kingsley, P. R. (1968). Labeling effects in short-term memory. *Child Development, 39,* 113–121.

Hagen, J. W., & Stanovich, K. G. (1977). Memory: Strategies of acquisition. In R. V. Kail & J. W. Hagen (Eds.), *Perspectives on the development of memory and cognition* (pp. 89–111). Hillsdale, NJ: Lawrence Erlbaum Associates.

Hale, G. A., & Lewis, M. (1979). *Attention and cognitive development.* New York: Plenum.

Harnishfeger, K. K. (1995). The development of cognitive inhibition: Theories, definitions, and research evidence. In F. N. Dempster & C. J. Brainerd (Eds.), *Interference and inhibition in cognition* (pp. 175–204). San Diego: Academic Press.

Harnishfeger, K. K., & Bjorklund, D. F. (1993). The ontogeny of inhibition mechanisms: A renewed approach to cognitive development. In M. L. Howe & R. Pasnak (Eds.), *Emerging themes in cognitive development: Vol. 1. Foundations* (pp. 28–49). New York: Springer-Verlag.

Harnishfeger, K. K., & Bjorklund, D. F. (1994). The ontogeny of inhibition mechanisms: A renewed approach to cognitive development. In M. L. Howe & R. Pasnak (Eds.), *Emerging themes in cognitive development, Vol. 1. Foundations.* New York: Springer-Verlag.

Harris, G. J., & Burke, D. (1972). The effects of grouping on short-term serial recall of digits by children: Developmental trends. *Child Development, 43,* 710–716.

Hasselhorn, M. (1986). *Differentielle Bedingungsanalyse verbaler Gedächtnisleistungen bei Schulkindern* [Differential conditions analysis of verbal memory performance in school children]. Frankfurt/Main: Lang.

Hasselhorn, M. (1990). The emergence of strategic knowledge activation in categorical clustering during retrieval. *Journal of Experimental Child Psychology, 50,* 59–80.

Hasselhorn, M. (1992). Task dependency and the role of category typicality and metamemory in the development of an organizational strategy. *Child Development, 63,* 202–214.

Hasselhorn, M. (1994). Zur Erfassung von Metagedächtnisaspekten bei Grundschulkindern [Assessment of metamemory in elementary school children]. *Zeitschrift für Entwicklungspsychologie und Pädagogische Psychologie, 26,* 71–78.

Hasselhorn, M. (1995). Beyond production deficiency and utilization inefficiency: Mechanisms of the emergence of strategic categorization in episodic memory tasks. In F. E. Weinert & W. Schneider (Eds.), *Memory performance and competencies: Issues in growth and development* (pp. 141–159). Mahwah: NJ: Lawrence Erlbaum Associates.

Hatano, G. (1982). Cognitive consequences of practice in cultural specific procedural skills. *Newsletter of the Laboratory of Comparative Human Cognition, 4,* 15–18.

Hayes, J. R., Waterman, D. A., & Robinson, C. S. (1977). Identifying relevant aspects of a problem text. *Cognitive Science, 1,* 297–313.

Haynes, C. R., & Kulhavy, R. W. (1976). Conservation level and category clustering. *Developmental Psychology, 12,* 179–184.

Heindel, P., & Kose, G. (1990). The effects of motoric action and organization on children's memory. *Journal of Experimental Child Psychology, 50,* 416–428.

Henry, L. A., & Millar, S. (1991). Memory span increases with age: A test of two hypotheses. *Journal of Experimental Child Psychology, 51,* 459–484.

Higbee, K. L. (1977). *Your memory: How it works and how to improve it.* Englewood Cliffs, NJ: Prentice-Hall.

Higbee, K. L. (1987). Process mnemonics: Principles, prospects, and problems. In M. A. McDaniel & P. Pressley (Eds.), *Imagery and related mnemonic processes: Theories, individual differences, and applications* (pp. 407–427). New York: Springer-Verlag.

Hinsley, D., Hayes, J. R., & Simon, H. A. (1977). From words to equations. In P. Carpenter & M. Just (Eds.), *Cognitive processes in comprehension.* Hillsdale, NJ: Lawrence Erlbaum Associates.

Hitch, G. J., Halliday, M. S., Schaafstal, A. M., & Heffernan, T. M. (1991). Speech, "inner speech," and the development of short-term memory: Effects of picture-labeling on recall. *Journal of Experimental Child Psychology, 51,* 220–234.

Holt, J. H. (1964). *How children fail.* New York: Dell.

Hoppe-Graff, S., & Schöler, H. (1980). *Wie gut verstehen und behalten Kinder einfache Geschichten?* [How well do children understand and memorize simple stories?] (Arbeiten der Forschungsgruppe Sprache und Kognition, Ber. Nr. 17) [Reports from the research group on language and cognition, No. 17]. Mannheim, Germany: Universität Mannheim.

Howe, M. L., & Courage, M. L. (1993). On resolving the enigma of infantile amnesia. *Psychological Bulletin, 113,* 305–326.

Howe, M. L., Courage, M. L., & Bryant-Brown, L. (1993). Reinstating preschoolers' memories. *Developmental Psychology, 29,* 854–869.

Hudson, J. A. (1986). Memories are made of this: General event knowledge and the development of autobiographical memory. In K. Nelson (Ed.), *Event knowledge: Structure and function in development* (pp. 87–118). Hillsdale, NJ: Lawrence Erlbaum Associates.

Hudson, J. A. (1988). Children's memory for atypical actions in script based stories: Evidence for a disruption effect. *Journal of Experimental Child Psychology, 46,* 159–173.

Hudson, J. A. (1990). Constructive processes in children's event memory. *Developmental Psychology, 26,* 180–187.

Hudson, J. A., & Fivush, R. (1991). As time goes by: Sixth graders remember a kindergarten experience. *Applied Cognitive Psychology, 5,* 347–360.

Hudson, J. A., Fivush, R., & Kuebli, J. (1992). Scripts and episodes: The development of event memory. *Applied Cognitive Psychology, 6,* 483–505.

Hudson, J., & Nelson, K. (1983). Effects of script structure on children's story recall. *Developmental Psychology, 19,* 625–635.

Hudson, J. A., & Shapiro, L. (1991). Effects of task and topic on children's narratives. In A. McCabe & C. Peterson (Eds.), *New directions in developing narrative structure* (pp. 59–136). Hillsdale, NJ: Lawrence Erlbaum Associates.

Hudson, J. A., & Slackman, E. A. (1990). Children's use of scripts in inferential text processing. *Discourse Processes, 13,* 375–385.

Hulme, C., & MacKenzie, S. (1992). *Working memory and severe learning difficulties.* Hillsdale, NJ: Lawrence Erlbaum Associates.

Hulme, C., Thomson, N., Muir, C., & Lawrence, A. (1984). Speech rate and the development of short-term memory span. *Journal of Experimental Child Psychology, 38,* 241–253.

Hulme, C., & Tordoff, V. (1989). Working memory development: The effects of speech rate, word length, and acoustic similarity on serial recall. *Journal of Experimental Child Psychology, 47,* 72–87.

Huttenlocher, J., & Burke, D. (1976). Why does memory span increase with age? *Cognitive Psychology, 8,* 1–31.

Inhelder, B., & Piaget, J. (1964). *The early growth of logic in the child.* New York: Norton.

Jackson, J. V., & Gildemeister, J. (1991). Effects of strategy training on Black children's free recall, strategy maintenance, and transfer. *Contemporary Educational Psychology, 16,* 183–191.

Jenkins, J. J. (1974). Remember that old theory of memory? Well, forget it! *American Psychologist, 29,* 785–795.

Jensen, A. R. (1981). Reaction time and intelligence. In M. P. Freidman, J. P. Das, & N. O'Connor (Eds.), *Intelligence and learning.* New York: Plenum.

Johnson, C. J. (1994). Inhibitory mechanisms in selection among multiple object names. *Cognitive Development, 9,* 293–309.

Justice, E. M. (1985). Categorization as a preferred memory strategy: Developmental changes during elementary school. *Developmental Psychology, 21,* 1105–1110.

Justice, E. M. (1986). Developmental changes in judgements of relative strategy effectiveness. *British Journal of Developmental Psychology, 4,* 75–81.

Justice, E. M., & Bray, N. W. (1979). *The effects of context and feedback on metamemory in young children.* Unpublished manuscript, Old Dominion University, Norfolk.

Kail, R. (1988). Developmental functions for speeds of cognitive processes. *Journal of Experimental Child Psychology, 45,* 339–364.

Kail, R. (1991). Processing time declines exponentially during childhood and adolescence. *Developmental Psychology, 27,* 259–266.

Kail, R. (1992a). Evidence for global developmental change is intact. *Journal of Experimental Child Psychology, 54,* 308–314.

Kail, R. (1992b). Processing speed, speech rate, and memory. *Developmental Psychology, 28,* 899–904.

Kail, R. (1993). Processing time decreases globally at an exponential rate during childhood and adolescence. *Journal of Experimental Child Psychology, 56,* 254–265.

Kail, R., & Park, Y. (1994). Processing time, articulation time, and memory span. *Journal of Experimental Child Psychology, 57,* 281– 291.

Kearins, J. M. (1981). Visual spatial memory in Australian aboriginal children of desert regions. *Cognitive Psychology, 13,* 434–460.

Kearins, J. M. (1983). A quotient of awareness. *Education News, 18,* 18–22.

Keating, D. P., & Bobbitt, B. L. (1978). Individual and developmental differences in cognitive-processing components of mental ability. *Child Development, 49,* 155–167.

Kee, D. W. (1995). Developmental differences in associative memory: Strategy use, mental effort, and knowledge-access interactions. In H. W. Reese (Ed.), *Advances in child development and behavior* (Vol. 25). New York: Academic Press.

Kee, D. W., & Bell, T. S. (1981). The development of organizational strategies in the storage and retrieval of categorical items in free-recall learning. *Child Development, 52,* 1163–1171.

Kee, D. W., & Davies, L. (1988). Mental effort and elaboration. A developmental analysis. *Contemporary Educational Psychology, 13,* 221–228.

Kee, D. W., & Davies, L. (1990). Mental effort and elaboration: Effects of accessibility and instruction. *Journal of Experimental Child Psychology, 49,* 264–274.

Kee, D. W., & Davies, L. (1991). Mental effort and elaboration: A developmental analysis of accessibility effects. *Journal of Experimental Child Psychology, 52,* 1–10.

Keeney, F. J., Cannizzo, S. R., & Flavell, J. H. (1967). Spontaneous and induced verbal rehearsal in a recall task. *Child Development, 38,* 953–966.

Kelly, M., Scholnick, E. K., Travers, S. H., & Johnson, J. W. (1976). Relations among memory, memory appraisal, and memory strategies. *Child Development, 47,* 648–659.

Kemler, D. G., & Jusczyk, P. W. (1975). A developmental study of facilitation by mnemonic instruction. *Journal of Experimental Child Psychology, 20,* 400–410.

Kendall, P. C., & Braswell, L. (1985). *Cognitive-behavioral therapy for impulsive children.* New York: Guilford.

Keniston, A. H., & Flavell, J. H. (1979). A developmental study of intelligent retrieval. *Child Development, 50,* 1144–1152.

Kennedy, B. A., & Miller, D. J. (1976). Persistent use of verbal rehearsal as a function of information about its value. *Child Development, 47,* 566–569.

Kennedy, S. P., & Suzuki, N. S. (1977). Spontaneous elaboration in Mexican-American and Anglo-American high school seniors. *American Educational Research Journal, 14,* 383–388.

Kesselring, M. (1911). Experimentelle Untersuchungen zur Theorie des Stundenplans [Experimental studies of the theory of times tables]. *Zeitschrift für Pädagogische Psychologie und Experimentelle Pädagogik, 12,* 314–324.

Khalaf, A. S. S., & Hanna, G. S. (1992). The impact of classroom testing frequency on high school students' achievement. *Contemporary Educational Psychology, 17,* 71–77.

King, M. A., & Yuille, J. C. (1986). *An investigation of the eyewitness abilities of children.* Unpublished manuscript, University of British Columbia.

Kingsley, P. R., & Hagen, J. W. (1969). Induced versus spontaneous rehearsal in short-term memory in nursery school children. *Developmental Psychology, 1,* 40–46.

Kintsch, W., & Greene, E. (1978). The role of culture-specific schemata in the comprehension and recall of stories. *Discourse Processes, 1,* 1–13.

Kintsch, W., Mandel, T. S., & Kozminsky, E. (1977). Summarizing scrambled stories. *Memory & Cognition, 5,* 547–552.

Kintsch, W., & van Dijk, T. A. (1978). Toward a model of text comprehension and production. *Psychological Review, 85,* 363–394.

Klausmeier, H. J. (1990). Conceptualizing. In B. F. Jones & L. Idol (Eds.), *Dimensions of thinking and cognitive instruction* (pp. 93–138). Hillsdale, NJ: Lawrence Erlbaum Associates.

Kluwe, R. H., & Schiebler, K. (1984). Entwicklung exekutiver Prozesse und kognitiver Leistungen [The development of executive processes and cognitive performance]. In F. E. Weinert & R. H. Kluwe (Eds.), *Metakognition, Motivation und Lernen* (pp. 31–60). Stuttgart: Kohlhammer.

Kobasigawa, A. (1974). Utilization of retrieval cues by children in recall. *Child Development, 45,* 127–134.

Kobasigawa, A. (1977). Retrieval strategies in the development of memory. In R. V. Kail & J. W. Hagen (Eds.), *Perspective on the development of memory and cognition* (pp. 177–201). Hillsdale, NJ: Lawrence Erlbaum Associates.

Kobasigawa, A., & Metcalf-Haggert, A. (1993). Spontaneous allocation of study time by first- and third-grade children in a simple memory task. *Journal of Genetic Psychology, 154,* 223–235.

Körkel, J. (1987). *Die Entwicklung von Gedächtnis- und Metagedächtnisleistungen in Abhängigkeit von bereichsspezifischen Vorkenntnissen* [The development of memory and metamemory as a function of domain-specific knowledge]. Frankfurt/Main, Germany: Lang.

Kosslyn, S. M. (1980). *Image and mind.* Cambridge, MA: Harvard University Press.

Kosslyn, S. M. (1994). *Image and brain: The resolution of the imagery debate.* Cambridge MA: MIT Press.

Kosslyn, S. M., Margolis, J. A., Barrett, A. M., Goldknopf, E. J., & Daly, P. F. (1990). Age differences in imagery abilities. *Child Development, 61,* 995–1010.

Kreutzer, M. A., Leonard, C., & Flavell, J. H. (1975). An interview study of children's knowledge about memory. *Monographs of the Society for Research in Child Development, 40* (Serial No. 159).

Kunzinger, E. L. (1985). A short-term longitudinal study of memorial development during early grade school. *Developmental Psychology, 21,* 642–646.

Kunzinger, E. L., & Witryol, S. L. (1984). The effects of differential incentives on second-grade rehearsal and free recall. *The Journal of Genetic Psychology, 144,* 19–30.

Kurtz, B. E. (1990). Cultural influences on children's cognitive and metacognitive development. In W. Schneider & F. E. Weinert (Eds.), *Interactions among aptitudes, strategies, and knowledge in cognitive performance* (pp. 177–199). New York: Springer-Verlag.

Kurtz, B. E., & Borkowski, J. G. (1984). Children's metacognition: Exploring relations among knowledge, process, and motivational variables. *Journal of Experimental Child Psychology, 37*, 335–354.

Kurtz, B. E., & Borkowski, J. G. (1987). Development of strategic skills in impulsive and reflective children: A developmental study of metacognition. *Journal of Experimental Child Psychology, 43*, 129–148.

Kurtz, B. E., Borkowski, J. G., & Deshmukh, K. (1988). Metamemory development in Maharashtrian children: Influences from home and school. *Journal of Genetic Psychology, 149*, 363–376.

Kurtz, B. E., Carr, M., & Schneider, W. (1988, April). *Development of attributional beliefs and self-concept in German and American children.* Paper presented at the annual meeting of the American Educational Research Association, New Orleans.

Kurtz, B. E., Reid, M. K., Borkowski, J. G., & Cavanaugh, J. C. (1982). On the reliability and validity of children's metamemory. *Bulletin of the Psychonomic Society, 19*, 137–140.

Kurtz, B. E., & Schneider, W. (1988). The effects of age, study time, and importance of text units on strategy use and memory for texts. *European Journal of the Psychology of Education*, 191–199.

Kurtz, B. E., Schneider, W., Carr, M., Borkowski, J. G., & Rellinger, E. (1990). Strategy instruction and attributional beliefs in West Germany and the United States: Do teachers foster metacognitive development? *Contemporary Educational Psychology, 15*, 268–283.

Kurtz, B. E., Schneider, W., Turner, L., & Carr, M. (1986, March). *Memory performance in German and American children: Differing roles of metacognitive and motivational variables.* Paper presented at the annual meeting of the American Educational Research Association, San Francisco.

Kyllonen, P. C., & Stephens, D. L. (1990). Cognitive abilities as determinants of success in acquiring logic skill. *Learning and Individual Differences, 2*, 129–160.

Lane, D. M., & Pearson, D. A. (1982). The development of selective attention. *Merrill-Palmer Quarterly, 28*, 317–337.

Lane, M. K., & Hodkin, B. (1985). Role of atypical exemplars of social and nonsocial superordinate categories within the class inclusion paradigm. *Developmental Psychology, 21*, 909–915.

Lange, G. (1973). The development of conceptual and rote recall skills among school age children. *Journal of Experimental Child Psychology, 15*, 394–406.

Lange, G. (1978). Organization-related processes in children's recall. In P. A. Ornstein (Ed.), *Memory development in children* (pp. 101–128). Hillsdale, NJ: Lawrence Erlbaum Associates.

Lange, G., Guttentag, R. E., & Nida, R. E. (1990). Relationships between study organization, retrieval organization, and general and strategy-specific memory knowledge in young children. *Journal of Experimental Child Psychology, 49*, 126–146.

Lange, G., MacKinnon, C. E., & Nida, R. E. (1989). Knowledge, strategy, and motivational contributions to preschool children's object recall. *Developmental Psychology, 25*, 772–779.

Lange, G., & Pierce, S. H. (1992). Memory-strategy learning and maintenance in preschool children. *Developmental Psychology, 28*, 453–462.

Lawson, M. J., & Fuelop, S. (1980). Understanding the purpose of strategy training. *British Journal of Educational Psychology, 50*, 175–180.

Leal, L., Crays, N., & Moely, B. E. (1985). Training children to use a self-monitoring study strategy in preparation for recall: Maintenance and generalization effects. *Child Development, 56*, 643–653.

Leontjev, A. N. (1931). *Development of memory.* Moscow: Uchpedgiz.

Leontjev, A. N. (1977). *Probleme der Entwicklung des Psychischen* [Problems regarding the development of psychological functions]. Kronberg, Ts.: Athenäum.

Levie, W. H. (1987). Research on pictures: A guide to the literature. In D. M. Willows & H. A. Houghton (Eds.), *Illustrations, graphs, and diagrams: Psychological theory and educational practice* (pp. 1– 50). New York: Springer-Verlag.

Levin, J. R. (1976). What have we learned about maximizing what children can learn? In J. R. Levin & V. L. Allen (Eds.), *Cognitive learning in children* (pp. 105–134). New York: Academic Press.

Levin, J. R. (1981). The mnemonic '80s: Keywords in the classroom. *Educational Psychologist, 16*, 65–82.

Levin, J. R. (1983). Pictorial strategies for school learning: Practical illustrations. In M. Pressley & J. R. Levin (Eds.), *Cognitive strategy research: Educational applications* (pp. 213–237). New York: Springer-Verlag.

Levin, J. R., Anglin, G. J., & Carney, R. N. (1987). On empirically validating functions of pictures in prose. In D. M. Willows & H. A. Houghton (Eds.), *Illustrations, graphs, and diagrams: Psychological theory and educational practice* (pp. 51–85). New York: Springer-Verlag.

Levin, J. R., McCabe, A. E., & Bender, B. G. (1975). A note on imagery-inducing motor activity in young children. *Child Development, 46,* 263–266.

Levin, J. R., & Pressley, M. (1981). Improving children's prose comprehension: Selected strategies that seem to succeed. In C. Santa & E. Bittayes (Eds.), *Children's prose comprehension: Research and practice* (pp. 44–71). Newark, DE: International Reading Association.

Levin, J. R., Yussen, S. R., DeRose, T. M., & Pressley, M. (1977). Developmental changes in assessing recall and recognition memory capacity. *Developmental Psychology, 13,* 608–615.

Liberman, I. Y., Mann, V. A., Shankweiler, D., & Werfelman, M. (1982). Children's memory for recurring linguistic and nonlinguistic material in relation to reading ability. *Cortex, 18,* 367–375.

Lindberg, M. A. (1980). Is knowledge base development a necessary and sufficient condition for memory development? *Journal of Experimental Child Psychology, 30,* 401–410.

Lipson, M. Y. (1982). Learning new information from text: The role of prior knowledge and reading ability. *Journal of Reading Behavior, 14,* 243–261.

List, J. (1986). Age and schematic differences in the reliability of eyewitness testimony. *Developmental Psychology, 22,* 50–57.

Lobsien, M. (1902). Experimentelle Untersuchungen über die Gedächtnisentwicklung bei Schulkindern [Experimental studies concerning memory development of schoolchildren]. *Zeitschrift für Psychologie und Physiologie der Sinnesorgane, 27,* 34–76.

Lobsien, M. (1911). Zur Entwicklung des akustischen Wortgedächtnisses der Schüler [The development of acoustic word memory in schoolchildren]. *Zeitschrift für Pädagogische Psychologie und Experimentelle Pädagogik, 12,* 238–245.

Lodico, M. G., Ghatala, E. S., Levin, J. R., Pressley, M., & Bell, J. A. (1983). The effects of strategy-monitoring on children's selection of effective memory strategies. *Journal of Experimental Child Psychology, 35,* 263–277.

Lovett, S. B., & Flavell, J. H. (1990). Understanding and remembering: Children's knowledge about the differential effects of strategy and task variables on comprehension and memorization. *Child Development, 61,* 1842–1858.

Luria, A. R. (1961). *The role of speech in the regulation of normal and abnormal behavior.* New York: Pergamon.

Lyon, T. D., & Flavell, J. H. (1993). Young children's understanding of forgetting over time. *Child Development, 64,* 789–800.

Lyon, T. D., & Flavell, J. H. (1994). Young children's understanding of "remember" and "forget." *Child Development, 65,* 1357–1371.

MacDonald, M. C., Just, M. A., & Carpenter, P. A. (1992). Working memory constraints on the processing of syntactic ambiguity. *Cognitive Psychology, 24,* 56–98.

Mandler, J. M. (1978). A code in the node: The use of a story scheme in retrieval. *Discourse Processes, 1,* 14–35.

Mandler, J. M. (1984). *Stories, scripts and scenes: Aspects of schema theory.* Hillsdale, NJ: Lawrence Erlbaum Associates.

Mandler, J. M. (1987). On the psychological reality of story structure. *Discourse Processes, 10,* 1–29.

Mandler, J. M., & DeForest, M. (1979). Is there more than one way to recall a story? *Child Development, 50,* 886–889.

Mandler, J. M., & Johnson, N. S. (1977). Remembrance of things parsed: Story structure and recall. *Cognitive Psychology, 9,* 111–151.

Mandler, J. M., Scribner, S., Cole, M., & De Forest, M. (1980). Cross-cultural invariance in story recall. *Child Development, 51,* 19–26.

Markman, E. M. (1973). *Factors affecting the young child's ability to monitor his memory.* Unpublished doctoral dissertation, University of Pennsylvania.

Markman, E. M. (1989). *Categorization and naming in children.* Cambridge, MA: MIT Press.

Marmor, G. S. (1975). Development of kinetic images: When does the child first represent movement in mental images? *Cognitive Psychology, 7,* 548–559.

Marshall, G. R., & Cofer, C. N. (1970). Single-word free-association norms for 328 responses from the Connecticut cultural norms for verbal items in categories. In L. Postman & G. Keppel (Eds.), *Norms of word association* (pp. 321–360). New York: Academic Press.

Mastropieri, M. A., Scruggs, T. E., & Levin, J. R. (1987). Mnemonic instruction in special education. In M. A. McDaniel & M. Pressley (Eds.), *Imagery and related mnemonic processes: Theories, individual differences, and applications* (pp. 358–376). New York: Springer-Verlag.

Masur, E. F., McIntyre, C. W., & Flavell, J. H. (1973). Developmental changes in apportionment of study time among items in a multitrial free recall task. *Journal of Experimental Child Psychology, 15*, 237–246.

Mayer, R. E. (1982). Memory for algebra story problems. *Journal of Educational Psychology, 74,* 199–216.

Mayer, R. E., Larkin, J. H., & Kadane, J. (1984). A cognitive analysis of mathematical problem solving ability. In R. Sternberg (Ed.), *Advances in the psychology of human intelligence* (pp. 231–273). Hillsdale, NJ: Lawrence Erlbaum Associates.

McCabe, A., & Peterson, C. (Eds.). (1991). *Developing narrative structure.* Hillsdale, NJ: Lawrence Erlbaum Associates.

McCarthy, K. A., & Nelson, K. (1981). Children's use of scripts in story recall. *Discourse Processes, 4,* 59–70.

McClure, E., Mason, J., & Barnitz, J. (1979). An exploratory study of story structure and age effects on children's ability to sequence stories. *Discourse Processes, 2,* 213–249.

McGarry-Roberts, P. A., Stelmack, R. M., & Campbell, K. B. (1992). Intelligence, reaction time, and event related potentials. *Intelligence, 16,* 289–313.

McGilly, K., & Siegler, R. S. (1989). How children choose among serial recall strategies. *Child Development, 60,* 172–182.

McKoon, G., & Ratcliff, R. (1992). Inference during reading. *Psychological Review, 99,* 440–466.

Meacham, J. A. (1977). Soviet investigations of memory development. In R. V. Kail & J. W. Hagen (Eds.), *Perspectives on the development of memory and cognition* (pp. 273–295). Hillsdale, NJ: Lawrence Erlbaum Associates.

Meichenbaum, D. M. (1977). *Cognitive behavior modification. An integrative approach.* New York: Plenum Press.

Merritt, K. A., Ornstein, P. A., & Spicker, B. (1994). Children's memory for a salient medical procedure: Implications for testimony. *Pediatrics, 94,* 17–23.

Meumann, E. (1907). Sechste Vorlesung: Entwicklung der einzelnen geistigen Fähigkeiten beim Kinde (Fortsetzung) [Sixth lecture: Development of the various mental abilities in children]. *Vorlesungen zur Einführung in die Experimentelle Pädagogik (Bd. 1).* Leipzig: Wilhelm Engelmann.

Meumann, E. (1912). Beobachtungen über differenzierte Einstellung bei Gedächtnisversuchen [Observations on differential attitudes regarding memory tests]. *Zeitschrift für Pädagogische Psychologie, 13,* 456–463.

Milgram, N. A. (1967). Verbal context versus visual compound in paired-associate learning in children. *Journal of Experimental Child Psychology, 5,* 597–603.

Miller, C. A. (1956). The magical number seven, plus or minus two: Some limits on our capacity for processing information. *Psychological Review, 63,* 81–97.

Miller, G. E., & Pressley, M. (1989). Picture versus question elaboration on young children's learning of sentences containing high- and low-probability content. *Journal of Experimental Child Psychology, 48,* 431–450.

Miller, P. H. (1990). The development of strategies of selective attention. In D. F. Bjorklund (Ed.), *Children's strategies: Contemporary views of cognitive development.* Hillsdale, NJ: Lawrence Erlbaum Associates.

Miller, P. H. (1994). Individual differences in children's strategic behavior: Utilization deficiencies. *Learning and Individual Differences, 6,* 285–307.

Miller, P. H., Haynes, V. F., DeMarie-Dreblow, D., & Woody-Ramsey, J. (1986). Children's strategies for gathering information in three tasks. *Child Development, 57,* 1429–1439.

Miller, P. H., & Seier, W. L. (1994). Strategy utilization deficiencies in children: When, where, and why. In H. W. Reese (Ed.), *Advances in child development and behavior,* (Vol. 25, pp. 105–156). San Diego: Academic Press.

Miller, P. H., Seier, W. L., Barron, K. L., & Probert, J. S. (1994). What causes a memory strategy deficiency? *Cognitive Development, 9,* 77–101.

Miller, P. H., Seier, W. L., Probert, J. S., & Aloise, P. A. (1991). Age differences in the capacity demands of a strategy among spontaneously strategic children. *Journal of Experimental Child Psychology, 52,* 149–165.

Miller, P., & Sperry, L. (1988). Early talk about the past: The origins of conversational stories of personal experiences. *Journal of Child Language, 15,* 292–315.

Miller, P. H., Woody-Ramsey, J., & Aloise, P. A. (1991). The role of strategy effortfulness in strategy effectiveness. *Developmental Psychology, 27,* 738–745.

Minsky, M. (1975). A framework for representing knowledge. In P. H. Winston (Ed.), *The psychology of computer vision* (pp. 211–277). New York: McGraw-Hill.

Misciones, J. L., Marvin, R. S., O'Brien, R. G., & Greenburg, M. T. (1978). A developmental study of preschool children's understanding of the words "know" and "guess." *Child Development, 48,* 1107–1113.

Mistry, J. J., & Lange, G. W. (1985). Children's organization and recall of information in scripted narratives. *Child Development, 56,* 953–961.

Moely, B. E. (1977). Organizational factors in the development of memory. In R. V. Kail & J. W. Hagen (Eds.), *Perspectives on the development of memory and cognition* (pp. 203–236). Hillsdale, NJ: Lawrence Erlbaum Associates.

Moely, B. E., Hart, S. S., Leal, L., Santulli, K. A., Rao, N., Johnson, T., & Hamilton, L. B. (1992). The teacher's role in facilitating memory and study strategy development in the elementary school classroom. *Child Development, 63,* 653–672.

Moely, B. E., Olson, F. A., Halwes, T. G., & Flavell, J. H. (1969). Production deficiency in young children's clustered recall. *Developmental Psychology, 1,* 26–34.

Monroe, E. K., & Lange, G. (1977). The accuracy with which children judge the composition of their free recall. *Child Development, 48,* 381–387.

Morra, S., Moizo, C., & Scopesi, A. (1988). Working memory (or the M operator) and the planning of children's drawings. *Journal of Experimental Child Psychology, 46,* 41–73.

Moynahan, E. D. (1978). Assessment and selection of paired associate strategies: A developmental study. *Journal of Experimental Child Psychology, 26,* 257–266.

Murphy, M. D. (1979). Measurement of category clustering in free recall. In C. R. Puff (Ed.), *Memory, organization, and structure* (pp. 51–83). New York: Academic Press.

Murphy, M. D., & Puff, C. R. (1982). Free recall: Basic methodology and analyses. In C. R. Puff (Ed.), *Handbook of research methods in human memory and cognition* (pp. 99–128). New York: Academic Press.

Myers, M., & Paris, S. G. (1978). Children's metacognitive knowledge about reading. *Journal of Educational Psychology, 70,* 680–690.

Myers, N. A., & Perlmutter, M. (1978). Memory in the years from two to five. In P. A. Ornstein (Ed.), *Memory development in children* (pp. 191–218). Hillsdale, NJ: Lawrence Erlbaum Associates.

Naus, M. J., & Ornstein, P. A. (1983). Development of memory strategies: Analysis, questions, and issues. In M. T. H. Chi (Ed.), *Trends in memory development research* (Vol. 9, pp. 1–30). Basel: Karger.

Naus, M. J., Ornstein, P. A., & Aivano, S. (1977). Developmental changes in memory: The effects of processing time and rehearsal instructions. *Journal of Experimental Child Psychology, 23,* 237–251.

Neimark, E., Slotnick, N. S., & Ulrich, T. (1971). Development of memorization strategies. *Developmental Psychology, 5,* 427–432.

Nelson, K. (1978). How young children represent knowledge of their world in and out of language. In R. Siegler (Ed.), *Children's thinking: What develops?* (pp. 255–273). Hillsdale, NJ: Lawrence Erlbaum Associates.

Nelson, K. (1986). *Event knowledge: Structure and function in development.* Hillsdale, NJ: Lawrence Erlbaum Associates.

Nelson, K. (1988). The ontogeny of memory for real events. In U. Neisser & E. Winograd (Eds.), *Remembering reconsidered: Ecological and traditional approaches to memory* (pp. 244–276). New York: Cambridge University Press.

Nelson, K. (1993a). Events, narratives, and memory: What develops? In C. A. Nelson (Ed.), *Memory and affect in development: Minnesota symposium on child psychology,* (Vol. 26, pp. 1–24). Hillsdale, NJ: Lawrence Erlbaum Associates.

Nelson, K. (1993b). Explaining the emergence of autobiographical memory in early childhood. In A. F. Collins, S. E. Gathercole, M. A. Conway, & P. E. Morris (Eds.), *Theories of memory* (pp. 355–385). Hillsdale, NJ: Lawrence Erlbaum Associates.

Nelson, K., & Gruendel, J. (1981). Generalized event representations. Basic building blocks of cognitive development. In M. E. Lamb & A. L. Brown (Eds.), *Advances in developmental psychology* (Vol. 1, pp. 131–158). Hillsdale, NJ: Lawrence Erlbaum Associates.

Nelson, K., & Hudson, J. (1988). Scripts and memory: Functional relationship in development. In F. E. Weinert & M. Perlmutter (Eds.), *Memory development: Universal changes and individual differences* (pp. 147–167). Hillsdale, NJ: Lawrence Erlbaum Associates.

Nelson, K., & Ross, G. (1980). The generalities and specifics of long-term memory in infants and young children. In M. Perlmutter (Ed.), *New directions for child development: Children's memory* (pp. 87–101). San Francisco: Jossey-Bass.

Nelson, T. O., & Narens, L. (1980). Norms of 300 general-information questions: Accuracy of recall, latency of recall, and feeling-of-knowing ratings. *Journal of Verbal Learning and Behavior, 19,* 338–368.

Netschajeff, A. (1900). Experimentelle Untersuchungen über die Gedächtnisentwicklung bei Schulkindern [Experimental studies regarding the development of memory in schoolchildren]. *Zeitschrift für Psychologie und Physiologie der Sinnesorgane, 24,* 322–351.

Newman, L. S. (1990). Intentional and unintentional memory in young children. *Journal of Experimental Child Psychology, 50,* 243–258.

Nicolson, R. (1981). The relationship between memory span and processing speed. In M. J. Friedman, J. P. Das, & N. O'Connor (Eds.), *Intelligence and learning* (pp. 179–183). New York: Plenum Press.

Norman, D. A., & Rumelhart, D. E. (1975). *Explorations in cognition.* San Francisco: Freeman.

O'Brien, E. J., & Myers, J. L. (1985). When comprehension difficulty improves memory for text. *Journal of Experimental Psychology: Learning, Memory, and Cognition, 11,* 12–21.

Ormrod, J. E., & Cochran, K. F. (1988). Relationships of verbal ability and working memory to spelling achievement and learning to spell. *Reading Research and Instruction, 28,* 33–43.

Ornstein, P. A., Baker-Ward, L., & Naus, M. J. (1988). The development of mnemonic skill. In F. E. Weinert & M. Perlmutter (Eds.), *Memory development: Universal changes and individual differences* (pp. 31–50). Hillsdale, NJ: Lawrence Erlbaum Associates.

Ornstein, P. A., Medlin, R. G., Stone, B. P., & Naus, M. J. (1985). Retrieving for rehearsal: An analysis of active rehearsal in children's memory. *Developmental Psychology, 21,* 633–641.

Ornstein, P. A., & Naus, M. J. (1978). Rehearsal processes in children's memory. In P. A. Ornstein (Ed.), *Memory development in children* (pp. 69–99). Hillsdale, NJ: Lawrence Erlbaum Associates.

Ornstein, P. A., & Naus, M. J. (1985). Effects of the knowledge base on children's memory strategies. In H. W. Reese (Ed.), *Advances in child development and behavior* (Vol. 19, pp. 113–148). Orlando, FL: Academic Press.

Ornstein, P. A., Naus, M. J., & Liberty, C. (1975). Rehearsal and organizational processes in children's memory. *Child Development, 46,* 818–830.

Ornstein, P. A., Naus, M. J., & Stone, B. P. (1977). Rehearsal training and developmental differences in memory. *Developmental Psychology, 13,* 15–24.

Ornstein, P. A., Shapiro, L. R., Clubb, P. A., & Follmer, A. (1996). The influence of prior knowledge on children's memory for salient medical experiences. In N. Stein, P. A. Ornstein, C. J. Brainerd, & B. Tversky (Eds.), *Memory for everyday and emotional events.* Mahwah, NJ: Lawrence Erlbaum Associates.

O'Sullivan, J. T. (1993). Preschoolers' beliefs about effort, incentives, and recall. *Journal of Experimental Child Psychology, 55,* 396–414.

O'Sullivan, J. T., & Pressley M. (1984). Completeness of instruction and strategy transfer. *Journal of Experimental Child Psychology, 38,* 275–288.

Paivio, A. U. (1971). *Imagery and verbal processes.* New York: Holt, Rinehart, & Winston.

Paivio, A. U. (1986). *Mental representation: A dual-coding approach.* New York: Oxford University Press.

Palermo, D. S., Flamer, G. B., & Jenkins, J. J. (1964). Association value of responses in the paired-associate learning of children and adults. *Journal of Verbal Learning and Verbal Behavior, 3*, 171–175.

Paris, S. G. (1975). Integration and inference in children's comprehension and memory. In F. Restle, R. M. Shiffrin, J. Castellan, H. Lindman, & D. Pisoni (Eds.), *Cognitive theory* (Vol. 1, pp. 223–246). Hillsdale, NJ: Lawrence Erlbaum Associates.

Paris, S. G. (1978). Coordination of means and goals in the development of mnemonic skills. In P. Ornstein (Ed.), *Memory development in children* (pp. 259–273). Hillsdale, NJ: Lawrence Erlbaum Associates.

Paris, S. G., & Carter, A. Y. (1973). Semantic and constructive aspects of sentence memory in children. *Developmental Psychology, 9*, 109–113.

Paris, S. G., & Lindauer, B. K. (1976). The role of inference in children's comprehension and memory for sentences. *Cognitive Psychology, 8*, 217–227.

Paris, S. G., & Lindauer, B. K. (1977). Constructive aspects of children's comprehension and memory. In R. V. Kail & J. W. Hagen (Eds.), *Perspectives on the development of memory and cognition* (pp. 35–60). Hillsdale, NJ: Lawrence Erlbaum Associates.

Paris, S. G., & Lindauer, B. K. (1982). The development of cognitive skills during childhood. In B. Wolman (Ed.), *Handbook of developmental psychology* (pp. 333–349). Englewood Cliffs, NJ: Prentice-Hall.

Paris, S. G., Lipson, M. Y., & Wixson, K. K. (1983). Becoming a strategic reader. *Contemporary Educational Psychology, 8*, 293–316.

Paris, S. G., Newman, R. S., & McVey, K. A. (1982). Learning the functional significance of mnemonic actions: A microgenetic study of strategy acquisition. *Journal of Experimental Child Psychology, 34*, 490–509.

Paris, S. G., & Upton, L. R. (1976). Children's memory inferential relationships in prose. *Child Development, 47*, 660–668.

Parker, J. F., & Carranza, L. E. (1989). Eyewitness testimony of children in target-absent lineups. *Law and Human Behavior, 13*, 133–149.

Parker, J. F., Haverfield, E., & Baker-Thomas, S. (1986). Eyewitness testimony of children. *Journal of Applied Social Psychology, 16*, 287–302.

Pearson, P. D., Hansen, J., & Gordon, C. (1979). The effect of background knowledge on young children's comprehension of explicit and implicit information. *Journal of Reading Behavior, 11*, 201–209.

Peeck, J. (1987). The role of illustrations in processing and remembering illustrated text. In D. M. Willows & H. A. Houghton (Eds.), *Illustrations, graphs, and diagrams: Psychological theory and educational practice* (pp. 115–151). New York: Springer-Verlag.

Peeck, J., van den Bosch, A. B., & Kreupeling, W. J. (1982). Effect of mobilizing prior knowledge in learning from text. *Journal of Educational Psychology, 74*, 771–777.

Pellegrino, J. W., & Hubert, J. L. (1982). The analysis of organization and structure in free recall. In C. R. Puff (Ed.), *Handbook of research methods in human memory and cognition* (pp. 129–172). New York: Academic Press.

Perlmutter, M., Hazen, N., Mitchell, D. B., Grady, J. G., Cavanaugh, J. C., & Flook, J. P. (1981). Picture cues and exhaustive search facilitate very young children's memory for location. *Developmental Psychology, 17*, 104–110.

Peterson, C., & McCabe, A. (1983). *Developmental psycholinguistics: Three ways of looking at a child's narrative.* New York: Plenum.

Piaget, J., & Inhelder, B. (1971). *Mental imagery in the child.* New York: Basic Books.

Pichert, J. W., & Anderson, R. C. (1977). Taking different perspectives on a story. *Journal of Educational Psychology, 69*, 309–315.

Pillemer, D. B., & White, S. H. (1989). Childhood events recalled by children and adults. In H. W. Reese (Ed.), *Advances in child development and behavior* (Vol. 21, pp. 297–340). San Diego, CA: Academic Press.

Pohlmann, A. (1906). *Einfluss der Lokalisation auf das Behalten. Experimentelle Beiträge zur Lehre vom Gedächtnis* [On the impact of localization on memory: Experimental contributions to the investigation of memory]. Berlin: Gerdes & Hödel.

Poole, D., & White, L. (1991). Effects of question repetition on the eyewitness testimony of children and adults. *Developmental Psychology, 27*, 975–986.

Poole, D., & White, L. (1995). Tell me again and again: Stability and change in the repeated testimonies of children and adults. In M. S. Zaragoza, J. R. Graham, C. N. Gordon, R., Hirschman, & Y. Ben Porath (Eds.), *Memory and testimony in the child witness* (pp. 24–43). Newbury Park, CA: Sage.

Posnansky, C. J. (1978a). Age- and task-related differences in the use of category-size information for the retrieval of categorized items. *Journal of Experimental Child Psychology, 26,* 373–382.

Posnansky, C. J. (1978b). Category norms for verbal items in 25 categories for children in grades 2–6. *Behavior Research Methods & Instruments, 10,* 819–832.

Pressley, M. (1977). Imagery and children's learning: Putting the picture in developmental perspective. *Review of Educational Research, 47,* 586–622.

Pressley, M. (1979). Increasing children's self-control through cognitive interventions. *Review of Educational Research, 49,* 319–370.

Pressley, M. (1982). Elaboration and memory development. *Child Development, 53,* 296–309.

Pressley, M. (1986). The relevance of the good strategy user model to the teaching of mathematics. *Educational Psychologist, 21,* 139–161.

Pressley, M., Borkowski, J. G., & Johnson, C. J. (1987). The development of good strategy use: Imagery and related mnemonic strategies. In M. A. McDaniel & M. Pressley (Eds.), *Imagery and related mnemonic processes: Theories, individual differences, and applications* (pp. 274–301). New York: Springer-Verlag.

Pressley, M., Borkowski, J. G., & O'Sullivan, J. T. (1984). Memory strategy instruction is made of this: Metamemory and durable strategy use. *Educational Psychologist, 19,* 94–107.

Pressley, M., Borkowski, J. G., & O'Sullivan, J. T. (1985). Children's metamemory and the teaching of memory strategies. In D. L. Forrest-Pressley, G. E. MacKinnon, & T. G. Waller (Eds.), *Metacognition, cognition, and human performance* (Vol. 1, pp. 111–153). Orlando, FL: Academic Press.

Pressley, M., Borkowski, J. G., & Schneider, W. (1987). Cognitive strategies: Good strategy users coordinate metacognition and knowledge. In R. Vasta & G. Whitehurst (Eds.), *Annals of Child Development* (Vol. 5, pp. 89–129). New York: JAI Press.

Pressley, M., Borkowski, J. G., & Schneider, W. (1989). Good information processing: What it is and what education can do to promote it. *International Journal of Educational Research, 13,* 857–867.

Pressley, M., Cariglia-Bull, T., Deane, S., & Schneider, W. (1987). Short-term memory, verbal competence, and age as predictors of imagery instructional effectiveness. *Journal of Experimental Child Psychology, 43,* 194–211.

Pressley, M., & Dennis-Rounds, J. (1980). Transfer of a mnemonic keyword strategy at two age levels. *Journal of Educational Psychology, 72,* 575–582.

Pressley, M., El-Dinary, P. B., Gaskins, I., Schuder, T., Bergman, J. L., Almasi, J., & Brown, R. (1992). Beyond direct explanation: Transactional instruction of reading comprehension strategies. *Elementary School Journal, 92,* 513–556.

Pressley, M., & Ghatala, E. S. (1988). Delusions about performance on a multiple-choice comprehension test. *Reading Research Quarterly, 23,* 454–464.

Pressley, M., Goodchild, F., Fleet, J., Zajchowski, R., & Evans, E. D. (1989). The challenges of classroom strategy instruction. *Elementary School Journal, 89,* 301–342.

Pressley, M., Johnson, C. J., & Symons, S. (1987). Elaborating to learn and learning to elaborate. *Journal of Learning Disabilities, 20,* 76–91.

Pressley, M., & Levin, J. R. (1977a). Developmental differences in subjects' associative-learning strategies and performance: Assessing a hypothesis. *Journal of Experimental Child Psychology, 24,* 431–439.

Pressley, M., & Levin, J. R. (1977b). Task parameters affecting the efficacy of a visual imagery learning strategy in younger and older children. *Journal of Experimental Child Psychology, 24,* 53–59.

Pressley, M., & Levin, J. R. (1978). Developmental constraints associated with children's use of the keyword method for foreign language vocabulary learning. *Journal of Experimental Child Psychology, 26,* 359–372.

Pressley, M., Levin, J. R., & Bryant, S. L. (1983). Memory strategy instruction during adolescence: When is explicit instruction needed? In M. Pressley & J. R. Levin (Eds.), *Cognitive strategy research: Psychological foundations* (pp. 25–49). New York: Springer-Verlag.

Pressley, M., Levin, J. R., & Delaney, H. D. (1982). The mnemonic keyword method. *Review of Educational Research, 52,* 61–92.

Pressley, M., Levin, J. R., & Ghatala, E. S. (1984). Memory strategy monitoring in adults and children. *Journal of Verbal Learning and Verbal Behavior, 23,* 270–288.

Pressley, M., Levin, J. R., Ghatala, E. S., & Ahmad, M. (1987). Test monitoring in young grade school children. *Journal of Experimental Child Psychology, 43,* 96–111.

Pressley, M., with McCormick, C. B. (1995). *Advanced educational psychology for educators, researchers, and policymakers.* New York: HarperCollins.

Pressley, M., & Miller, G. E. (1987). The effects of illustrations on children's listening comprehension and oral prose memory. In D. M. Willows & H. A. Houghton (Eds.), *Illustrations, graphs, and diagrams: Psychological theory and educational practice* (pp. 87–114). New York: Springer-Verlag.

Pressley, M., Ross, K. A., Levin, J. R., & Ghatala, E. S. (1984). The role of strategy utility knowledge in children's strategy decision making. *Journal of Experimental Child Psychology, 38,* 491–504.

Price, D. W. W., & Goodman, G. S. (1990). Visiting the wizard: Children's memory for a recurring event. *Child Development, 61,* 664–680.

Pritchard, R. (1990). The effects of cultural schemata on reading processing strategies. *Reading Research Quarterly, 25,* 273–295.

Rabinowitz, M. (1984). The use of categorical organization: Not an all-or-none situation. *Journal of Experimental Child Psychology, 38,* 338–351.

Rabinowitz, M. (1988). On teaching cognitive strategies: The influence of accessibility of conceptual knowledge. *Contemporary Educational Psychology, 13,* 229–235.

Rabinowitz, M., & Chi, M. T. H. (1987). An interactive model of strategic processing. In S. J. Ceci (Ed.), *Handbook of the cognitive, social, and physiological characteristics of learning disabilities* (Vol. 2, pp. 83–102). Hillsdale, NJ: Lawrence Erlbaum Associates.

Rabinowitz, M., Freeman, K., & Cohen, S. (1992). Use and maintenance of strategies: The influence of accessibility to knowledge. *Journal of Educational Psychology, 84,* 211–218.

Rabinowitz, F. M., Howe, M. L., & Lawrence, J. A. (1989). Class inclusion and working memory. *Journal of Experimental Child Psychology, 48,* 379–409.

Rabinowitz, M., & Kee, D. (1994). A framework for understanding individual differences in memory: Strategy-knowledge interactions. In P. A. Vernon (Ed.), *The neuropsychology of individual differences* (pp. 135–148). San Diego: Academic Press.

Rabinowitz, M., & McAuley, R. (1990). Conceptual knowledge processing: An oxymoron? In W. Schneider & F. E. Weinert (Eds.), *Interactions among aptitudes, strategies, and knowledge in cognitive performance* (pp. 117–133). New York: Springer-Verlag.

Raine, A., Hulme, C., Chadderton, H., & Bailey, P. (1991). Verbal short-term memory span in speech-disordered children: Implications for articulatory coding in short-term memory. *Child Development, 62,* 415–423.

Rao, N., & Moely, B. E. (1989). Producing memory strategy maintenance and generalization by explicit or implicit training of memory knowledge. *Journal of Experimental Child Psychology, 48,* 335–352.

Ratner, H. H. (1980). The role of social context in memory development. In M. Perlmutter (Ed.), *Children's memory: New directions for child development* (Vol. 10, pp. 49–67). San Francisco: Jossey-Bass.

Ratner, H. H. (1984). Memory demands and the development of young children's memory. *Child Development, 55,* 2173–2191.

Recht, D. R., & Leslie, L. (1988). Effect of prior knowledge on good and poor readers' memory of text. *Journal of Educational Psychology, 80,* 16–20.

Reese, E., Haden, C., & Fivush, R. (1993). Mother–child conversations about the past: Relations of style and memory over time. *Cognitive Development, 8,* 141–148.

Reese, H. W. (1962). Verbal mediation as a function of age level. *Psychological Bulletin, 59,* 502–509.

Renninger, K. A., & Wozniak, R. H. (1985). Effect of interest on attentional shift, recognition, and recall in young children. *Developmental Psychology, 21,* 624–632.

Reyna, V. F. (1995). Interference effects in memory and reasoning: A fuzzy-trace theory analysis. In F. N. Dempster & C. J. Brainerd (Eds.), *Interference and inhibition in cognition* (pp. 29–59). San Diego: Academic Press.

Reyna, V. F., & Brainerd, C. J. (1995). Fuzzy-trace theory: An interim synthesis. *Learning and Individual Differences, 7*, 1–75.

Reynolds, R. E., Shephard, C., Lapan, R., Kreek, C., & Goetz, E. T. (1990). Differences in the use of selective attention by more successful and less successful tenth-grade readers. *Journal of Educational Psychology, 82*, 749–759.

Rickards, J. P. (1976). Interaction of position and conceptual level of adjunct questions on immediate and delayed retention of text. *Journal of Educational Psychology, 68*, 210–217.

Rickards, J. P., & DiVesta, F. J. (1974). Type and frequency of questions in processing text material. *Journal of Educational Psychology, 66*, 354–362.

Ringel, B. A., & Springer, C. J. (1980). On knowing how well one is remembering: The persistence of strategy use during transfer. *Journal of Experimental Child Psychology, 29*, 322–333.

Ritter, K. (1978). The development of knowledge of an external retrieval cue strategy. *Child Development, 49*, 1227–1230.

Ritter, K., Kaprove, B. H., Fitch, J. P., & Flavell, J. H. (1973). The development of retrieval strategies in young children. *Cognitive Psychology, 5*, 310–321.

Robinson, C. S., & Hayes, J. R. (1978). Making inferences about relevance in understanding problems. In R. Revlin & R. E. Mayer (Eds.), *Human reasoning*. Washington, DC: Winston.

Roehler, L. R., & Duffy, G. G. (1984). Direct explanation of comprehension processes. In G. G. Duffy, L. R. Roehler, & J. Mason (Eds.), *Comprehension instruction: Perspectives and suggestions* (pp. 265–280). New York: Longman.

Roenker, D. L., Thompson, C. P., & Brown, S. C. (1971). Comparisons of measures for the estimation of clustering in free recall. *Psychological Bulletin, 76*, 45–48.

Rogoff, B. (1981). Schooling and development of cognitive skills. In H. C. Triandis & A. Heron (Eds.), *Handbook of cross-cultural psychology* (Vol. 4, pp. 233–294). Boston: Allyn & Bacon.

Rogoff, B. (1990). *Apprenticeship in thinking: Cognitive development in social context*. New York: Oxford University Press.

Rogoff, B., & Mistry, J. (1985). Memory development in cultural context. In M. Pressley & C. J. Brainerd (Eds.), *Cognitive learning and memory in children* (pp. 117–142). New York: Springer-Verlag.

Rohwer, W. D., Jr. (1973). Elaboration and learning in childhood and adolescence. In H. W. Reese (Ed.), *Advances in child development and behavior* (Vol. 8, pp. 1–57). New York: Academic Press.

Rohwer, W. D., Jr., & Bean, J. P. (1973). Sentence effects and noun-pair learning: A developmental interaction during adolescence. *Journal of Experimental Child Psychology, 15*, 521–533.

Rohwer, W. D., Jr., Rabinowitz, M., & Dronkers, N. F. (1982). Event knowledge, elaborative propensity, and the development of learning proficiency. *Journal of Experimental Child Psychology, 33*, 492–503.

Roodenrys, S., Hulme, C., & Brown, G. (1993). The development of short-term memory span: Separable effects of speech rate and long-term memory. *Journal of Experimental Child Psychology, 56*, 431–442.

Ross, B. M., & Millsom, C. (1970). Repeated memory of oral prose in Ghana and New York. *International Journal of Psychology, 5*, 173–181.

Rossi, S., & Wittrock, M. C. (1971). Developmental shifts in verbal recall between mental ages two and five. *Child Development, 42*, 333–338.

Roth, C. (1983). Factors affecting developmental changes in speed of processing. *Journal of Experimental Child Psychology, 35*, 509–528.

Rudy, L., & Goodman, G. S. (1991). Effects of participation on children's reports: Implications for children's testimony. *Developmental Psychology, 27*, 527–538.

Ryan, E. B., Weed, K. A., & Short, E. J. (1986). Cognitive behavior modification: Promoting active, self-regulatory learning styles. In J. K. Torgeson & B. Y. L. Wong (Eds.), *Psychological and educational perspectives on learning disabilities* (pp. 367–397). Orlando, FL: Academic Press.

Sadoski, M., Paivio, A., Goetz, E. T. (1991). A critique of schema theory in reading and a dual coding alternative. *Reading Research Quarterly, 26*, 463–486.

Salatas, H., & Flavell, J. H. (1976). Retrieval of recently learned information: Development of strategies and control skills. *Child Development, 47*, 941–948.

Saltz, E., Soller, E., & Sigel, I. (1972). The development of natural language concepts. *Child Development, 43,* 1191–1202.

Saywitz, K., Goodman, G., Nicholas, G., & Moan, S. (1991). Children's memory for genital exam: Implications for child sexual abuse. *Journal of Consulting and Clinical Psychology, 59,* 682–691.

Schank, R. C. (1982). *Dynamic memory: A theory of reminding and learning in computers and people.* New York: Cambridge University Press.

Schlagmüller, M., Visé, M., Büttner, G., & Schneider, W. (1995, September). *Zum Einfluss verschiedener kognitiver und motivationaler Variablen auf die Gedächtnisleistung bei Sort-Recall-Aufgaben* [The effects of cognitive and motivational variables on memory performance in sort-recall tasks]. Paper presented at the biennial meeting of the German Developmental Psychology Association, Leipzig.

Schmidt, C. R., Paris, S. G., & Stober, S. (1979). Inferential distance and children's memory for pictorial sequences. *Developmental Psychology, 15,* 395–405.

Schneider, W. (1985). Developmental trends in the metamemory-memory behavior relationship: An integrative review. In D. L. Forrest-Pressley, G. E. MacKinnon, & T. G. Waller (Eds.), *Metacognition, cognition, and human performance* (Vol. 1, pp. 57–109). Orlando, FL: Academic Press.

Schneider, W. (1986). The role of conceptual knowledge and metamemory in the development of organizational processes in memory. *Journal of Experimental Child Psychology, 42,* 218–236.

Schneider, W. (1993). Domain-specific knowledge and memory performance in children. *Educational Psychology Review, 5,* 257–273.

Schneider, W., & Bjorklund, D. F. (1992). Expertise, aptitude, and strategic remembering. *Child Development, 63,* 461–473.

Schneider, W., & Bjorklund, D. F. (in press). Memory. In D. Kuhn & R. Siegler (Volume Eds.), *Handbook of child psychology: Vol. 2. Cognition, perception, and language* (5th ed.). New York: Wiley.

Schneider, W., Bjorklund, D. F., & Maier-Brückner, W. (1996). The effects of expertise and IQ on children's memory: When knowledge is, and when it is not enough. *International Journal of Behavioral Development.*

Schneider, W., Borkowski, J. G., Kurtz, B. E., & Kerwin, K. (1986). Metamemory and motivation: A comparison of strategy use and performance in German and American children. *Journal of Cross-Cultural Psychology, 17,* 315–336.

Schneider, W., Gruber, H., Gold, A., & Opwis, K. (1993). Chess expertise and memory for chess positions in children and adults. *Journal of Experimental Child Psychology, 56,* 328–349.

Schneider, W., & Körkel, J. (1989). The knowledge base and text recall: Evidence from a short-term longitudinal study. *Contemporary Educational Psychology, 14,* 382–393.

Schneider, W., Körkel, J., & Vogel, K. (1987). Zusammenhänge zwischen Metagedächtnis, strategischem Verhalten und Gedächtnisleistungen im Grundschulalter: Eine entwicklungspsychologische Studie [Relationships among metamemory, strategy development, and memory performance in elementary school children: A developmental study]. *Zeitschrift für Entwicklungspsychologie und Pädagogische Psychologie, 19,* 99–115.

Schneider, W., Körkel, J., & Weinert, F. E. (1987). The effects of intelligence, self-concept, and attributional style on metamemory and memory behavior. *International Journal of Behavioral Development, 10,* 281–299.

Schneider, W., Körkel, J., & Weinert, F. E. (1989). Domain-specific knowledge and memory performance: A comparison of high- and low-aptitude children. *Journal of Educational Psychology, 81,* 306–312.

Schneider, W., Körkel, J., & Weinert, F. E. (1990). Expert knowledge, general abilities, and text processing. In W. Schneider & F. E. Weinert (Eds.), *Interactions among aptitudes, strategies, and knowledge in cognitive performance* (pp. 235–251). New York: Springer-Verlag.

Schneider, W., & Näslund, J. C. (1992). Cognitive prerequisites of reading and spelling. In A. Demetriou, M. Shayer, & A. Efklides (Eds.), *Neo-Piagetian theories of cognitive development* (pp. 256–274). London: Routledge.

Schneider, W., & Pressley, M. (1997). *Memory development between two and twenty* (2nd ed.). Mahwah, NJ: Lawrence Erlbaum Associates.

Schneider, W., & Sodian, B. (1988). Metamemory-memory behavior relationships in young children: Evidence from a memory-for-location task. *Journal of Experimental Child Psychology, 45,* 209–233.

Schneider, W., & Sodian, B. (1991). A longitudinal study of young children's memory behavior and performance in a sort-recall task. *Journal of Experimental Child Psychology, 51,* 14–29.

Schneider, W., & Uhl, C. (1990). Metagedächtnis, Strategienutzung und Gedächtnisleistung: Vergleichende Analysen bei Kindern, jüngeren Erwachsenen und alten Menschen [Metamemory, strategy use, and memory performance: A comparison among children, young adults, and the elderly]. *Zeitschrift für Entwicklungspsychologie und Pädagogische Psychologie, 22,* 22–41.

Schneider, W., & Weinert, F. E. (1995). Memory development during early and middle childhood: Findings from the Munich Longitudinal Study (LOGIC). In F. E. Weinert & W. Schneider (Eds.), *Memory performance and competencies: Issues in growth and development* (pp. 263–279). Mahwah, NJ: Lawrence Erlbaum Associates.

Schumaker, J. B., Deshler, D. D., & Ellis, E. S. (1986). Intervention issues related to the education of LD adolescents. In J. K. Torgeson & B. Y. L. Wong (Eds.), *Psychological and educational perspectives on learning disabilities* (pp. 329–365). Orlando, FL: Academic Press.

Schunk, D. H., & Zimmerman, B. J. (1994). *Self-regulation of learning and performance.* Hillsdale, NJ: Lawrence Erlbaum Associates.

Schwanenflugel, P. J., Fabricius, W. V., & Alexander, J. (1994). Developing theories of mind: Understanding concepts and relations between mental activities. *Child Development, 65,* 1546–1563.

Scribner, S., & Cole, M. (1972). Effects of constrained recall training on children's performance in a verbal memory task. *Child Development, 43,* 845–857.

Shepard, R. N., & Metzler, J. (1971). Mental rotation of three-dimensional objects. *Science, 171,* 701–703.

Siegel, L. S., & Ryan, E. B. (1989). The development of working memory in normally achieving and subtypes of learning disabled children. *Child Development, 60,* 973–980.

Siegler, R. S. (1983). Information processing approaches to development. In P. H. Mussen (Ed.), *Handbook of child psychology: History, theory, and methods* (Vol. 1, pp. 129–211). New York: John Wiley & Sons.

Siegler, R. S. (1986). *Children's thinking.* Englewood Cliffs, NJ: Prentice-Hall.

Simon, H. A. (1974). How big is a chunk? *Science, 183,* 482–488.

Singer, M. (1979a). Processes of inference in sentence encoding. *Memory & Cognition, 7,* 192–200.

Singer, M. (1979b). Temporal locus of inference in the comprehension of brief passages: Recognizing and verifying implications about instruments. *Perceptual and Motor Skills, 49,* 539–550.

Small, M. Y., Lovett, S. B., & Scher, M. S. (1993). Pictures facilitate children's recall of unillustrated prose. *Journal of Educational Psychology, 85,* 520–528.

Smirnov, A. A. (1973). *Problems of the psychology of memory.* New York: Plenum.

Smirnov, A. A., & Zinchenko, P. I. (1969). Problems in the psychology of memory. In M. Cole & J. Maltzman (Eds.), *A handbook of contemporary Soviet psychology* (pp. 452–502). New York: Basic Books.

Smith, C. L. (1979). Children's understanding of natural language categories. *Journal of Experimental Child Psychology, 30,* 191–205.

Smith, L. C., Readence, J. E., & Alvermann, D. E. (1984). Effects of activating background knowledge on comprehension of expository prose. *33rd Yearbook of the National Reading Conference.* Rochester, NY: National Reading Conference, 188–192.

Sodian, B., & Schneider, W. (1990). Children's understanding of cognitive cuing: How to manipulate cues to fool a competitor. *Child Development, 61,* 697–704.

Sodian, B., & Schneider, W. (in press). Memory strategy development: Gradual increase, sudden insight, or roller coaster? In F. E. Weinert & W. Schneider (Eds.), *Individual development from 3 to 12: Findings from the Munich Longitudinal Study.* Cambridge, England: Cambridge University Press.

Sodian, B., Schneider, W., & Perlmutter, M. (1986). Recall, clustering, and metamemory in young children. *Journal of Experimental Child Psychology, 41,* 395–410.

Somerville, S. C., Wellman, H. M., & Cultice, J. C. (1983). Young children's deliberate reminding. *The Journal of Genetic Psychology, 143,* 87–96.

Sophian, C., Larkin, J. H., & Kadane, J. B. (1985). A developmental model of search: Stochastic estimation of children's rule use. In H. M. Wellman (Ed.), *Children's searching: The development of search skill and spatial representation* (pp. 185–214). Hillsdale, NJ: Lawrence Erlbaum Associates.

Speer, J. R., & Flavell, J. H. (1979). Young children's knowledge of the relative difficulty of recognition and recall memory tasks. *Developmental Psychology, 15*, 214–217.

Spiker, C. C. (1960). Associative transfer in verbal paired-associate learning. *Child Development, 31*, 73–87.

Spring, C., & Capps, C. (1974). Encoding speed, rehearsal, and probed recall of dyslexic boys. *Journal of Educational Psychology, 66*, 780–786.

Stein, N. L., & Glenn, C. G. (1975, March). *A developmental study of children's recall of story material.* Paper presented at the biennial meeting of the Society for Research in Child Development, Denver, CO.

Stein, N. L., & Glenn, C. G. (1979). An analysis of story comprehension in elementary school children. In R. Freedle (Ed.), *New directions in discourse processing* (pp. 53–120). Norwood, NJ: Ablex.

Stein, N. L., & Nezworski, T. (1978). The effects of organization and instructional set on story memory. *Discourse Processes, 1*, 177–193.

Steinberg, E. R., & Anderson, R. C. (1975). Hierarchical semantic organization in 6-year-olds. *Journal of Experimental Child Psychology, 19*, 544–553.

Stevens, K. (1980). The effect of topic interest on the reading comprehension of higher ability students. *Journal of Educational Research, 73*, 365–368.

Stevenson, H. W. (1992). Learning from Asian schools. *Scientific American, 267*(6), 70–76.

Stewart, L., & Pascual-Leone, J. (1992). Mental capacity constraints and the development of moral reasoning. *Journal of Experimental Child Psychology, 54*, 251–287.

Stigler, J. W., Lee, S., & Stevenson, H. W. (1986). Digit memory in Chinese and English: Evidence for a temporarily limited store. *Cognition, 23*, 1–20.

Strage, A., Tyler, A. B., Rohwer, W. D., Jr., & Thomas, J. W. (1987). An analytic framework for assessing distinctive course features with and across grade levels. *Contemporary Educational Psychology, 12*, 280–302.

Strutt, G. F., Anderson, D. R., & Weil, A. D. (1975). A developmental study of the effects of irrelevant information of speeded classification. *Journal of Experimental Child Psychology, 20*, 127–135.

Suzuki-Slakter, N. S. (1988). Elaboration and metamemory during adolescence. *Contemporary Educational Psychology, 13*, 206–220.

Swanson, H. L. (1992). Generality and modifiability of working memory among skilled and less skilled readers. *Journal of Educational Psychology, 84*, 473–488.

Swanson, H. L. (1993). Working memory in learning disability subgroups. *Journal of Experimental Child Psychology, 56*, 87–114.

Swanson, H. L., & Cooney, J. B. (1991). Learning disabilities and memory. In B. Y. L. Wong (Ed.), *Learning about learning disabilities* (pp. 104–127). San Diego: Academic Press.

Swimney, D. A., & Prather, P. (1989). On the comprehension of lexical ambiguity by young children: Investigation into the development of mental modularity. In D. S. Gorfein (Ed.), *Resolving semantic ambiguity* (pp. 225–238). New York: Springer-Verlag.

Symons, S., & Greene, C. (1993). Elaborative interrogation and children's learning of unfamiliar facts. *Applied Cognitive Psychology, 7*, 219–228.

Tajika, H., Taniguchi, A., Yamamoto, K., & Mayer, R. E. (1988). Effects of pictorial advance organizers on passage retention. *Contemporary Educational Psychology, 13*, 133–139.

Tatarsky, J. H. (1974). The influence of dimensional manipulations on class-inclusion performance. *Child Development, 45*, 1173–1175.

Tessler, M. (1986). *Mother–child talk in a museum: The socialization of a memory.* New York: City University of New York, Graduate Center.

Thomas, J. W. (1988). Proficiency at academic studying. *Contemporary Educational Psychology, 13*, 265–275.

Thomas, J. W., Bol, L., Warkentin, R. W., Wilson, M., Strage, A., & Rohwer, W. D., Jr. (1993). Interrelationships among students' study activities, self-concept of academic ability, and achievement as a function of characteristics of high-school biology courses. *Applied Cognitive Psychology, 7*, 499–532.

Tierney, R. J., & Cunningham, J. W. (1984). Research on teaching reading comprehension. In P. D. Pearson (Ed.), *Handbook of reading research* (pp. 609–655). New York: Longman.

Tipper, S. P., Bourque, T. A., Anderson, S. H., & Brehaut, J. (1989). Mechanisms of attention: A developmental study. *Journal of Experimental Child Psychology, 48,* 353–378.

Tobey, A., & Goodman, G. S. (1992). Children's eyewitness memory: Effects of participation and forensic context. *Child Abuse & Neglect, 16,* 779–796.

Trabasso, T., & Nicholas, D. W. (1980). Memory and inferences in the comprehension of narratives. In F. Wilkening, J. Becker, & T. Trabasso (Eds.), *Information integration by children* (pp. 215–242). Hillsdale, NJ: Lawrence Erlbaum Associates.

Tulving, E. (1972). *Episodic and semantic memory.* New York: Academic Press.

Turnure, J. E., & Lane, J. F. (1987). Special educational applications of mnemonics. In M. A. McDaniel & M. Pressley (Eds.), *Imagery and related mnemonic processes: Theories, individual differences, and applications* (pp. 329–357). New York: Springer-Verlag.

Van Meter, P., & Pressley, M. (1994). The encoding of instruments when 10- to 14-year-old process isolated instrument-implicit sentences: More evidence of improved encoding during childhood due to elaborative instructions. *Journal of Educational Psychology, 86,* 402–412.

Varnhagen, C. K., Morrison, F. J., & Everall, R. (1994). Aging and schooling effects in story recall and story production. *Developmental Psychology, 30,* 969–979.

Vertes, J. O. (1913). Das Wortgedächtnis im Schulkindesalter [Memory for words in schoolchildren]. *Zeitschrift für Psychologie, 63,* 19–128.

Vertes, J. O. (1931). Behalten und Vergessen des Kindes [Memory and forgetting in children]. *Zeitschrift für Psychologie und Physiologie der Sinnesorgane, 121,* 241–354.

Vosniadou, S., & Brewer, W. F. (1992). Mental models of the earth: A study of conceptual change in childhood. *Cognitive Psychology, 24,* 535–585.

Wagenaar, W. A. (1986). My memory: A study of autobiographic memory over six years. *Cognitive Psychology, 18,* 225–252.

Wagner, D. A. (1974). The development of short-term and incidental memory: A cross-cultural study. *Child Development, 45,* 389–396.

Wagner, D. A. (1978). Memories of Morocco: The influence of age, schooling, and environment on memory. *Cognitive Psychology, 10,* 1–28.

Wagner, D. A., & Spratt, J. E. (1987). Cognitive consequences of contrasting pedagogies: The effects of Quranic preschooling in Morocco. *Child Development, 58,* 1207–1219.

Waters, H. S. (1982). Memory development in adolescence: Relationships between metamemory, strategy use, and performance. *Journal of Experimental Child Psychology, 33,* 183–195.

Watts, G. H., & Anderson, R. C. (1971). Effects of three types of inserted questions on learning from prose. *Journal of Educational Psychology, 62,* 387–394.

Waugh, N. C., & Norman, D. A. (1965). Primary memory. *Psychological Review, 72,* 89–104.

Weaver, P. A., & Dickinson, D. K. (1984). Scratching below the surface structure: Exploring the usefulness of story grammars. *Discourse Processes, 5,* 225–243.

Weed, K., Ryan, E. B., & Day, J. (1990). Metamemory and attributions as mediators of strategy use and recall. *Journal of Educational Psychology, 82,* 849–855.

Weinert, F. E., Knopf, M., Körkel, J., Schneider, W., Vogel, K., & Wetzel, M. (1984). Die Entwicklung einiger Gedächtnisleistungen bei Kindern und älteren Erwachsenen in Abhängigkeit von kognitiven, metakognitiven und motivationalen Einflussfaktoren [On the development of memory performance in children and the elderly, as a function of cognitive, metacognitive, and motivational impact factors]. In K. E. Grossmann & P. Lütkenhaus (Eds.), *Bericht über die 6. Tagung Entwicklungspsychologie in Regensburg* (pp. 313–326). Regensburg, Germany: Universitäts-Druckerei.

Weinert, F. E., & Schneider, W. (Eds.). (1986). *First report on the Munich Longitudinal Study on the Genesis of Individual Competencies (LOGIC).* Munich, Germany: Max Planck Institute for Psychological Research.

Weinert, F. E., & Schneider, W. (Eds.). (1987). *The Munich Longitudinal Study on the Genesis of Individual Competencies (LOGIC), Report No. 2: Documentation of assessment procedures used in waves one to three* (Tech. Rep.). Munich, Germany: Max Planck Institute for Psychological Research.

Weinert, F. E., & Schneider, W. (Eds.). (1992). *The Munich Longitudinal Study on the Genesis of Individual Competencies (LOGIC). Report No. 8: Results of wave 6* (Tech. Rep.). Munich, Germany: Max Planck Institute for Psychological Research.

Weinert, F. E., & Schneider, W. (Eds.). (1995). *Memory performance and competencies: Issues in growth and development.* Mahwah, NJ: Lawrence Erlbaum Associates.

Weinert, F. E., Schneider, W., & Knopf, M. (1988). Individual differences in memory development across the life-span. In P. B. Baltes, D. L. Featherman, & R. M. Lerner (Eds.), *Life-span development and behavior* (Vol. 9, pp. 39–85). Hillsdale, NJ: Lawrence Erlbaum Associates.

Wellman, H. M. (1977a). The early development of intentional memory behavior. *Human Development, 20,* 86–101.

Wellman, H. M. (1977b). Preschooler's understanding of memory-relevant variables. *Child Development, 48,* 1720–1723.

Wellman, H. M. (1978). Knowledge of the interaction of memory variables: A developmental study of metamemory. *Developmental Psychology, 14,* 24–29.

Wellman, H. M. (1979). *The role of metamemory in memory behavior: A developmental demonstration.* Unpublished manuscript, University of Michigan, Ann Arbor.

Wellman, H. M. (1983). Metamemory revisited. In M. T. H. Chi (Ed.), *Trends in memory development research* (pp. 31–51). Basel, Switzerland: Karger.

Wellman, H. M. (1985). A child's theory of mind: The development of conceptions of cognition. In S. R. Yussen (Ed.), *The growth of reflection in children* (pp. 169–206). New York: Academic Press.

Wellman, H. M. (1988). The early development of memory strategies. In F. E. Weinert & M. Perlmutter (Eds.), *Memory development: Universal changes and individual differences.* Hillsdale, NJ: Lawrence Erlbaum Associates.

Wellman, H. M. (1990). *The child's theory of mind.* Cambridge, MA: MIT Press.

Wellman, H. M., & Johnson, C. N. (1979, April). *Children's conception of the mental world.* Paper presented at the biennial meeting of the Society for Research in Child Development, San Francisco.

Wellman, H. M., Ritter, K., & Flavell, J. H. (1975). Deliberate memory behavior in the delayed reactions of very young children. *Developmental Psychology, 11,* 780–787.

Wellman, H. M., & Somerville, S. C. (1982). The development of human search ability. In M. E. Lamb & A. L. Brown (Eds.), *Advances in developmental psychology* (Vol. 2, pp. 41–84). Hillsdale, NJ: Lawrence Erlbaum Associates.

Wellman, H. M., Somerville, S. C., & Haake, R. J. (1979). Development of search procedures in real-life spatial enviroment. *Developmental Psychology, 15,* 530–542.

Wetzler, S. E., & Sweeney, J. A. (1986). Childhood amnesia: An empirical demonstration. In D. C. Rubin (Ed.), *Autobiographical memory* (pp. 191–201). Cambridge, England: Cambridge University Press.

Whipple, G. M. (1912). Psychology of testimony and report. *Psychological Bulletin, 9,* 264–269.

Whitney, D., & Williams-Whitney, D. (1990). Toward a contextualist view of elaborative inferences. In A. C. Graesser & G. H. Bower (Eds.), *Inferences in text comprehension* (pp. 279–293). San Diego, CA: Academic Press.

Whittaker, S., McShane, J., & Dunn, D. (1985). The development of cueing strategies in young children. *British Journal of Developmental Psychology, 3,* 153–161.

Williams, K. G., & Goulet, L. R. (1975). The effects of cueing and constraint instructions on children's free recall performance. *Journal of Experimental Child Psychology, 19,* 464–475.

Willoughby, T., Wood, E., & Khan, M. (1994). Isolating variable that impact on or detract from the effectiveness of elaborative strategies. *Journal of Educational Psychology, 86,* 279–289.

Wimmer, H. (1980). Children's understanding of stories: Assimilation by a general schema for actions or coordination of temporal relations. In F. Wilkening, J. Becker, & T. Trabasso (Eds.), *Information integration by children* (pp. 267–290). Hillsdale, NJ: Lawrence Erlbaum Associates.

Winch, W. H. (1906). Immediate memory in school children. No. II. Auditory. *British Journal of Psychology, 2,* 1906–1908.

Winer, G. A. (1974). An analysis of verbal facilitation of class-inclusion reasoning. *Child Development, 45,* 224–227.

Winer, G. A. (1980). Class-inclusion reasoning in children: A review of the empirical literature. *Child Development, 51,* 309–328.

Wippich, W. (1980). Meta-Gedächtnis und Gedächtnis-Erfahrung [Metamemory and memory experience]. *Zeitschrift für Entwicklungspsychologie und Pädagogische Psychologie, 12*, 40–43.

Wolff, P., & Levin, J. R. (1972). The role of overt activity in children's imagery production. *Child Development, 43*, 537–547.

Wolff, P., Levin, J. R., & Longobardi, E. T. (1972). Motoric mediation in children's paired-associate learning: Effects of visual and tactile contact. *Journal of Experimental Child Psychology, 14*, 176–183.

Woloshyn, V. E., Paivio, A., & Pressley, M. (1994). Use of elaborative interrogation to help students acquire information consistent with prior knowledge and information inconsistent with prior knowledge. *Journal of Educational Psychology, 86*, 79–89.

Woloshyn, V. E., Wood, E., & Willoughby, T. (1994). Considering prior knowledge when using elaborative interrogation. *Applied Cognitive Psychology, 8*, 25–36.

Wood, E., Willoughby, T., Bolger, A., Younger, J., & Kaspar, V. (1993). Effectiveness of elaboration strategies for grade school children as a function of academic achievement. *Journal of Experimental Child Psychology, 56*, 240–253.

Woody-Ramsey, J., & Miller, P. H. (1988). The facilitation of selective attention in preschoolers. *Child Development, 59*, 1497–1503.

Worden, P. E. (1974). The development of the category-recall function under three retrieval conditions. *Child Development, 45*, 1054–1059.

Worden, P. E., & Sladewski-Awig, L. J. (1982). Children's awareness of memorability. *Journal of Educational Psychology, 74*, 341–350.

Yendovitskaya, T. V. (1971). Development of memory. In A. V. Zaporozhets & D. B. Elkonin (Eds.), *The psychology of preschool children* (pp. 89–110). Cambridge, MA: MIT Press.

Yoshida, M., Fernandez, C., & Stigler, J. W. (1993). Japanese and American students' differential recognition memory for teachers' statements during a mathematics lesson. *Journal of Educational Psychology, 85*, 610–617.

Young, D. R., & Schumacher, G. M. (1983). Context effects in young children's sensitivity to the importance level of prose information. *Child Development, 54*, 1446–1456.

Yuill, N., & Oakhill, J. (1991). *Children's problems in text comprehension: An experimental investigation.* Cambridge, England: Cambridge University Press.

Yuille, J. C., Cutshall, J. L., & King, M. A. (1986). *Age related changes in eyewitness accounts and photo identification.* Unpublished manuscript, University of British Columbia, Vancouver.

Yussen, S. R., & Bird, J. E. (1979). The development of metacognitive awareness in memory, communication, and attention. *Journal of Experimental Child Psychology, 28*, 300–313.

Yussen, S. R., Gagné, E., Gargiulo, R., & Kunen, S. (1974). The distinction between perceiving and memorizing in elementary school children. *Child Development, 45*, 547–551.

Yussen, S. R., Kunen, S., & Buss, R. (1975). The distinction between perceiving and memorizing in the presence of category cues. *Child Development, 46*, 763–768.

Yussen, S. R., & Levy, V. M. (1975). Developmental changes in knowledge about different retrieval problems. *Journal of developmental psychology, 19*, 502–508.

Yussen, S. R., Mathews, S. R., Buss, R. R., & Kane, P. T. (1980). Developmental change in judging important and critical elements of stories. *Developmental Psychology, 16*, 213–219.

Zimmerman, B. J., & Martinez-Pons, M. (1988). Construct validation of a strategy model of student self-regulated learning. *Journal of Educational Psychology, 80*, 284–290.

Zimmermann, B. J., & Pons, M. M. (1986). Development of a structured interview for assessing student use of self-regulated learning strategies. *American Educational Research Journal, 23*, 614–628.

Author Index

151

Misciones, J. L., 95
Mistry, J. J., 12, 65, 89
Mitchell, D. B., 61
Moan, S., 17
Moely, B. E., 49, 59, 71, 103, 106, 111, 117, 118
Moizo, C., 28
Monroe, E. K., 101, 102
Montague, W. E., 72
Morra, S., 28
Morrison, F. J., 38
Moynahan, E. D., 96
Muir, C., 26
Murphy, M. D., 71
Myers, J. L., 56
Myers, M., 97
Myers, N. A., 61, 72

N

Nakamura, G. V., 56
Narens, L., 93
Näslund, J. C., 28
Naus, M. J., 67, 68, 69, 70, 74
Neimark, E., 71
Nelson, K., 8, 9, 10, 11, 12, 35, 36, 38, 39, 40, 61
Nelson, T. O., 93, 94
Netschajeff, A., 2
Newman, L. S., 65
Newman, R. S., 19
Nezworski, T., 37, 38
Nicholas, D. W., 51
Nicholas, G., 17
Nicolson, R., 25
Nida, R. E., 17, 19, 65, 92
Nitchell, D. B.,
Norman, D. A., 23, 32

O

O'Brien, E. J., 56
O'Brien, R. G., 95
O'Sullivan, J. T., 20, 78, 93, 98, 108
Oakhill, J., 53
Olsen, D. R., 95
Olsen, S. F., 64
Olson, F. A., 59, 71
Olver, R. R., 34, 77
Opwis, K., 47
Ormrod, J. E., 28
Ornstein, P. A., 15, 16, 17, 50, 64, 65, 67, 68, 69, 70, 71, 74, 92

P

Paivio, A., 40, 45, 56, 57
Palermo, D. S., 72
Paris, S. G., 19, 51, 52, 93, 97
Park, Y., 26
Parker, J. F., 13
Pascual-Leone, J., 28
Pearson, D. A., 29
Pearson, P. D., 46, 55
Peck, J., 94
Peck, V. A., 92, 99
Peeck, J., 42, 56
Peleg-Bruckner, Z., 48
Pellegrino, J. W., 71
Perlmutter, M., 61, 72, 92, 98
Peterson, C., 10
Piaget, J., 32, 42, 77
Pichert, J. W., 56
Pierce, S. H., 83
Pilek, E., 2, 3, 4
Pillemer, D. B., 8, 10
Pohlmann, A., 2, 3, 4
Pons, M. M., 113, 115
Poole, D., 16
Posnansky, C. J., 71, 94
Prather, P., 29
Pressley, M., 19, 20, 27, 28, 29, 42, 52, 53, 55, 56, 57, 75, 76, 77, 78, 79, 80, 93, 101, 102, 103, 104, 106, 107, 108, 113, 115, 117, 120
Price, D. W. W., 36
Pritchard, R., 50
Probert, J. S., 82, 83
Puff, C. R., 71
Putnam, J.,

Q

Quinan, J. R., 39

R

Rabinowitz, M., 28, 45, 49, 50, 74, 78, 80
Rack, J., 26
Rackliffe, G., 19
Raine, A., 26
Rao, N., 106, 120
Ratcliff, R., 52
Ratner, H. H., 10
Raugh, M. R., 75
Readence, J. E., 56
Recht, D. R., 48
Reed, R. S., 16, 17

Subject Index

A

Academic achievement and memory, 3, 113–116
Attentional capacity, 21–31
Autobiographical memory, 1, 8–19, 110

C

Capacity, basic memory, 21–31, 109–110
Case-based knowledge, 39–40, 110
Categorizable knowledge, 33–34
Chunking, 23–24
Classification tasks, 33–34
Comprehension and memory, 4, 28
Concepts, 32–34
Consciousness, 7
Cross-cultural studies, 83–89

D

Deafness, 86–87
Declarative knowledge, 7
Depth of processing, 60
Dialogical experiences, 10–11
Dual coding, 40–44

E

Elaboration, 75–80, 115–116
Elaborative interrogation, 54–55
Episodic vs. semantic memory, 60, 110
Expert–novice differences, 24, 46–47, 111
Eyewitness memory, 12–19

F

Face memory, 12–14
Fast finish strategy, 115
Feeling of knowing, 93–94
Fuzzy traces, 30, 44–45

G

German contributions, 2–3
Gifted students, 28
Good information processing, 1, 19–20, 113–120

H

High achievement, 113–116
History of memory development, 1–19

I

Imagery, 28–29, 40–44, 75–80, 88
Incidental learning, 60
Individual differences, 2–3, 27–29
Infantile amnesia, 8–12
Inferencing, 51–53
Information processing, 7
Inhibition, 29–30
Instructional experiments, 70, 75–80
Intelligence and memory, 3
Intelligence vs. prior knowledge, 48
Intentional memory behaviors, 5–6, 60
Interest, 48–49
Interference by prior knowledge, 55–57
Involuntary memory, 4–5
Item sequencing, 24–25

K

Keyword method, 75–79
Knowledge, 7, 19–20, 32–58, 89, 110–113

L

Learning disabilities, 28
List learning, 64–75, 84–87
Logical memory, 3
Long-term memory, 7, 32–58

M

Meaning and memory, 2–6
Mediation deficiencies, 59
Medical procedures, memory of, 15–18
Memory span, 2, 21–27, 109–110
Mental verbs, 94–95, 100
Metacognitive knowledge, 7, 19–20
Metamemory, 7, 91–108, 111–113
Metamemory–memory relationships, 107–108